Sven Lindqvist was born in 1932 in Stockholm, where he still lives. Since 1955 he has published more than thirty books of essays, aphorisms, autobiography, documentary prose, travel and literary reportage. He is the author of *Bench Press*, an autobiographical essay on gym culture, ending with the protagonist leaving for the Sahara. His intellectual adventures in the desert are followed up in the highly acclaimed *Desert Divers* and '*Exterminate All the Brutes*', a book-length study of a single sentence in Joseph Conrad's *Heart of Darkness* and a journey to the roots of European racism; these titles are published by Granta Books in a single volume as *Saharan Journey*. He is also the author of *Terra Nullius: A Journey Through No One's Land*.
www.svenlindqvist.net

'A fascinating read . . . you can't fail to be impressed by his erudition. Drawing on a variety of sources, from popular fiction to first-hand accounts by victims and perpetrators, he creates a work of astonishing range, verve and inventiveness' *Literary Review*

'A history that feels uniquely fresh' *Independent*

'Lindqvist's innovative, impassioned approach to history makes his books both an education and a literary experience' *Scotland on Sunday*

'This thought-provoking little history of the weapon which so influenced the twentieth century is especially welcome just now' *Sunday Times*

'Shockingly original' *Scotsman*

'A scholarly work drawing on an eclectic well of memories, arguments, fiction, biography, history and newspaper accounts . . . the book is compelling' *Sunday Tribune*

'*A History of Bombing* is continuously interesting, often fascinating . . . we need writers like Sven Lindqvist to expose the brutality of warfare and to challenge the need for it' *Financial Times*

ALSO BY SVEN LINDQVIST AND AVAILABLE FROM GRANTA BOOKS

'Exterminate All the Brutes'

Desert Divers

Saharan Journey (omnibus)

Bench Press

Terra Nullius: A Journey Through No One's Land

A HISTORY OF BOMBING

SVEN LINDQVIST

TRANSLATED BY

LINDA HAVERTY RUGG

GRANTA

Granta Publications, 12 Addison Avenue, London W11 4QR

First published in Great Britain by Granta Books 2001
Previous paperback edition published by Granta Books 2002
This paperback edition with afterword published by Granta Books 2012

Originally published in Sweden as *Nu Dog du* by Albert Bonniers Förlag, 1999
Published in the United States by The New Press, 2001

A CIP catalogue record for this book is available from the British Library.

1 3 5 7 9 10 8 6 4 2

ISBN 978 1 84708 501 6

Printed and bound by CPI Group (UK) Ltd, Croydon, CR0 4YY

HOW TO READ THIS BOOK

This book is a labyrinth with twenty-two entrances and no exit. Each entrance opens into a narrative or an argument, which you then follow by going from text to text according to the arrow (➤) indicating the number of the section where the narrative is continued. So from entrance 1 you proceed to section 166 and continue reading section by section until you come to 173, where another arrow (➤) takes you back to entrance 2.

If you get lost, you can find your way again with the assistance of the table of entrances (Ways into the Book) at the beginning of the book.

In order to move through time, you also have to move through the book, often forward, but sometimes backward. Wherever you are in the text, events and thoughts from that same period surround you, but they belong to narratives other than the one you happen to be following. That's the intention. That way the text emerges as what it is—one of many possible paths through the chaos of history.

So welcome to the labyrinth! Follow the threads, put together the horrifying puzzle, and, once you have seen my century, build one of your own from other pieces.

WAYS INTO THE BOOK

Numbers refer to section numbers.

CHRONOLOGY

The following chronology shows which sections correspond to the years indicated.

YEAR	SECTIONS
762–1910	**23–74**
1911–1939	**75–176**
1940–1945	**177–245**
1946–1955	**246–291**
1956–1965	**292–327**
1966–1975	**328–351**
1976–1985	**352–365**
1986–1995	**366–380**
1996–1999	**381–399**

A HISTORY OF BOMBING

1 BANG, YOU'RE DEAD

"Bang, you're dead!" we said. "I got you!" we said. When we played, it was always war. A bunch of us together, one-on-one, or in solitary fantasies – always war, always death.

"Don't play like that," our parents said, "you could grow up that way." Some threat – there was no way we would rather be. We didn't need war toys. Any old stick became a weapon in our hands, and pinecones were bombs. I cannot recall taking a single piss during my childhood, whether outside or at home in the outhouse, when I didn't choose a target and bomb it. At five years of age I was already a seasoned bombardier.

"If everyone plays war," said my mother, "there will be war." And she was quite right – there was. ➤ **166**

2 IN THE BEGINNING WAS THE BOMB

In the beginning was the bomb. It consisted of a pipe, like a bamboo pipe of the type abundant in China, filled with an explosive, like gunpowder, which the Chinese had discovered as early as the ninth century. If one closed this pipe at both ends, it became a bomb.

When the pipe was opened at one end, it was blown forward by the explosion. The bomb then became a rocket. It soon developed into a two-stage rocket – a large rocket that rose into the air and released a shower of small rockets over the enemy. The Chinese used rockets of this type in their defense of Kaifeng in 1232. The rocket weapon spread via the Arabs and Indians to Europe around 1250 – but it was forgotten again until the English rediscovered it at the beginning of the 19th century.

If the rocket was opened at the other end the bomb became a gun or a cannon. The explosion blew out whatever had been tamped into the pipe, like a bullet or another, smaller bomb, called a shell. Both the gun and the cannon had been fully developed in China by 1280, and they reached Europe thirty years later. ➤ **24**

3 THE HISTORY OF THE FUTURE

1880–1910

Good morning! My name is Meister. Professor Meister. I will be lecturing today on the history of the future as depicted in *Three Hundred Years Hence* by William D. Hay. When this book came out in 1881, my time lay three hundred years ahead of the reader's. Today the society of United Man, in which I live, has drawn much closer to you. But my situation as narrator is essentially unchanged. I am speaking of your future, which for me is history. I know what is going to happen to you, since for me it has already happened. ➤ **46**

4 DEATH COMES FLYING

The first bomb dropped from an airplane exploded in an oasis outside Tripoli on November 1, 1911.

"The Italians have dropped bombs from an airplane," reported the Swedish newspaper

Dagens Nyheter the next day. "One of the aviators successfully released several bombs in the camp of the enemy, with good results."

It was Lieutenant Giulio Cavotti who leaned out of his delicate monoplane and dropped the bomb – a Danish Haasen hand grenade – on the North African oasis Tagiura, near Tripoli. Several moments later, he attacked the oasis Ain Zara. Four bombs in total, each weighing two kilos, were dropped during this first air attack. ➤ 76

5 WHAT IS PERMISSIBLE IN WAR?

The laws of war have always answered two questions: When may one wage war? What is permissible in war?

And international law was always given two completely different answers to these questions, depending on who the enemy is. The laws of war protect enemies of the same race, class, and culture. The laws of war leave the foreign and the alien without protection.

When is one allowed to wage war against savages and barbarians? Answer: always. What is permissible in wars against savages and barbarians? Answer: anything. ➤ 26

6 BOMBING THE SAVAGES

In an illustration in Jules Verne's *The Flight of Engineer Robur* (1886), the airship glides majestically over Paris, the capital of Europe. Powerful searchlights shine on the waters of the Seine, over the quays, bridges, and façades. Astonished but unperturbed, the people gaze up into the sky, amazed at the unusual sight but without fear, without feeling the need to seek cover. In the next illustration the airship floats just as majestically and inaccessibly over Africa. But here it is not a matter merely of illumination. Here the engineer intervenes in the events on the ground. With the natural authority assumed by the civilized to police the savage, he stops a crime from taking place. The airship's weapons come into play, and death and destruction rain down on the black criminals, who, screaming in terror, try to escape the murderous fire. ➤ 74

7 BOMBED INTO SAVAGERY

THE HISTORY OF THE FUTURE (2)

Jeremy Tuft is an overprotected, middle-aged, middle-class man, helpless without his privileges. In Edward Shanks's novel of the future, *People of the Ruins* (1920), his London is bombed and gassed. When Jeremy miraculously comes to life in the ruins, he finds himself in a new Middle Ages. The English have become savages who live among the ruins of the 20th century, a civilization incomprehensible to them.

Shanks's novel employs a thoroughly modern theme. In 1920, British planes bombed the "Mad Mullah" in Somaliland, thus beginning the systematic bombardment of savages and barbarians in the interwar period. In precisely that same year, 1920, the first of a long series of novels was published in which England is bombed back to barbarism, and the English themselves become savages. ➤ 109

Engineer Robur illuminates the Parisians . . .

… and bombs the savages.

8 THE LAW AND THE PROPHETS

The First World War killed ten million people and wounded twenty million. Was it a crime against humanity? Or was it quite all right, as long as the dead and wounded were young, armed men?

An unknown number of children and the elderly died of hunger and disease as a consequence of the British naval blockade against Germany. Was that a crime against humanity? Or was it quite all right, since the English couldn't help the fact that the Germans sent the little food they had to the front, letting the children and elderly starve?

The slaughter at the front seemed meaningless even as it was going on. The war had dug in and got stuck, and the military looked desperately for a new, more mobile way to wage war. Aerial combat seemed to offer the most obvious solution; attacks against the civilian population would force rapid results and ultimate victories.

But "the colonial shortcut" was forbidden in Europe. Here it was a crime against humanity to save the lives of soldiers by bombing women, children, and old people. Human rights seemed to forbid what military necessity seemed to demand – a contradiction that has colored the entire 20th century. ➤ 93

9 FROM CHECHAOUEN TO GUERNICA

Everyone in Chechaouen knows about Guernica. In Guernica no one has ever heard of Chechaouen. And yet they are sister cities. Two small cities, clinging to mountainsides, a few miles from the northern coasts of Spain and Morocco, respectively. Both of them are very old – Guernica was founded in 1366, and Chechaouen in 1471. Both are holy places – Guernica has the sacred oak of the Basque people, and Chechaouen has Moulay Abdessalam Ben Mchich's sacred grave. Both are capitals – Guernica for the Basques, and Chechaouen for the Jibala people. Both had populations of about 6,000 when they were bombed, Guernica in 1937 and Chechaouen in 1925. Both were bombed by legionnaires – Guernica by Germans serving under Franco, and Chechaouen by Americans under French command, serving the interests of the Spanish colonial power. Both had their turn to be "discovered" by a London *Times* correspondent – Guernica by George Steer, Chechaouen by Walter Harris, who wrote: ➤ 119

10 THE SPLENDID DECISION

On May 10, 1940, Churchill became Prime Minister of England. On May 11, he gave the order to bomb Germany.

"It was a splendid decision," writes J. M. Spaight, expert on international law and Secretary of the British Air Ministry. Thanks to that decision, the English today can walk with their heads held high. When Churchill began to bomb Germany, he knew that the Germans did not want a bombing war. Their air force, unlike that of the British, was not made for heavy bombs. Churchill went on bombing, even though he knew that reprisals were unavoidable. He consciously sacrificed London and other English cities for the sake of freedom and civilization. "It was a splendid decision." ➤ 178

11 HAMBURG, AUSCHWITZ, DRESDEN

During the summer of 1948 I lived with a working-class family in St. Albans, outside London. It was a cold summer, and when we sat and drank tea in the evenings we often lit the electric heater, which was made to look like a glowing heap of coal. Somehow my thoughts flew to the burned-out cities of Germany, and I told them how on my trip across the country the train had struggled, hour after hour, to make its way through the blackened ruins of what were once the homes of human beings.

"We were bombing the military transports on the railways," my host family said. If some houses by the side of the railway were damaged it was unfortunate but unavoidable. "It was war, you know."

"This is not a question of 'a few houses,' " I said. "Hamburg was razed by British bombs. This was the third time I've traveled through the city, and I have seen nothing but ruins."

"That must have been the Americans," said my host. "The British bombers never attacked civilians."

"I am sorry to contradict you, but it was the other way around. The Americans bombed the industries by day, and the British the residential areas by night. That was the general pattern, I'm afraid."

"I am not going to listen to any more German war propaganda in my house," my host said, cutting me short. "The British bombers attacked military targets, period." ➤ **391**

12 TOKYO

In the spring of 1941, a series of mysterious explosions occurred at a DuPont factory for the production of synthetic dyes. The Harvard chemist Louis Fieser was assigned to investigate the cause and he found, more or less by chance, that when burned, the fluid divinylacetylene converted into to a sticky goo with an unusually strong adhesive power. It occurred to him that such a liquid, if it were enclosed in a bomb, could be spread in the form of burning, sticky lumps that would cling to buildings and people and could be neither extinguished nor removed. ➤ **197**

13 THE DREAM OF A SUPERWEAPON

THE HISTORY OF THE FUTURE (3)

On December 10, 1903 (a week before the first airplane left the ground), the Curies accepted the Nobel Prize for Physics. They had shown that radioactive material could release enormous amounts of energy.

The series of discoveries had unfolded at a dizzying speed. The radiation that Röntgen had discovered by chance in 1895 led Becquerel to the discovery of radioactivity in uranium the very next year, then to Thomson's discovery of the "planets" around the nucleus of the atom – the electrons – and finally in 1898 to Marie Curie's discovery of radium and polonium. And in 1903, the future Nobel laureate in physics Frederick Soddy was already giving a talk before the Royal Corps of Engineers on atomic power as the superweapon of the future. The idea of an atomic weapon seems not to have been particularly frightening since weapons in general were something used primarily in the colonies, and thus posed no threat to ordinary well-behaved European citizens. An imagination unworried by fear could play with the idea. ➤ **69**

14 HIROSHIMA

The Smithsonian Institution is the collective name of a group of museums that constitute the national memory of the United States. The most beloved of these is the National Air and Space Museum in Washington, D.C. About 8,000,000 people visit it each year, making it the world's most visited museum.

The only possible rival is the famous Shinto temple Yasukuni and its museum in Tokyo. There, too, about 8,000,000 people come each year. And Yasukuni, too, serves as the memory of a nation – or more precisely, the Japanese nation's memory of its wars. ➤ **371**

15 LIVING WITH THE SUPERWEAPON

THE HISTORY OF THE FUTURE (4)

"In Hiroshima, everything was over in a second. But the bomb itself is not over. It is still here, awaiting its next opportunity," says Faos Cheeror, an Eastern European refugee whom South African writer Horace Rose met in London, late in the summer of 1945.

"Truman says that atomic power is much too terrible to be unleashed in a lawless world."

"Truman said that after he had already unleashed it."

"He used the bomb to shorten the war and save lives."

"You belong to a nation of hypocrites, my friend," says Faos. "I am thinking of the victims of the bomb in all those future wars, the wars that have already begun in the dreams of maniacs."

In *The Maniac's Dream, A Novel of the Atomic Bomb* (1946) we are allowed a look into those dreams, and we see the atom bomb destroy New York and London. But actually it is not the Londoners the Maniac hates and reviles, but the blacks of his own country. They are subhuman apes, whose existence is justified only by their service to whites. To attribute human desires and feelings to them would be ridiculous. When they rise up against their oppressors, he doesn't hesitate for a moment to let the atom bomb destroy them.

"A land which had been brilliantly alive with colour, movement and activity was utterly and completely motionless, utterly and completely dumb." ➤ **246**

16 BOMBS AGAINST INDEPENDENCE

While everyone's attention was diverted by the superweapon and the necessity of avoiding total destruction, bombing took up its old role of securing European colonial power. The same old bombs were dropped, the same old villages burned. The wars were reported as "police actions" to "reinstate order" or fight "terrorists." Only slowly and reluctantly did Europe admit that these wars were wars and concerned the right to independence. ➤ **97**

17 KOREA

On June 25, 1950, I found myself in the gallery at the United Nations Security Council. I was a year away from high-school graduation and was going to enter compulsory military service the following fall. I had received a scholarship to study "international relations." That was why I was sitting there listening as the Security Council decided to intervene in the Korean War.

What would Sweden's position be? Strong forces demanded that we should participate. I was constantly asked about it in New York. Suddenly international relations were no longer something that concerned only adults, way above my head. The demand was being made of me. It was I, personally, who would have to shoot and bomb. I, who at this point, at the beginning of the war, had scarcely heard of Korea.

I sat down in the U.N. library and tried to figure out why I should kill or be killed. ➤ 267

18 MASSIVE RETALIATION

THE HISTORY OF THE FUTURE (5)

On January 27, 1796, the young researcher Charles Cuvier gave his first public lecture at the Institute de France in Paris. Before a deeply shocked audience he proved that the species created by God were not eternal. They could, he said, "become extinct" in a kind of "revolution of the earth." And we, the new tribes that have taken their place, could ourselves be destroyed one day, and replaced by others. ➤ 36

19 FLEXIBLE RETALIATION

MEIDIGUOZHUYI SHI QUAN SHIJIE RENMINDE ZUI XIONGEDE DIREN.

Those were the first words I had to learn when I was studying Chinese at Peking University in the winter of 1961. The phrase was terribly difficult, partially because I considered the statement false. "American imperialism is the most evil enemy of all the world's people." I found myself constantly protesting the Chinese government's distorted image of American policies.

"Throughout its history, the U.S. has defended the right of peoples to self-determination," I said. "That will be the case in Vietnam, as well."

"You underestimate the free press in America," I said. "The facts always come out, sooner or later. You can't overrule public opinion in a democracy. You won't get reelected that way."

"Only Congress can declare war," I explained to my Chinese hosts. Do you think that Congress, only ten years after Korea, will send its constituents and their children to die in a new Asian war? Never. It will never happen. There will be no war in Vietnam. ➤ 322

20 SURGICAL PRECISION

Once upon a time there were a Frenchman, an American, and a German. The Frenchman wanted to prove that the world turns. The American wanted to fly to Mars in a spaceship.

The German wanted to go to the North Pole in a submarine. Along with some other monomaniac dreamers, they created an instrument that could aim a rocket out into space and get it to deliver a dozen hydrogen bombs, each to its own separate address on the other side of the globe, more accurately than the postal service, faster than flight, and with the proverbial surgical precision. ➤ **38**

21 THE BOMB ON TRIAL

If the dum-dum bullet is forbidden by the rules of war on account of the unnecessary pain it causes (it has been and it continues to be), how can the hydrogen bomb be legal? If the rules of war forbid weapons that do not distinguish between noncombatants and combatants, how could weapons that spread uncontainable radioactivity over large areas be legal? How could military strategies that cold-bloodedly calculate tens or hundreds of millions of civilian victims be legal?

And if through the use of precise weapon systems one could reduce the number of victims in the first round to just a few million while holding the enemies' big cities hostage – would the weapons become more legal? If the "surgical" attacks then escalated to a general atomic war that destroyed all of humankind – could those who made the decisions declare with good conscience that they had, in any case, remained within the bounds of the law? ➤ **239**

22 NOTHING HUMAN

THE HISTORY OF THE FUTURE (6)

"War," said the great military theoretician Karl von Clausewitz, "is nothing but a duel on a larger scale."

That was at the beginning of the 19th century. Today we are no longer dueling. That two grown men would believe their honor demanded that they meet at dawn in order to give one of them the opportunity to murder the other in a ceremonial ritual – the mere thought has become absurd, even ridiculous.

And war? Will it one day be equally absurd? ➤ **367**

To the reader who has come this far without entering one of the narratives: now you have seen the beginning of them all.

Nothing can prevent you from continuing to read the book page after page as if it were a normal book. That will work, too.

*But this is not a normal book. I am trying to give you a new kind of reading experience and therefore ask you to turn back. Choose one of the entrances and read on to the section in which that narrative is taken up again – for example, from entrance **1** to section **166**.*

23

762 It was Abu Hanifa, an influential legal expert of Persian origin, the founder of a school of law in Baghdad, who first forbade the killing of women, children, the

elderly, the sick, monks, and other noncombatants. He also condemned rape and the killing of captives. We do not know much about him other than that he himself was captured after an attempted coup and died five years later in prison.[1]

The moral sense to which Charlton appealed had been formulated in Iraq long before civilization reached the British Isles. As early as the 8th century, when Islam had conquered Asia Minor and north Africa and pushed into Europe from two directions – that is, at the peak of Islam's power – a legal expert in Baghdad attempted to make war more humane by setting forth rules that were not accepted in Europe until several centuries later.

Rules that were still not accepted, or in any case not practiced, when colored people were involved. ➤ **113**

24

1044 But in the beginning was the bomb. It began to be used in warfare around the same time that the chemical equation for gunpowder was first published, in 1044. The bombs were dropped from the tops of city walls or slung from catapults at the enemy.

The first technical description of a bomb, made in China during the 12th century, shows the bomb filled with thirty-odd thin slivers of porcelain, which were flung out in the explosion. Starting in 1412, there are descriptions of "fragmentation bombs" filled with iron shot or shards of porcelain inside a thin cast-iron shell, which blew to bits with the explosion. The jagged shards of metal were intended to "wound the skin and break the bones." Thus the first bombs were what we call antipersonnel bombs today, intended for battling so-called "soft targets."[2]

25

1207 The first depiction of war to describe the use of bombs dates from 1207. It emphasizes what would later be called the "morale effect" or the "terror effect." When the bombs exploded, "the [enemy] wretches were terrified and quite lost their senses, men and horses running away as fast as they could..."[3] ➤ **28**

26

During the Middle Ages, a distinction was drawn between *bellum hostile*, war between Christian knights, and *bellum romanum*, war waged against outsiders, infidels, barbarians, or insurgent peasants. *Bellum hostile* was conducted according to chivalric code and followed strict rules. *Bellum romanum* was lawless war.

It was called "Roman" because the Roman Empire was held to have been especially merciless in war. The Romans killed or enslaved their captives, they plundered and destroyed their enemies' cities, they slaughtered entire populations without distinguishing between combatants and noncombatants.[4]

"Roman war" was the medieval term for what the 20th century would call "total war."

27

1625 At the age of 36, the Dutchman Hugo Grotius (1583–1645) was captured after a military coup and condemned to life in prison and the loss of his entire fortune. After two years he managed to flee to France, where he eventually became Sweden's ambassador, one of the few non-Swedes ever to serve in such a capacity. During his time in prison and exile he wrote the work that forms the basis for the modern rules of war: *Three Books about Law in War and Peace* (1625).

While he was writing, the Thirty Years' War between Catholics and Protestants laid waste to Europe. Grotius coolly asserts what everyone already knew – that in this war, everything was allowed. No law protected anyone, even children and old people, from slaughter.

But, he continues, everyone also knows that there is much the law permits that nevertheless is wrong. First of all, anything that happens in an unjust war is naturally unjust. And even in a just war, "One must take care, so far as is possible, to prevent the death of innocent persons, even by accident." Children and the elderly should always be spared, and women as well, as long as they do not take the place of men as soldiers. Grotius created the vision of an international law that as yet did not exist.[5] ➤ **30**

28

1670 For a long time the bomb was considered a primitive forerunner to the rocket or cannon. But the early theoreticians of flight realized that the bomb would be a terrible weapon if it could be thrown from the air.

In his *Prodromo overo Saggio* (*The Aerial Ship*) of 1670, Francesco Lana de Terzi already warned of airships that from an appropriate height could drop "artificial fire, bullets, and bombs" at "houses, castles, or cities," without placing themselves in the least danger. Defying his own warning, he himself tried to construct such an airship, built on the vacuum principle.[6]

29

1710 In 1710 Gottfried Zeidler published *Der fliegende Wandersmann* (*The Flying Wanderer*). He dreamed of flight as a way to make travel easier and cheaper. Like storks and swallows, everyone would be able to take off for warmer lands when winter came. But he also realized the lack of security that flight would create. "No country, no city would ever be safe from attacks from above." ➤ **32**

30

1762 The Enlightenment expanded Grotius's vision of protection for civilian populations. Charles de Montesquieu in his *The Spirit of Laws* (1748) and Jean-Jacques Rousseau in *The Social Contract* (1762) maintained that war is a contest between states and not between individuals. The violence of war ought therefore to be aimed exclusively at the state and its military, not at the peaceful inhabitants of the country. The ideal would be for the people in warring countries to be able to go on living as before, leaving war to their respective ruler and his soldiers. This thesis goes on the assumption that the rulers are the type of despot that ruled the continent at that time, and not the government by the people that was developing in England. It also assumes a conflict involving the land armies of the continent, rather than Great Britain's most important weapons: the navy and trade blockades. The effects of a blockade could not be limited to the enemies' armed forces. Thus the English considered peaceful trade and unhampered production to be military goals.

There were horrifying exceptions to the 18th-century humanization of war. In particular, three types of opponents were excluded from the process: rebels, infidels, and savages. According to the English, the Irish belonged to all three categories. A number of scholars have pointed out the connection between the merciless methods used by the English to put down rebellion in Ireland and those used by English colonists against the natives of North America. French and English soldiers treated one another as equals when they fought over their American claims – but Indians could be put down by any means necessary.[7]

31

The Puritans arrived in Ireland and America with the Bible in hand. The Bible backed them up. They simply acted in accordance with the commandments of the Lord as stated in the verses of chapter 7 of Deuteronomy:

> 1 When the LORD your God brings you into the land which you are entering to take possession of it, and clears away many nations before you, the Hittites, the Girgashites, the Amorites, the Canaanites, the Perizzites, the Hivites, and the Jebusites, seven nations greater and mightier than yourselves,
>
> 2 And when the LORD your God gives them over to you, and you defeat them; then you must utterly destroy them; you shall make no covenant with them, and show no mercy to them...
>
> 16 And you shall destroy all the peoples that the LORD your God will give over to you, your eye shall not pity them...
>
> 24 And he will give their kings into your hand, and you shall make their name perish from under heaven; not a man shall be able to stand against you, until you have destroyed them.

From the beginning, genocide is inscribed in our culture's earliest and holiest texts. Read the Old Testament. Read the *Iliad*. Read the *Aeneid*. There are your instructions.[8] ➤ **35**

32

1781 A French printer, Restif de la Bretonne, travelled far into the future in *La découverte australe par un homme-volant (The Astral Discovery of a Flying Man,*

1781). There he foresaw interplanetary rocket trips and fleets of bombers leaving "in the immense space of future time a trail of infamy, fear and horror."

33

1783 The year after that, the Montgolfier brothers in Avignon began to experiment with hot-air balloons. Ascents were first attempted with unmanned balloons, since no one knew what would happen to a human being who left the earth and rose into the unknown. The balloon was also tested with a duck and a sheep as passengers before the Montgolfier brothers took off in an unanchored balloon on November 21, 1783, and flew for twenty-five minutes.

Among the audience was a Prussian lieutenant engineer by the name of J. C. G. Heyne. He was impressed by the military possibilities of the balloon, and a few months later had already published the first book about flight as a weapon. The balloon could, he wrote, "rain down fire and destruction on whole towns with catastrophic results for the inhabitants." But since this threat would hover over all the countries at war, they would, Heyne believed, soon agree on rules that would prevent flying machines from being used for purposes of terror or mass destruction.

Balloons proved to be so vulnerable and difficult to steer that they lacked significant military value. A hundred years later, in 1899 at The Hague, the great powers could therefore agree to follow Heyne's recommendation and forbid bombardment from balloons.[9]

➤ **62**

34

1784 As early as the Middle Ages, the Chinese loaded their bombs with sharp shards of porcelain or pieces of scrap iron that were thrown out in every direction upon explosion. The method was rediscovered in 1784 by Lieutenant Henry Shrapnel, who loaded a bomb with gunpowder and scrap iron. This was called a case shot or a "shrapnel bomb," and was the forerunner of the bombs designed especially to kill humans, which were used on such a large scale in Vietnam.

➤ **88**

35

1803 The conquest of the American continents became a model for European expansion in other regions suitable for white settlement – from Siberia in the north to Patagonia and Australia in the south.

This expansion served to relieve the pressure of population in Europe for a time. Thomas Malthus was among the first to realize this. In the second edition of his most important work, *Principles of Population* (1803), he writes that it is quite possible to solve Europe's food shortages temporarily by exterminating the native populations of other continents; but that it would be morally indefensible to repeat what was happening in America: "If the United States of America continue increasing, which they certainly will do, though not with the same rapidity as formerly, the Indians will be driven further and further back into the country, till the whole race is ultimately exterminated, and the territory is incapable of further extension."

Would the same thing happen in Asia and Africa? No, that must not be allowed to happen, wrote Malthus: "To exterminate the inhabitants of the greatest part of Asia and Africa is a thought that could not be admitted for a moment."[10] ➤ 45

36

1806 Cuvier's notion of extinction captured the imagination of his contemporaries.[11] It was the French author Cousin de Grainville who wrote the first *The Last Man* (*Le dernier homme*, 1806). In his novel the sun grows pale, the earth ages, and human beings become more and more exhausted and used up. The last fertile man is taken by airship to Brazil to mate with the last fertile woman. But the final bell has already tolled for civilization. Its heart, Paris, has stopped. Everything collapses and turns into desert. The two lovers see the futility in bringing a child into a dying world and so the last human beings sadly refrain from a union with each other. God is involved. But there is no hint that humankind itself might have brought about its own demise.[12]

37

1826 When Mary Wollstonecraft Shelley wrote her *The Last Man* (1826), her husband Percy Shelley had drowned, her friend Byron was dead, and she herself was left alone. And in addition, all of Europe at the time lived in fear of the Bengali cholera, a deadly epidemic disease that came wandering slowly from the East and reached England in 1831. The general Romantic *Weltschmerz* of the period suddenly acquired a motivation.

Her novel takes place during the 2090s. People can travel wherever they like in balloons, poverty and disease have been eliminated, machines take care of every imaginable need, peace and prosperity reign everywhere. "The energies of man were before directed to the destruction of his species; they now aim at its liberation and preservation."[13]

Suddenly this happy world is stricken with an epidemic that drives humanity back to violence, barbarism, and superstition. Science and politics are helpless in the face of nature's power. Slowly and painfully, humankind becomes extinct.

The alienation that usually characterizes the Romantic hero is taken a step farther than usual here – the very existence of humankind becomes problematic. But there is no hint that the plague has been intentionally set loose. No one is consciously trying to "annihilate his race." ➤ 61

38

1852 The Frenchman was Léon Foucault (1819–1868), best known for his pendulum. But that was just one of many methods he invented to show that the world turns. In 1852 he invented the gyroscope – the name comes from the Greek *gyros*, ring, circle, rotation, and *skopein*, show. The gyroscope consists of a rapidly rotating top, suspended so that it can turn in any direction. In relation to the stars it maintains its original direction and therefore shows, like the pendulum, that the world is turning.[14]

Foucault's experiment failed because friction caused the top to stop before the rotation of the earth became visible. But in the 1860s the gyroscope was outfitted with an electric motor. Now the top could spin forever. It turned out that its axis pointed north–south, like the needle in a magnetic compass. ➤ **51**

39

1854–1856 The air force could and did point to many models they might follow in the traditional service branches' practice of warfare.[15] On July 13, 1854, the American navy bombarded and destroyed the undefended city of San Juan del Norte in Nicaragua. It was claimed that the American ambassador had been insulted and abused. The population was warned in advance. After several hours of firing, the American captain sent in a detachment of marines, who completed the destruction by setting fire to the city.

The British protested the bombardment of an undefended city, something "without precedent among civilized nations."

No, such behavior was no longer tolerated among civilized nations. But Nicaragua and China did not belong to that club.

Two years later the British navy burned down Canton in ten days of firing with no return fire from the Chinese. A large number of civilians were killed.

In the debate in the House of Commons afterward, one defense of the action was that only Chinese had been killed in the shelling. The idea that they, too, should come under the protection of international law was considered absurd. "Talk of applying the pedantic rules of international law to the Chinese!"

But the British government never maintained that the shelling of an undefended population was justified. Instead they claimed that it had never occurred. The shelling had been aimed, they said, at the city wall, and it was only by mistake that adjacent buildings had been damaged. A pity that the whole city had burned. ➤ **41**

40

1863 At the same time, the tradition of Grotius and Rousseau lived on and became valid law in the United States as General Order No. 100, which was passed on April 24, 1863. One of the essential paragraphs states: "The unarmed citizen is to be spared in person, property, and honour as much as the exigencies of war will admit."[16]

The paragraph became a model piece of legislation. It formed the basis for the Geneva Convention in 1864, the Brussels Conference in 1874, and the Oxford Manual of Wars in 1880. Similar laws were passed in Germany in 1870, the Netherlands in 1871, France and Russia in 1877, Great Britain in 1883, and Spain in 1893.

And in practice?

In practice, the reservation expressed by "as much as the exigencies of war will admit" was the sticking point.

Just a year after the passing of General Order No. 100, the Union General Sherman burned the city of Atlanta, and that act touched off a trail of devastation through the southern states that spared neither persons, property, nor honor. "War is cruel and you cannot refine it," said Sherman.

And when the rebellious South was defeated, Sherman continued to use the same methods against the Indians. In practice the old exceptions were still in force: the rules of war give no quarter to rebels and savages.[17] ➤ 43

41

1863 In August of 1863 it was time for another round. An Englishman had been murdered in Kagoshima, Japan, and the British navy arrived to claim damages. The shelling was aimed at the city's fortifications, but because of rough seas it was difficult to contain the effects of the fire to military targets.

"Over half of the town was in flames and entirely destroyed," wrote Admiral Kuper in his report. "The fire, which is still raging, affords reasonable grounds for believing that the entire town of Kagoshima is now a mass of ruins," he concludes.

In the House of Commons debate, Kuper received the full support of the government. Kuper would have acted unjustifiably, said a representative speaker, had he intentionally aimed his guns at civilians. But this was not the case. It would be absurd if military installations were to be rendered immune to acts of war simply by placing them so near to civilian structures that they could not be attacked without damaging civilian life and property.

That was the principle. The British Foreign Ministry added that there had to be a certain proportion between "loss of life and property of innocent persons" and "any military advantage likely to be secured by the operation." This sense of proportion seems to have been somewhat less well developed in Kuper.

42

1866 In March of 1866, the Spaniards bombarded the undefended city of Valparaiso in Chile. Since it was mostly British property that was damaged, the bombardment excited great indignation in England. In the House of Commons debate, the Foreign Minister did not want to dispute the fact that warring countries had the right to bombard one another's cities, whether they were defended or not. But it was not quite civilized. Only one speaker was sufficiently boorish to bring up what the English had done in Kagoshima three years earlier. That was immediately set aside. William Hall, an expert in international law, designated Valparaiso as "the sole instance in which a commercial town had been attacked as a simple act of devastation." Other jurists allied themselves with Hall, and in their textbooks, Valparaiso stood as the black example of impermissible bombardment of a city, until that honor was taken over by Guernica in 1937. ➤ 47

43

1868 Taking the 1863 American rules of war as a point of departure, the Swiss Johann Caspar Bluntschli wrote the first international "law book" set down as a legal code, *Das moderne Völkerrecht der zivilisierten Staaten als Rechtsbuch dargestellt* (*Modern International Law of the Civilized Nations*, 1868). There was as yet no international body that could pass these laws, but they had great impact nevertheless. The book was translated into French, Spanish, Russian, and Chinese, and remained in print for thirty years through nine editions.[18]

Bluntschli was of course quite aware that up to that time non-Europeans had been considered outside the protection of international law. This was the defect he aimed to correct. "International law is not limited to the European family of nations, but is valid wherever people live. Since savages are human beings, they must be treated humanely, and their human rights must not be denied." (paragraph 535)

He condemns the extermination of the native peoples of the North American colonies, and expressly compares it with the persecution suffered by Jews in many European countries. (paragraph 25)

He also condemns the genocidal campaign conducted by the ancient Jews against the original inhabitants of Palestine. The commandments issued in Deuteronomy conflict with his day's more humane legal concepts and "no longer should be praised as a worthy example." (paragraph 535) By 1868 it had become more important than ever to warn about the dangers of Deuteronomy.

44

1868 The first edition of Bluntschli's legal code had just come out when seventeen states, representing "the civilized world," signed the so-called Petersburg Declaration of 1868. A key passage states: "The only legitimate object which states should endeavour to accomplish during war is to weaken the military forces of the enemy."[19]

But the declaration applied only to the signatories. Savages and barbarians were not invited. Nor were they invited to the Berlin Conference of 1884–1885, which sought to ensure peace in Europe by slicing up Africa and parceling it out among the European powers. ➤ 48

45

1869 But the thought of extermination, which in 1803 "could not be admitted for a moment," began to seem more and more natural and unavoidable as the 19th century wore on. In 1869, a British imperialist like Charles Dilke could maintain in his best-seller *Greater Britain* that "The gradual extinction of the inferior races is not only a law of nature, but a blessing to mankind."[20]

Genocide now emerged as a source of pride: "The Anglo-Saxon is the only extirpating race on earth." "The Portuguese in Ceylon, the Dutch in Java, the French in Canada and Algeria, have conquered but not killed off the native peoples."

"Up to the commencement of the now-inevitable destruction of the Red Indians of Central North America, of the Maoris, and of the Australians by the English colonists, no numerous race had ever been blotted out by an invader."

Dilke is hardly justified in granting the English such a special distinction. But that is not what is strange. What is strange is the change that had taken place in the attitude about the blotting out of numerous races.[21] ➤ 40

46

1880 The major difference between 1880 and 2180, says Professor Meister, is that the population of the earth has increased enormously. But the rise in population has not been distributed equally. Certain races, the Polynesian and aboriginal Australians, for example, have died out for some mysterious reason. Others, the Indians and Malaysians, for example, survived for a long time as an underclass in white colonial society before they gradually faded away and disappeared. Actually, how such considerable populations as that of India became lost, we do not know in detail.

The increase in population occurred most significantly in the white nations that made up United Man. There the English, Americans, Germans, and Slavs predominated, and taken as a group they now made up more than half of the earth's population.

The Chinese Empire and black Africa made up the largest groups outside the White Commonwealth. When the earth's population rose to twenty-three billion, everyone realized that food production would not be able to keep up with another doubling of the population. The fertility of the yellow and black races in particular seemed so threatening that the old idea of brotherhood went by the board.

To White Man, the inferior races seemed to sink out of Humanity and appear nearer and nearer to the brutes. It was agreed that their power of reasoning was of a lower order than that of white men, and that their capacity for intellectual development was limited. Even the vaunted culture of China proved to be, on closer inspection, only an elaborate form of barbarism, incapable of assimilating the higher civilization of United Man.

The Japanese had – somewhat prematurely – been admitted to United Man. But for them, Western civilization proved to be nothing more than a veneer. As an ape can be taught to wield a sword but never to read and write, so the Japanese learned to use the weapons of civilization without mastering the science that had made them possible.

Once these matters had been publicly canvassed, an astonishingly rapid reversal in public opinion occurred. A low murmur was heard, soon rising into a formidable outcry: "Why do we wait?...Let us seize upon these countries! Let the inferior give place to the superior! ...There is now no other way! Death to the Negro! Annihilation to the Chinaman!"

What happened? Well, the Japanese began the war that spread to the Asian continent and led to the extinction of the slant-eyes. Close your eyes and imagine the great fleets of airships called lucogenostats, as they draw near to the Chinese coast. Now they are already hovering over the land of the doomed race. We see the wild attempt of the Yellow man to measure his puny strength against the irresistible dominion of the White. But the Mongolian air fleet succumbs to the silent, almost regretful, but intractably determined Caucasian executioners of Destiny's decree.

The battle was already decided at its inception. And then the white avengers swept onward, silent and terrible. From their airplanes "falls a rain of awful death to every breathing thing, a rain that exterminates the hopeless race..."

What need is there to say more? You know the awful story – for awful it undoubtedly is – the destruction of a thousand millions of beings who once were held to be the equals of intellectual men. We look back upon the yellow race with pitying contempt, for to us they can but seem mere anthropoid animals, not to be regarded as belonging to the race that is summed up and glorified in United Man. Yet in your day these creatures were held to be an important and integral part of the human family.

Once the Chinese were exterminated, the future of the Africans became the topic of the day. Reluctant to take their lives, United Man sought a way to sterilize them. But when rumors of this led to a black revolt against the whites, things took a different turn. The representatives of United Man felt forced to decide on a complete destruction of the black race as well.

With the entire armament of humankind at their disposal and with airplanes to carry them, the parliament soon had reached a decision. All of the member states took part with aircraft, men, and equipment when the unwelcome but unavoidable task was carried out. The Black Man ceased to be.

A few million blacks and Orientals were living in the member nations of United Man. They were of course not killed, but effectual means were taken in each individual case to prevent propagation. A half-century has passed since the Great Extermination, and now even these favored lingerers are a thing of the past. The lower races are nothing but a memory.

In the countries where they once lived, white immigrants have moved in. "The face of Africa changed like a dream..." Today the whole world belongs to United Man.[22] ➤ **55**

47

1882 Rarely has a city been bombarded under more bombastic pretexts than when the British reduced Alexandria to rubble and ash in 1882. Prime Minister Gladstone cited a fundamental right of the global community (as we would put it today) to intervene in the affairs of other states in the name of peace, humanity, and progress, by, for example, bombarding their cities and occupying their territory.

The British navy shelled Alexandria from sunrise to sunset. During the night the city was transformed into a sea of fire. The foreign press held that the fire was caused by the shelling, but the British denied this; they claimed that the Egyptians had set fire to the city during their retreat. Both sides found eyewitnesses to support their positions.

The intention behind the bombardment was to put down a nationalist uprising against combined British and French forces; the result was that for the next half-century, Egypt became a British colony. The British may have planned a humanitarian intervention, but it was not entirely without self-interest.

The most serious problem from the point of view of international law was the precedent that was created in Alexandria. "Is it now fair game," asked Admiral Aube in *Révue des deux Mondes*, "for the navy to bombard the enemies' undefended coastal cities?"[23] By 1911 one could add, "If what the navy has already done will determine what the air force will be permitted to do in the future, is any city safe from destruction?" ➤ **50**

48

1885 "International law exists only for the powerful. Up to now they have shown no consideration for the weak. The other peoples, who make up three-quarters of humanity, have no recourse against injustice," writes Joseph Hornung, scholar of international law, in an unusual and groundbreaking series of articles entitled "The Civilized and the Barbarians" in *Révue de droit international* in 1885. "The principle of international law that war is to be waged only between states and armies and not between nationals and civilian societies, this principle we do not apply to conflicts with barbarians.

"Among civilized states, warfare is limited to states and their armies. But the civilized states deem such considerations unnecessary in warfare against the so-called inferior nations. In those cases the entire nation must be punished.

"We burn their poor villages, we cut down their fruit trees, we massacre their women and children. Is this, I ask of you, the best way to teach them to love civilization?"[24]

49

1885 And what happened to those who burned the villages of the savages, massacring their women and children? What did they learn? How could one keep the lawlessness of the wars outside Europe from seeping into wars between Europeans?

One person who asked that question early on was James Anson Farrer. In his classic *Military Manners and Customs* (1885), he says that war between peoples with different standards of civilization "does more to barbarise the civilised than to civilise the barbarous population."[25]

Farrer considers it a proven fact that European wars became more lawless as a result of the habits acquired by the troops on the other side of the Atlantic. There the ties of common humanity had been cut by differences in race and religion. There all inhibitions fell away. We see the same phenomenon in Roman history. "The Roman annalists bear witness to the deterioration that ensued both in their modes of waging war and in the national character."

The colonial wars have accustomed European military men and politicians to see all warfare as a kind of punitive expedition against rebels and criminals, writes Farrer. They have learned to view the enemy as a criminal and demand unconditional surrender under humiliating terms, which unnecessarily embitters and prolongs the conflicts. They have learned to burn cities and villages. "An English commander, for instance, should no more set fire to the capital of Ashantee or Zululand for so paltry a pretext as the display of British power than he would set fire to Paris or Berlin."

Once a commander has set fire to an African capital, might he have learned to burn Paris or Berlin? The type of war that Europe had allowed itself to wage for so long against three-quarters of humanity – was that what came back to haunt us in the 20th century? ➤ 53

50

1896 During the long period of comparative peace that Europe enjoyed between 1815 and 1914, the area under European control grew from 35% of the earth to 85%.[26]

Shelling of undefended cities such as Canton and Alexandria was the favored form of warfare for the European navies during this period. They had no need to "fear vengeance in their homeland from the peoples whose homelands were their theaters of war," writes Eberhard Spetzler, a German expert in international law. "Unassailable naval powers such as the United States and England were seduced by their military victories against primitive opponents into mistaken ideas about the value of destroying homes and attacking peaceful civilians."[27] The European armies reached the same false conclusion through their experience of "small wars." Until the First World War, the standard British text on that sort of conflict was Colonel C. E. Caldwell's *Small Wars, Their Principle and Practise* (1896, 1906, 1990). Caldwell was an Irishman who had been educated in England and had served as an artilleryman in India and South Africa. After the singular success of his book, he retired to become a professional writer.

"The small war" arises, according to Caldwell, "whenever a regular army finds itself engaged upon hostilities against irregular force, or forces, which in their armament, their organisation, and their discipline are palpably inferior to it." Small wars can be conquests, as "when a Great Power adds the territory of barbarous races to its possessions," or they can be punitive expeditions against bellicose neighbors, or expeditions intended to put down continued resistance in already occupied regions.

In these conflicts there is often no enemy army to vanquish, no capital city to occupy, no government with which to sign a treaty. One must steal the enemy's cattle, destroy his stores of food, and burn his villages, even if sensitive individuals might find this objectionable.

"The crushing of a populace in arms and the stamping out of widespread disaffection by military methods, is a harassing form of warfare...and [is] always most trying to the troops. As a general rule the quelling of rebellion in distant colonies means protracted, thankless, inveterate war.

"A 'real' war can end with the capitulation of the enemy leader, but when one is dealing with a rebellion, the entire population must be chastised and subdued.

"The main points of difference between small wars and regular campaigns...are that, in the former, the beating of the hostile armies is not necessarily the main object even if such armies exist, that moral effect is often far more important than material success, and that the operations are sometimes limited to committing havoc which the laws of regular warfare do not sanction."[28]

Several years later, when it became evident that modern weapons had made it almost impossible to achieve victory against an enemy of equal power, it was tempting to take the colonial shortcut: to try to achieve by terror a devastating effect on morale, to allow in Europe the "havoc" that had until then been forbidden by the laws of war. ➤ 6

51

1897 The American was Robert Goddard (1882–1945). One day when he was fifteen years old he was perched in a cherry tree, dreaming of the planet Mars.

Mars was a topic of current interest because of a mistranslation from Italian that had led people to believe that there were "canals" on Mars. The immensely rich amateur astronomer Percival Lowell had an observatory built in Arizona and thought he had found close to 200 canals, which he described in *Mars* (1895). From the existence of the canals he concludes that there are Martians, and he depicts imaginatively their struggle against extinction on a dying planet. All remaining water is bound up in the polar ice, and the canals serve to carry the melt-off to the oases where life still flickers. The Martians' superior civilization is doomed to go under because we Earthlings can not reach them to rescue them in time.[29]

That is why little Robert Goddard, sitting in the tree, made himself a solemn promise to go to Mars himself. His whole life long he returned to the cherry tree every year on that same day, October 19, to renew his promise.[30]

52

The rocket had been invented in China in the 13th century, but it was in India that the British rediscovered it at the end of the 18th century and took it home to Europe. The first thing they did was burn down Copenhagen in 1807. But rockets fell into disrepute because of their lack of precision. You never knew precisely where they would land.

They were reserved for savages and barbarians – in Algeria in 1816, Burma in 1825, Ashante in 1826, Sierra Leone in 1831, Afghanistan in 1837–1842, China in 1839–1842 and 1856–60, against Shimonoseki in 1864, in Central America in 1867, Abyssinia in 1868, against the Zulus of South Africa in 1879, against the Nagas on the Afghani border in 1880, against Alexandria in 1882, and against rebellious subjects in Sudan, Zanzibar, and East and West Africa in 1894 – just to name a few of the most prominent occasions when the British used rockets to demoralize "native" enemies.[31]

This was the primitive weapon of terror that Robert Goddard wanted to develop into a rocket that could carry his spaceship to Mars. ➤ 63

53

1898 The machine gun was the weapon of choice in colonial wars. It was used throughout the world to educate uppity natives. The climax came at the battle at Omdurman in 1898. There the English lost forty-eight men, while more than 10,000 Sudanese were left on the battlefield, mowed down by the rapid fire of the British rifles and machine guns.

So as early as 1898 it was possible to anticipate Verdun and Sedan. But Europeans, especially the British, did not want to admit that they had the machine gun to thank for their "sickeningly total victories," as John Ellis writes in *The Social History of the Machine Gun* (1976). The core of European imperialist ideology was an unquestioning belief in the superiority of the white race. It took several million corpses to convince Europe's officers that the machine gun had the same effect on European soldiers as it did on "dirty niggers" in Africa.[32]

54

1898 In the same year as the battle at Omdurman, the Polish-born banker Jean de Bloch, active as a financier and railway entrepreneur in Russia, published a six-volume study of the future of war, in which he made a detailed forecast of what would happen in the First World War.

"The spade will be as indispensable to the soldier as his rifle....There will be increased slaughter...on so terrible a scale as to render it impossible to get troops to push the battle to a decisive issue. They will try to, thinking that they are fighting under the old conditions, and they will learn such a lesson that they will abandon the attempt forever."

The firepower of the new weapons had made defense vastly more effective than attack. The defense could lay down an impassable barrage of fire. The armies would get mired in interminable, siegelike battles, which would be decided finally not by the bayonet, but by the economic resources required to support these armies of millions.

Bloch's work came out simultaneously in all of the major European languages and was refuted by military experts in every country. The offense would be able to overcome machine-gun fire with three methods: (1) through initiative and enthusiasm, (2) by accepting initial losses that would prove to be profitable in the end, and (3) by building the morale necessary to get soldiers to advance despite heavy losses. Victory would come to those who had learned not to avoid death, but to allow themselves to be killed.[33]

All three of the methods recommended by the military were essentially the same and had already been tested – in Omdurman. ➤ **58**

55

1898 In *The Last War, or the Triumph of the English Tongue* (1898) by Samuel W. Odell, there is another professor who lectures on the history of the future. He lives in the year 2600, when the U.S. has 185 states and is a member of a worldwide federation of English-speaking nations that have long since done away with such minor languages as French, German, and Italian. "At the dawn of history there were many races," lectures the professor, but now the Chinese, Malaysians, and blacks have fallen under the rule of their white brothers and have disappeared as peoples or been allowed to survive on mercy. The white race has spread across the globe without resistance. Some of the conquerors let themselves be pulled down to an inferior plane by mixing with the conquered. But not the English-speaking peoples. "Here the evil was destroyed, not absorbed."[34]

The violence with which the Europeans conducted their colonial business for a time proved to be advantageous to the progress of the world. And sometimes no violence was necessary – the blacks of the U.S. emigrated to Africa as early as 1950, in order to settle peacefully and voluntarily in the Sudan.

The conflict with Russia united the Western countries all the more closely. As they were approaching human perfection, the gulf between good and evil widened to such an extent that war became inevitable – war to the finish – war which could only result in the annihilation of the forces of evil. The 1,500 airships of the allies were armed with bombs of unparalleled explosive power and some sort of napalm – "a fire that [could not] be quenched."[35]

Nine million corpses later, the victory was won and the occupation began – an occupation that would teach Eastern Europe and East Asia what true freedom and civilization mean. First the local languages were forbidden, and English was introduced into the entire conquered area. All land not reserved for the original inhabitants was handed over to immigrants from the civilized world. The colonists "acted as a restraining power upon the ignorant and savage inhabitants as well as a guiding influence to their benighted minds."[36]

After thirty-five years of this education, the United States of the World could finally be formed in the year 2600, embracing all countries and peoples. "The dream of the ages had been realized and peace assured to the human race forever."

56

1898 In Stanley Waterloo's *Armageddon* (1898), the Anglo-Saxon alliance is forced to destroy a great many inferior races, particularly the Slavs – "these ignorant, helpless millions, hopelessly pauperized, alien in race, language, and affiliations."[37] The victory is assured by a single genius from America, whose invention for air warfare makes "war into suicide."

"To have a world at peace there must be massed in the controlling nations such power of destruction as may not even be questioned... When war means death to all, or the vast majority of all who engage in it, there will be peace."[38]

57

1898 But is that really so certain? Isn't it true that every superweapon actually tempts those who have it to be the first to strike?

Edison's Conquest of Mars (1898) by Garrett P. Serviss begins where H. G. Wells's *The War of the Worlds* (1897) leaves off. Edison has discovered an airplane that can be flown in outer space and a weapon – "the disintegrator" – that renders all other weapons obsolete. Why then wait for another attack from Mars? Why not take over the foreign planet and, if necessary, destroy it in order to wipe out the threat that now hangs over the Earth?

The Martians assemble a thousand spaceships to defend against the surprise attack from the Earth, but they don't have a chance against Edison's disintegrator. "It was like firing into a flock of birds... They were practically at our mercy. Shattered into unrecognizable fragments, hundreds of airships continually dropped from their great height to be swallowed up in the boiling waters."[39] The commander declares:

"We are prepared to complete the destruction, leaving not a living being in this world of yours."[40]

Edison stops him. "We can't possibly murder these people in cold blood."

But they had already done just that, by destroying the Martian dams. When Edison's men see the Martian people fighting for their lives in the waves, they recoil at what they have done: "How many millions would perish as a result of our deed we could not even guess. Many of the victims, so far as we knew, might be entirely innocent... It was an awful sight to look at them. We were all moved by a desire to help our enemies, for we were overwhelmed by feelings of pity and remorse, but to aid them was now utterly beyond our power.

"Probably more than nine-tenths of the inhabitants of Mars have perished in the deluge. Even if all the others survived ages would elapse before they could regain the power to injure us."

The preventative war has thus achieved its goal. Filled with noble sentiment, Edison returns to be hailed as the savior of the Earth.

➤ **59**

58

1899 The material gathered in Bloch's study was laid before the 1899 peace conference at The Hague. Here there were already some participants who had begun to realize that the greatest future threat to civilians would come from the air. The small countries wanted to be ahead of the game; they argued for a total prohibition of air war. The great powers, especially Great Britain, opposed prohibition. The English supreme commander Lord Wolseley argued the British position: "Dropping bombs from balloons would, if it proved possible, confer an enormous advantage on a power like Britain that possessed only a small army.

"Restrictions on scientific inventions deprive a nation of the advantages which accrue from its scientific men and from the productive capacity of its manufacturing establishments. It can be proved to the hilt that scientific development of engines of destruction had tended (a) to make nations hesitate before going to war; (b) to reduce the percentages of losses in war; (c) to shorten the length of campaigns, and thus to reduce to a minimum the sufferings endured by the inhabitants."[41]

Every country but Britain signed an American compromise, which for a period of five years temporarily prohibited "the dropping of projectiles or explosives from balloons or other airships."

➤ **64**

59

1900 In Robert W. Coles's first novel *The Struggle for Empire* (1900) the Anglo-Saxon race has reached its apex – London is not only the capital of the world, but of the entire universe as well. At the beginning of the 20th century, England and the United States reunite and enter into a union with Europe's Germanic states. The French, Italians, and other Mediterranean peoples die out quickly and handily, and their countries are taken over by the union. Russia and Turkey are reduced to insignificance. Soon the Anglo-Saxons have absorbed the remaining others and dominate the earth.

A decisive factor is the invention of spaceships that defy the law of gravity. The whole solar system is colonized, and by the year 2236 most planets are as densely populated as the earth.

The human race has gradually split into two classes – the talented, who have power, and the untalented, who descend into slavery. The ambition of the talented grows steadily. To rule a province or a country no longer counts for anything. Each and every one wants his own planet, his own solar system, his own universe.

The Anglo-Saxons construct spaceworthy war vessels, armed with terrible weapons, which patrol through space to conquer and plunder. Many crimes are committed out there in that darkness that never come to light. Intrepid scientists build bigger and bigger spaceships, venturing farther and farther into the abysses between the stars. There they finally encounter a worthy opponent, a people who have achieved the same level of civilization as themselves – the Sirians on planet Kairet.

War is inevitable. The Sirians bomb London, but the city is rescued through an invention that forces the Sirian spaceships to crash defenselessly to the ground. Now the Anglo-Saxons take a terrible revenge. They bomb the Sirian capital to dust and ashes, and when their government still refuses to surrender the Anglo-Saxons continue to destroy city after city until they finally get the unconditional surrender they want.[42]

London is once again the capital of the universe.

60

The evil Asian genius Dr. Yen How drools with lust for a British woman. When she rejects him, he decides to take his revenge by exterminating the white race. It is a simple matter for him to take power in China and surreptitiously arrange a war between the great powers of Europe. Then he turns to the Japanese:

"Look five hundred or a thousand years into the future, and what do you see? The white and the yellow locked in a life-and-death struggle for the Earth. The white and the yellow – there are no possible others. The blacks are the slaves of both, and the brown do not count. But these two do count – and when they one day stand face-to-face and say 'one of us must go,' who will triumph?

"Today the whites can mow down Japanese by the hundreds, but soon they will be able to do it by the millions. That is why," says Yen How, "you must take the initiative and surprise the Europeans, while they least expect it."[43]

And so, in Matthew P. Shiel's *The Yellow Danger* (1898), four hundred million Chinese, who rip open the belly of anyone they run across, flood the European continent. What makes this bloodbath particularly horrifying are all of the "sweating [Chinese] women, who, crazy with heat and lust, and the instinct of blood, and the ultimate wantonness of crime" satisfy their forbidden lusts and then, exhausted, go to sleep on the piles of corpses.[44]

The same fate awaits England. Perhaps the navy could hold the Chinese back from England's long coast. But "twenty million putrefying, derelict Chinese in barges floating at random in the Channel fair-way for the next year or two" is not a happy thought. The hero, Hardy, finds another solution.[45]

He selects one hundred and fifty Chinese, gives each of them a little injection in the upper arm, and lets them return to their countrymen. A black splotch emerges on their cheeks, a black foam forms on their lips. Soon the plague has liberated Europe from its yellow nightmare.

All's well that ends well. The extermination of the Chinese is no great loss, since their "dark and hideous instincts" lie beyond the grasp of even the most craven European. The continent falls to the English, Great Britain rules the world, and words like Germany, France, and Russia exist only as postal addresses. To be human now is to be English. ➤ **72**

61

1901 On his way to the North Pole, the protagonist of Matthew P. Shiel's *The Purple Cloud* (1901) releases a gas, the purple cloud of the title. When he returns, he finds that he has killed all of humankind except for himself.

He is the last man. He is all-powerful – but he has no one to rule. He can commit any crime he wants – but there is no one to commit crime against. He looks for someone to kill – but he has already killed everybody.

In desperation he sets fire to London and enjoys watching the city disappear into a sea of fire. Then he blissfully burns Paris, Calcutta, San Francisco, and countless other cities. He suspects that there might be someone left to kill in China and so he journeys there, but he finds no one, and so he burns Peking instead. When Constantinople, too, has gone up in flames, he finally finds a beautiful young Turkish woman who has escaped the gas. An inner voice whispers "Kill, kill – and wallow!"[46]

This peculiar paean to destruction stands as a portal to a century that would burn more cities and kill more people than any century before. Matthew Shiel's global arsonist is, as far as I could find out, the first fictional being who consciously and intentionally destroys the entire world. ➤ **277**

62

1903 On December 17, 1903, at 10:35 A.M. the first motor-driven airplane lifted off and flew. For only twelve seconds, and for only forty yards – but a dream of the millennia was fulfilled at that moment. Finally humans could fly! That humans could now bomb as well was forgotten in the excitement. All of the dangers associated with the conquest of the sky were blown away like mist in the tailwind of the first airplane.[47] ➤ **65**

63

1904 The German was Hermann Anschütz-Kaempfe (1872–1931). In order to realize his boyhood dream, he needed an instrument that could steer a submarine under the masses of ice beneath the North Pole, where neither sun nor stars shone. In which direction should he go? How would he know when he got there?

He attacked the problem by developing Foucault's gyroscope into a navigation instrument, the gyrocompass. At that time all modern navies were having problems with navigation due to the switch from wooden to steel ships. Steel confused the magnetic compasses. In 1904 Anschütz-Kaempfe had completed a functioning gyrocompass, and in 1908 it was installed on one of the most prestigious warships, the battleship *Deutschland*.[48] For the inventor himself it was only a way station. His boyhood dream was only realized a long time after his death, when the U.S.S. *Nautilus* navigated from the Pacific Ocean to the Atlantic under the polar ice of the North.[49] ➤ **86**

64

1907 The time limit on the prohibition of air warfare was extended by the second Hague Conference in 1907, but this was irrelevant since several of the great powers – Germany, France, Japan, and Russia – did not bother to sign.

The most important result of the conference was the fourth Hague Convention, which is still valid international law. Article 25 states that "bombardment, by whatever means, of towns, villages, dwellings, or buildings which are undefended, is prohibited."[50] The words "by whatever means" were added to make the prohibition apply to bombardment from the air.

➤ 75

65

1908 Dumbstruck crowds in New York and Paris saw an airplane for the first time in 1908. Every eye was fixed on the rubber wheels as if enchanted – would they really leave the ground? Yes, the miracle came to pass! "Never have I seen such a look of wonder in the faces of a multitude," wrote a Chicago newspaper reporter. "Everyone seemed to feel that it was a new day in their lives."[51]

Many Christians imagine that God can fly and lives in heaven. In other religions, too, flight is associated with divine power and immortality. So what people saw as they stood there with upturned faces was not merely a new means of transport. In the ability to fly they saw a sign of human perfection, and they received it with an almost religious ecstasy.

66

Flight seemed to be a step into a new element, a new world. People spoke of the "aerial age" and felt that we had now left behind our earlier, earthbound existence and were launched into a new way of life.

Soon human beings would be able to move freely in three dimensions. Flying would be as normal as riding a bicycle, as natural as walking. It was believed that the airborne equivalent to a Model T was just around the corner. Journalists speculated that the big cities would soon be connected by regular airlines, traveled by a kind of airbus that would carry more than a hundred passengers: a bold prediction in an age when airplanes could barely lift two or three people.

All good things would come with flight: democracy, equality, freedom. The air was freedom's realm, where travel went on unimpeded by rails, roadblocks, or stationmasters. Female flyers saw a great future in the air, where old gender differences would no longer apply. When cars were replaced by planes, black chauffeurs would train to be pilots and soon be the leaders of the air, according to another hopeful train of thought.

Mountain air and sunshine were thought to cure tuberculosis. So a period spent over the clouds should have therapeutic value. "Up, up into the pure microbeless air the sick and suffering will be carried and nursed back to health in private sanitoria and state and municipal air hospitals."[52]

Flight would lift humankind from the filth of the earth and create a new life form, according to Alfred W. Lawson, an early adherent of the gospel of flight. He believed in a new kind of human being, the "alti-man," who would be born in the air and live his whole life up there. In this future, the "ground-men" who continued to walk on the bottom of the air-sea would be regarded in much the way we regard oysters and crabs, prophesied Lawson. His alti-man would conquer all the limitations of the earth and become an angel or a god.

67

Other new means of transport met impassioned resistance from people who feared their social consequences. Not so the airplane. No one maintained that flight disfigured the landscape, as the railroad did, or that it destroyed the morals of the youth, as did the bicycle and the automobile.

New weapons – machine guns, tanks, poisonous gas – were sincerely detested by the general public. But not airplanes. The British sometimes feared that their hereditary foe, France, would invade England with troops sent in from the air. But their delight in airplanes conquered their fear. Even when airplanes were used to kill people on the ground, air war was generally considered "purer" and "nobler" than other forms of warfare. Pilots were seen as the duelists of the air, modern knights engaging in a heavenly tournament.

Airplanes were said to preserve the peace, mainly by democratizing the dangers of war. Up to this time, those who commanded others to do battle with each other could feel quite comfortable about their own safety. But in the age of flight they too would be exposed and therefore would be less inclined to begin a war.

People also believed that flight would do away with the very cause of national conflicts by bringing people closer to one another. People who flew would get to know and respect each other. Those who had been divisive and hostile on the ground would live peacefully together in the boundless heavens during the age of flight.

68

But beneath that gospel of peace there were other, darker dreams of the future, dreams of world domination and mass destruction, with the airplane as agent. ➤ 3

69

1908 Roy Norton's novel *The Vanishing Fleets* (1908) came out in the same year that the first exhibition of airplane flight took place over Paris and New York. The book depicts a future in which airplanes become gigantic and are propelled by the inexhaustible fuel of radioactivity.

Old Bill Roberts and his brilliant daughter Norma are drawing close to the discovery of the innermost secret of matter in their laboratory. Only the President of the United States knows about it. This news must not be made public, he says, "for if our secret becomes known, there will be no war, and war is a necessity for our purpose."

Ignorant of the existence of the superweapon, the Japanese and Chinese strike against the U.S. in a blitz attack. The American President knows what he must do: "In our hands has been given by a miracle the most deadly engine ever conceived, and we should be delinquent in our duty if we failed to use it as a means for controlling and thereby ending wars for all time. Let us bear with fortitude whatever reproaches may be heaped upon us, for we are the instruments of God, and the trial will last only a little longer."

Before a single human life is lost, Japan realizes that resistance is pointless in the face of such a weapon and gives up its vain attempt to compete with the Western powers. The unconditional surrender of Japan is a fact. "By the grace of God [the United States of America] has been placed in possession of such power that it could not only conquer the world, but destroy the inhabitants of all other nations."[53]

Of course this total power is never abused. In alliance with Britain, the United States determines that all countries will keep their present borders. No war is allowed. The radioactivity-powered giant airplanes, "the peacemakers," patrol the sky to ensure that the prohibition is followed. The superweapon has brought eternal peace to the world.

70

1908 Superweapons that put an end to war were popular in literature at the beginning of the 20th century. In Hollis Godfrey's *The Man Who Ended War* (1908), the final weapon is a beam of "radioactive waves," which has the immediate effect of disintegrating atoms in all metals, transforming them into subatomic particles.[54] Armed with his superweapon, the inventor, John King, demands total disarmament. Not surprisingly, the great powers refuse. Then King dissolves their navies, sinking them to the bottom of the sea. On one occasion he personally destroys no fewer than eighty-two vessels.

As in *The Vanishing Fleets*, the superweapon is aimed primarily at battleships. It is a uniquely humane weapon, ineffectual against the human body and no threat to civilization. Still, King is afraid that it will fall into the wrong hands. Thus once he has forced every country to disarm, he first destroys his weapon, then his secret, and finally himself.

71

1908 The road to peace is significantly bloodier in J. Hamilton Sedberry's *Under the Flag of the Cross*, published in the same year (1908). Here the superweapon consists of "wonderful electrobombs," which release matter's innermost powers, killing and destroying everything within a wide range. The inventor is Thomas Blake, who lives a hundred years into the future, when yellow and white are fighting for the domination of the world. In race biology of that period, the white race was called "Caucasian," and it is there, in the Caucasus, the homeland of the white race, that the war is now raging.

In September of 2007, the yellow armies of Heathendom launch their final attack against Christianity. But they had not reckoned with Thomas Blake's "inhuman machines of destruction," which kill them by the millions.[55]

With all deference to the superweapon, a real battle has to be won in the end by the bayonet. When the "sturdy sons of the Western hemisphere" come charging, the Mongolian bodies soon writhe like worms on the pointy steel.

The first person to imagine New York in flames after an air attack was A. C. Mitchell in this illustration for H. G. Wells's *The War in the Air* (1908).

The white victory is overwhelming. Millions of yellow men have fallen, yet more millions have been taken captive, and millions have spread over the face of the earth like withered leaves. No one will challenge white supremacy again. In the shadow of the electrobomb, eternal peace holds sway.

➤ **87**

72

One of Jack London's last short stories is called "The Unparalleled Invasion" (1910). Around 1970, the world suddenly discovers to its horror that China is populated by more than five hundred million Chinese. "This disgusting ocean of life" has already flooded Indochina and is now pressing against the northern border of India. Nothing seems capable of stemming the raging flood of humanity. But an American scientist by the name of Jacobus Laningdale has a fresh idea. One day in September, when the streets of Peking are as usual full of "jabbering Chinese," a little dark spot appears in the sky. It grows and grows, gradually revealing itself to be an airplane. It drops a few fragile glass tubes that cause no explosions, and merely are crushed in the streets and on the roofs of houses. But six weeks later, all of Peking's eleven million inhabitants are dead. Not a single person has escaped the combined effect of smallpox, yellow fever, cholera, and the plague. It was these bacteria, microbes, and bacilli that had rained down over China.

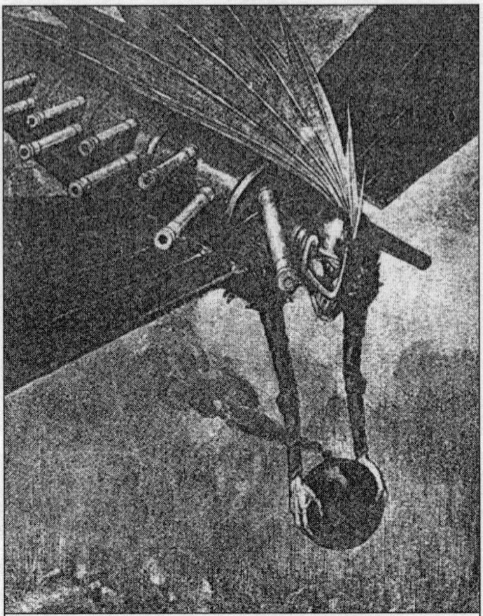

The bomb as the evil spirit of war. From *Conquête de l'Air vue par l'image 1495–1909*, Paris 1909.

The Chinese try to save themselves by escaping the country, but the fleeing millions are met at the borders of the empire by the armies of the Western powers. The slaughter of refugees is unprecedented. At regular intervals the troops have to draw back twenty or thirty miles to avoid contamination from the repulsive piles of corpses.

There is no hope for these millions of people who have lost all sense of organization, all initiative, and can do nothing but die. The modern instruments of war hold the terrified masses captive while the plague does its work. China becomes a hell on earth, where hundreds of millions of dead lie unburied and cannibalism, murder, and insanity reign unchecked.

Expeditions sent out in February of the following year find packs of wild dogs and isolated, nomadic groups of bandits. All survivors are killed instantly. The land is disinfected and new settlers move in from all over the world. A new era of peace and progress, art and science can begin.

73

Hay, Odell, Waterloo, Serviss, Cole, Shiel, London, and many other authors of the previous century – their fantasies of genocide lay in wait for the first airplane to arrive. The dream of solving all the problems of the world through mass destruction from the air was already in place before the first bomb was dropped. ➤ 4

74

1910 Pilot as policeman, bomb as baton – this thought was developed early by R. P. Hearne in *Airships in Peace and War* (1910). Punitive expeditions are costly and time-consuming. It can take months for them to reach their goal. But punishment from the air can be carried out immediately and at a much lower cost.

"In savage lands the moral effect of such an instrument of war is impossible to conceive," writes Hearne.[56] "The appearance of the airship would strike terror into the tribes." And in addition, one could avoid "the awful waste of life occasioned to white troops by expeditionary work."

The air force could simply patrol the land as the navy patrolled the sea. When necessary, bombers could mete out a "sharp, severe, and terrible punishment," which would nevertheless be more humane than a traditional punitive expedition. For the bombs would affect only the lawbreakers, and would leave the innocent unharmed.

This was of course pure fantasy. Hearne's idea demanded a precision that did not exist. When the French sent six planes to perform police actions in Morocco in 1912, the pilots chose large targets – villages, markets, grazing herds – otherwise their bombs would miss. And when the Spaniards began bombing "their" part of Morocco the next year, they used German cartouche bombs, filled with explosives and steel balls, bombs that were especially made not to focus their effect, but to spread it to as many living targets as possible.[57] ➤ 100

75

1911 When is a city undefended? How far away do its defenses have to be for the city not to become a permitted target for air attack? Are troop transports considered defense? Arms factories? Maybe the homes of the people who work in those factories? Or their children?

Paragraph 25 of the Hague Convention leaves innumerable questions unanswered. Since the distinction between a "defended" and an "undefended" city was unclear, the essential question once more arose: Should air attack against targets on the ground be allowed at all as a method of waging war?

In Madrid in April of 1911, the Institute for International Law convened some of Europe's foremost experts in the field to get an answer to that question. The discussion focused particularly on what kinds of injury could be expected when a population was bombed. Paul Fauchille averred that the weight of bombs an airplane could carry was still very small in comparison with a battleship's load. So the damage could hardly be larger than those already accepted in other forms of warfare, and air attack ought to be permitted.

The opposition, represented by von Bar, argued that air attacks were difficult to limit to a specified target. As long as precision was so low that civilian casualties were impossible to avoid, air attacks ought to be forbidden.

As a compromise between these two positions, the following recommendation was adopted: "Air warfare is allowed, but only on the condition that it does not expose the peaceful population to greater dangers than attacks on land or from the sea."[58] ➤ **79**

76

1911 Since the middle of the 16th century, North Africa had enjoyed a relatively independent position in the Turkish Empire. During the 19th century, the Turks lost possession after possession to the European powers, and by 1911 only a little strip of coastline remained to them, between British Egypt and French Tunisia.

Now the Italians wanted to celebrate the fiftieth anniversary of a united Italy by conquering that last piece of Turkish North Africa – the city of Tripoli with its 30,000 inhabitants, and a wide stretch of desert populated by about 600,000 Arab nomads. They thought it would be a military walkover.[59]

77

1911 The war was a godsend for the Italian pilots. Just three years after the first exhibition of flight in Paris, they would now have a chance to battle-test the new weapon.

Everything they did was wonderfully new. One of them mounted a camera in his airplane and took the first air photograph. Another made the first night raid, a third dropped the first firebomb, a fourth was the first to be shot down. Whatever they did, they were pioneers.

The pilots' war was also the poets'. For decades Gabriele D'Annunzio's gospel of violence had fallen on deaf ears. Now his *Canzoni delle geste d'Oltremare* (*Songs of Deeds Across the Sea*), set in boldface, covered whole pages of the Corriere della Sera. The little Satanist and *Übermensch*, whose immoral novels had always been regarded with great suspicion by the middle class, now stepped into the limelight as a national figurehead.

His young colleague Tommaso Marinetti, the founder of Futurism, vaunted the war as "hygienic" and "a moral education" in one provocative manifesto after another. Young poets found nothing more admirable than the love of violence, the symphony of explosions, and the "insane sculptures that our bullets carve out of the masses of our enemies." In "La Bataille de Tripoli" (October 26, 1911), soaring into the skies in Captain Piazza's airplane and observing the bloodbath from the safe distance of a half-mile above ground, Marinetti calls out his encouragement to the Italian troops: "Charge! Fix bayonets! Charge!"[60]

78

1911 Not everyone in Tripoli was so enchanted with the events of October 26, 1911. The day before, the Arabs had joined forces with the Turks in a counterattack that nearly drove the Italians back into the sea. The Italian army saw the Arabs as traitors, plain and simple, and struck back wildly against the Arab civilian population. "The floodgates of

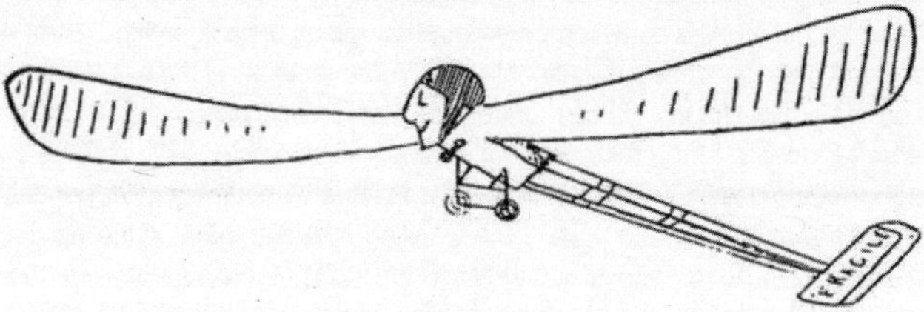

The winged D'Annunzio in a 1911 caricature.

blood and lust" were opened, according to the London *Times* (October 31). "This was not war. It was butchery," said the *Daily Chronicle* (November 6). "Noncombatants, young and old, were slaughtered ruthlessly, without compunction and without shame."

Those who found themselves beyond the reach of the bayonets were bombed instead. The first air attack was an act of revenge. It was directed at Tagiura and Ain Zara, since Arabs from these oases had distinguished themselves in battle. The first communiqué of the air force on November 6 proclaimed that the bombs had "a wonderful effect on the morale of the Arabs."

Three days later the Italians declared the end of the war – a bit prematurely, as time would tell.[61]

➤ 85

79

1911 Thus when the Italians, in bombing some oases outside of Tripoli, conducted the first air assault in 1911, they could refer to international law in defense of their actions. It could not be argued that the air force exposed the noncombatant population or its property to greater dangers than did the army (which had just carried out a merciless massacre of civilians) or the navy (which during the days before the air attack had dropped 152 heavy shells on the same oases). The danger in the principle adopted by the Institute for International Law in Madrid in 1911 was that the worse the attacks on civilians committed by the older branches of military service (and accepted by international law) became, the more – for the sake of consistency – one would have to allow the air force.[62]

➤ 39

80

1912 In the spring of 1912, Stockholm's *Dagens Nyheter* published Gustaf Janson's tales of the Tripoli war, which came out that fall as a book entitled *The Pride of War*.[63] It enjoyed great success internationally. Each chapter looks at the war from the point of view of an individual – for example, a Turkish peasant soldier's or an Italian infantryman's. The last chapter describes the rush of power that an Italian aviator gets from his bombs, soaring high over the desert, one of the elect, unassailable. "The empty earth beneath him, the empty sky above and he, the solitary man, sailing between them! A feeling of power seizes him. He was flying through space to assert the indisputable superiority of the white race. Within his reach he had the proof, seven high-explosive bombs. To be able to sling them from the heavens themselves – that was convincing and irrefutable."

81

It could not be denied that airplanes and bombs were examples of progress in military technology. And technology was civilization. Civilization brought with it the duty to expand civilization. By violent means, if necessary, even with war, if the uncivilized offered resistance.

To bomb a funeral or a hospital, as Gustaf Janson's pilot did, was naturally against the rules of war. But in their analyses of the Tripoli War, legal experts found a defense even for this type of action.

The civilizing mission of the technologically superior Italians was of a higher order, they said, than human laws and humanitarian rules. "When the highest principles of civilization contradict the written laws of humanity, the latter must give way – colonial law rests in its entirety on this assumption," wrote Dr. Tambaro in *Zeitschrift für internationales Recht*.[64] Nobody contradicted him.

82

1912 Bombs were a means of civilization. Those of us who were already civilized would not be bombed. Thus the bombing in Tripoli did not worry most people. The enchantment of the poets was predicated on a complete certainty that the bombs would never fall on Rome or Paris and strike at their own nearest and dearest. Janson was one of the first to see through that lie.

Only a few months after the first bomb had fallen on "some raging lunatics" in the African desert, he realized that even the inhabitants of Europe's capitals could be made into raging lunatics with the help of bombs. Within a few months after the first little explosion, he could already imagine a total catastrophe.

83

One has to admire the progress of technology, says Gustaf Janson's general in his speech of thanks to the pilot. Germany already has 300 airplanes that could drop 10,000 kilos of

RECONNAISSANCE IN ITS NEWEST FORM: THE FOURTH ARM AT TRIPOLI.

DRAWN BY H. W. KOEKKOEK FROM MATERIAL SUPPLIED BY FRANK MAGEE.

THE LAND-SCOUT WORKING WITH THE AIR-SCOUT: A CAVALRYMAN PICKING UP A DISPATCH JUST DROPPED BY THE AIRMAN, THAT HE MAY RIDE TO HEADQUARTERS WITH IT.

When the aeroplane takes flight for a scouting expedition, a cavalryman escorts it as far as he can with reasonable safety. It is his business to act as dispatch-rider between the airman and headquarters. The aviator, having scribbled his notes, makes a rough package of them, and drops them as nearly as possible at the cavalryman's feet. Then they are picked up and carried to their destination, while a second horseman takes the place of the first. Thus a series of messengers serve the airman, who is kept in close touch with his commanding officers. It may here be noted that the airman acting as bomb-dropper fills each bomb as he wants it while he is in flight, holding the case between his knees and the screw-cap between his teeth, and pouring the ingredients in as best he can. He does not start his flight with bombs loaded, lest, by mischance, he should fall to the ground, thus cause the bombs to explode, and so be hoist with his own petard. Each bomb is about the size of an orange, and is of steel.

Many saw the air force as a cavalry of the air. Here a flying cavalry soldier drops information to his comrade on horseback. *Illustrated London News*, November 11, 1911 dynamite on Paris in a half-hour. "In the middle of the night these three hundred airplanes take off from the border, and before morning Paris is a pile of rubble. Magnificent, gentlemen, magnificent!

"Unexpectedly, without warning, the dynamite begins to rain down on the city. Each explosion follows on the heels of the last. Hospitals, theaters, schools, museums, public buildings, private houses – all are demolished. Roofs collapse, floors falls into cellars, the streets are blocked with the ruins of houses. The sewer lines break and pour their stinking contents everywhere, everywhere. The water lines break, flooding begins. The gas lines burst, gas streams out, explodes, starts fires. The electric light goes out. One can hear the murmur of the mass of humanity, cries for help, screams of pain, the splash of water and the roar of fire. And loudest of all, at mathematically regular intervals, the uninterrupted detonations resound. Walls fall in, buildings disappear into the earth. Men, women, children, insane with terror, wander around among the ruins. They drown in filth, burn up, are torn apart by explosions, are destroyed, wiped out. Their blood flows among the garbage and the dirt, their cries for help are gradually smothered..."

84

"We have only to accept with gratitude," concludes the general, "the new and shining tasks that await us. In the face of the triumph of progress I have just described, I do not consider it an exaggeration to say: we are approaching perfection."

Janson knew what he was talking about. The general in question was still unknown outside Italy, but he would soon become the century's most influential military theoretician.[65]

➤ 5

85

1912 After another year of fighting, Turkey and Italy made peace in October of 1912. Europe declared the conclusion of the Tripoli War. But the Arab resistance continued. And the bombs were still falling. Their wonderful influence on morale seemed to take effect rather slowly. It took two decades to subjugate Libya, as the Italian colony was now called.

➤ 135

86

1912 In 1912, Robert Goddard was accepted at Princeton on a research scholarship, and while there he proved theoretically the amount of gunpowder needed to lift a rocket beyond the force of the earth's gravity. His research formed the basis for two patents on the principles of rocket propulsion. But he was diagnosed with advanced TB and could not work more than an hour a day. And the Russian scientist Konstantin Tsiolkovsky was already nose-to-nose with Goddard, publishing his *Exploration of Universal Space with Jet Devices* that same year.

➤ 99

87

1912 The peacekeeping superweapon, the mass destruction that delivers happiness, the total scientific power that, from the air, easily and playfully, finds the proper unsentimental solution to the problems of the world – these popular themes are elegantly joined in Nobel Prize-winner Rudyard Kipling's tale of the future, "As Easy as ABC" (1912).

"ABC" stands for Aerial Board of Control and is the name of a world council with total and universal power over all of humankind. With the help of sterilizing rays, this council has drastically reduced the population of the world to a half-billion – "but if next year's census shows more than 450 million, I myself will eat all the extra little babies," as one council member puts it.[66]

Who has been sterilized? And who has been allowed to continue reproducing? When ABC arrives in Chicago, it is stormed by Americans who beg to be allowed to retain their ability to reproduce. Answer: "Your birthrate is too high already as it is." The crowd can not be pacified. Their "serviles" even begin to talk about reinstating "popular government"! Imagine! They want the old voodoo-time back, when they used to put strips of paper with the names of windbag politicians into "ballot boxes"! But it won't be long before they ask for forgiveness and want to escape from democracy. "Administer us directly! Down with the People!"

➤ **183**

88

1913 The Spaniards dropped shrapnel bombs from the air to punish rebellious Moroccan villages. The premiere took place on December 17, 1913, when the captains Eduardo Barrón and Carlos Cifuentes attacked the village of Ben Carrich south of Tetuan, dropping four "Carbonit" bombs filled with explosives and steel balls intended to hit living targets.[67]

But what happened actually when a steel ball of this type drove into the body? Science took up this question. Experiments were conducted by shooting balls into tomato cans, model clay, soap, and other so-called "flesh simulants."[68] Some thought that the injury was caused by tissue pushed aside by the ball, which damaged adjacent tissue. Others argued that the ball created a cavity in the flesh or had a propeller effect in the fluid-filled tissue.

➤ **185**

89

1914 The first novel to give a more realistic picture of atomic energy and atomic weapons is H. G. Wells's *The World Set Free* (1914). Wells was quite simply better read than his colleagues. Most importantly, he had read Frederick Soddy's book *The Interpretation of Radium* (1909, 1912).[69]

In Wells's book, Soddy is called Professor Rufus, and like Soddy in his own book, he holds up a little bottle containing 500 grams of uraniumoxide. "Isn't it amazing that these 500 grams contain the same amount of energy as several hundred tons of coal?" he asks – just as Soddy does in his book. "If I could suddenly release the energy here and now, it would blow us and everything around us to pieces. If this same energy could be controlled and used as the energy from coal is used today, it would be worth thousands of times more than the substance that produces it."

In the first edition of the novel, Wells clearly identifies his source, and the entire book is dedicated to Soddy. But as Wells's own prophetic ambitions grew, Soddy's name disappeared and Wells claimed for himself the honor of having foreseen atomic power and atomic weapons. Soddy and Einstein had to be content with the Nobel Prize (1921).[70]

90

In Wells's novel, the world war breaks out in 1958. The great powers level each other's cities with atom bombs. Millions die. Out of the starvation and anarchy, a demand for peace grows. The powers gather for a conference in Italy and proclaim a world republic. War is done away with thanks to the superweapon, which has led to eternal peace via catastrophe.

The only unusual thing about Wells's variant of the story is that the Europeans use the superweapon against each other rather than against alien races.

But if you look more closely, you will see that the pilot who flies with the first atom bomb to attack Berlin is no ordinary Frenchman. He is "a dark young man" with "negroid" features. His face is "gleaming," there is an "exotic richness" in his voice, and his hands are unusually "hairy and exceptionally big." In his face shines "something of the happiness of an idiot child that has at last got hold of the matches."[71]

So the white man who attacks other whites with the atom bomb is not precisely white.

91

1915 When the First World War erupted, it appeared from the American perspective as a meaningless European civil war. Five million grown men destroyed by war, starvation, and disease. Ten million disabled. Fifteen million women and children widowed and orphaned. Thus the war is summed up as early as 1915 by Train and Wood in *The Man Who Rocked the Earth.* And still the starving armies go on slaughtering one another. They lie there like dying monsters, red with their own blood, incapable of raising an offensive, but still able to kill anyone who comes near.

The superweapon is the solution. In this case it is a radioactive beam strong enough to destroy a city. The weapon carrier is an atomic air vessel whose source of energy comes from rapidly disintegrating uranium.[72] The weapon's hero, Pax, wants to avoid using it in Europe, so he first demonstrates the power of his beam in North Africa. He levels the Atlas Mountains.

Many die in the explosion itself when the mountain range is turned to a crater, and people far from the target are affected by radiation sickness. After a few days, they "suffered excruciating torment from internal burns, the skin upon their heads and bodies began to peel off, and they died in agony within the week."

The result of the demonstration: the great powers pull their armies back to their own borders, destroy their weapons and ammunition, and create the United States of Europe.

All the resources that used to be invested in war are now devoted to hospitals and universities, schools and kindergartens, theaters and parks. The fear of war is past, and so the welfare of the nations rises beyond all human comprehension. By making peace, the superweapon has also created a paradise.

92

1915 But not everybody dreamed of the same paradise, of course. In his novel *L.P.M.: The End of the Great War* (1915), John Stuart Barney fantasizes about an atomic air-battleship weighing 40,000 tons, called the Little Peace Maker, which decides the war in favor of the Allies without the least exertion. There are no demonstrations of the weapon here – the enormous airplane rains down destruction over Germany day after day, until the exhausted Germans beg for peace.

After the war, the book's hero takes charge of a world organized along the lines of an American corporation.[73] He snorts at the idea of majority rule and equality: "Why should the majority rule if the minority were more intelligent?" He chooses a very limited number to make up the ruling class, called the Aristocracy of Intelligence, and gives them unrestricted powers. The race problem is solved by segregation – each race gets its own continent. If people choose to leave their own territory and settle in another, they "must bow absolutely to the will of those whose hospitality they were accepting." Does Barney think of the white Americans as living on the Indians' continent or white South Africans on the blacks'? No, it seems that it is the blacks and the Jews who will lose their rights. "Nations who had no home, and who had been parasites on the nations of the earth for thousands of years" shall, according to Barney, buy land in their country of origin and settle there.

Feminists are warmly welcomed – provided they have cropped their hair and borne and raised at least twelve children. As far as labor unions are concerned, the hero takes over their role himself. Good workers will be rewarded appropriately, lazy and ineffective ones will be treated like the worthless garbage they are.

This superweapon has not only given us world peace, but world fascism as well. ➤ **127**

93

1915 The principle for what was going to happen in Dresden and Tokyo at the end of the Second World War was already formulated at the beginning of the First.

"The critical point and the point to be aimed at as an act of war, is that at which the fire-extinguishing appliances of the community are beaten or overcome. Up to this point the damage done may be taken as roughly proportional to the means and cost of its accomplishment; beyond that point the damage is disproportionately great: the city may be destroyed in toto," wrote the British mathematician F. W. Lanchester in his book *Aircraft in Warfare* (1915).

But to burn down an entire city, an undefended city far behind the front lines – isn't that a crime against humanity? "There will always be sentimentalists," answers Lanchester. "To these the destruction of a city of 5,000,000 peaceable inhabitants by fire with the scenes of horror that would inevitably ensue, will be looked upon as the figment of a diseased imagination."

For his part, Lanchester considers the destruction of a city by firebombs as one of the possibilities every nation must prepare itself for in the name of military security. It cannot be considered more improbable "than any other hostile act of which an enemy might be capable."[74]

94

An enemy, yes...but what about you, Lanchester? Didn't you just write a moment ago that the destruction of the enemy's firefighting forces in order to accomplish total destruction was "the point to be aimed at"? So you are capable of the same evil as the enemy?

The ability to destroy the enemy's cities is required as intimidation, a "deterrent," replies Lanchester. And with that he introduces a concept that will be of central importance in the military thought of the 20th century. The threat of reprisal will always, he says, have a much stronger deterrent effect than some "pseudo-legal" regulation in international law.[75] But when you have the power of reprisal – won't you be tempted to use it, not only to deter attacks on your own cities, but also to conquer an enemy who cannot yet, or no longer can, carry out reprisals? Yes, certainly, that temptation will arise – properly masked, of course, as the desire to shorten the war and save the lives of soldiers.

95

1918 In September of 1918, the First World War had been at a standstill for four years and the British, in order to deter the Germans from bombing England, had built up a fleet of bombers that far outnumbered the Germans'. The British Air Ministry then wrote to the commander of the air force: "I would not be too exacting as regards accuracy in bombing railway stations in the middle of towns. The German is susceptible to bloodiness and I would not mind a few accidents due to inaccuracy. I would very much like it if you could start up a really big fire in one of the German towns." Firebombs, he added, could be used to advantage in older, more flammable residential areas.

The commander of the air force, Hugh Trenchard, offered some reassurance: "The accuracy is not great at present and all the pilots drop their eggs well into the middle of the town generally."[76]

96

1918 Several months later when the war was over, a demand was made that the German pilots who had bombed London be brought to trial as war criminals. The British Air Ministry protested. Trials of that sort "would be placing a noose round the necks of our airmen in future wars." Since the aim of the British air attacks against German cities had been "to weaken the morale of civilian inhabitants (and thereby their 'will to win') by persistent bomb attacks which would both destroy life (civilian and otherwise) and if possible originate a conflagration which should reduce to ashes the whole town," the application of the Hague Convention in these cases would defeat the very purpose of bombardment.

This was top secret. Publicly the air force continued to say something quite different, just as the navy had done throughout the 19th century. This was the best tack to take, wrote the air staff in 1921: "It may be thought better, in view of the allegations of the 'barbarity' of air attacks, to preserve appearances by formulating milder rules and by still nominally confining bombardment to targets which are strictly military in character...to avoid emphasizing the truth that air warfare has made such restrictions obsolete and impossible."[77]

➤ **103**

97

1918 The people's right to self-determination is a central principle of democracy. But the leading democracies were also leading colonial powers. Their power in the colonies depended on the right to occupy conquered territory, even against the will of the inhabitants.[78]

During the First World War, enemy territory was still considered fair game as war booty, to be disposed of by the victor as he pleased, without considering the wishes of the inhabitants. England, France, Italy, and Russia entered into agreements to divide the Ottoman Empire among themselves after their victory, and to annex large regions of the German and Austrian empires. After the March revolution of 1917, the Russians published the secret negotations and declared a new policy: "Free Russia does not aim at dominating other nations, at depriving them of their national patrimony, or at occupying by force foreign territories;... its object is to establish a durable peace on the basis of the rights of nations to decide their own destiny."[79]

It was the first time a European power had spoken out for national self-determination and against the right to conquest. This message exerted an enormous influence. Finland declared itself independent in 1917. The next year Estonia, Latvia, Lithuania, Poland, Byelorussia, the Ukraine, Georgia, Armenia, and Azerbaijan followed – countries that were then, however, soon integrated into the Soviet empire.[80] Russia retained its power over the Central Asian vassal states of the Czar and continued to extend its power in Europe.

98

The United States had its origins in a revolt against British rule. For Americans, the people's right to self-determination was a principal article of faith. The U.S. had no part in the secret negotiations that the Russians had unveiled.

On the contrary, for President Wilson the First World War was a crusade against the right of conquest. This war, he said in New York on September 27, 1917, is about "whether the military power of any nation or group of nations should be allowed to determine the fortunes of peoples over whom they had no right to rule except the right of force."

The need for economic and military support from the U.S. forced the other Allies into appearing to accept Wilson's view. But it was mere lip service. In practice the right of self-determination applied to Europe only. The U.S. retained power in Central America and the Philippines; the victorious European powers kept their colonies and were also given the colonies of their defeated opponents by a "mandate" of the League of Nations – it was all for the good of those natives. Even to people at the time, the whole thing reeked of hypocrisy.

➤ 184

99

1919 In October of 1919, twenty years after his promise in the cherry tree, Robert Goddard had completed his principal work: *A Method of Reaching Extreme Altitudes* (1920). It is a strictly scientific text, but in the conclusion Goddard cautiously points toward a practical application of his calculations – the possibility of sending a rocket to the moon. "These developments involve many experimental difficulties, to be sure; but they depend on nothing that is really impossible."

These lines sufficed to produce of storm of ridicule in the press. The reticent Goddard's home was besieged by reporters who called him "the Moon Man" and "the Modern Jules Verne." All of America was laughing at him.

On October 19, 1919, Robert stood a little longer by his cherry tree. He was in love, typically enough with the young woman who had typed out his manuscript. Two years later they were married and moved to 1 Tallawanda Drive. In their garden stood the cherry tree.

➤ 129

100

The First World War was waged on the ground. In four months in 1917, the British lost 324,000 soldiers on the Western front. During that same period London withstood two air attacks with a total of 216 dead. The total number of British deaths by air attack for the entire war was 1,400, a fraction of what a single day on the Western front could cost.[81] When the war was over, Great Britain had the world's only independent air force and a fleet of 3,300 planes, which had played an almost negligible role in the outcome of the war. Now the entire military was to be reduced to peacetime levels. Each branch of service would have to prove its indispensability. It was easier for the two traditional branches. They both agreed that the air force ought to be disbanded. Churchill was assigned the task of wielding the axe for the government.

At that point the commander-in-chief of the air force, Trenchard, bet everything on one card: the Mad Mullah in Somaliland.[82]

101

Mohammed Abdille Hassan, called "The Mad Mullah" by his enemies, had long been a thorn in the British lion's paw. Countless punitive expeditions had failed to punish him. Now the general staff wanted to engage two divisions for twelve months in a big offensive against the mullah. In addition, millions would be required to build the roads, railroads, and military bases necessary to occupy the country.

Trenchard proposed to fix the mullah from the air, with twelve airplanes and a maximum of 250 men. Squadron 221, which soon would bomb Tsaritsyn – later Stalingrad – on behalf of the British Empire, was first sent to Somaliland.

Mohammed A. Hassan had never seen an airplane, much less a bomb. He gave no evidence of fear. He did what he usually did when he had unexpected visitors: he dressed in his finest clothes and presented himself, surrounded by his most respected counselors, in front of his house under a white canopy that was used on ceremonial occasions. There he awaited the arrival of the foreign emissaries.

The first bomb almost put an end to the war. It killed Mohammed's counselors, and he himself had his clothes singed by the explosion. The next bombardment killed his sister and several of his immediate family members. Then for two days the British bombers attacked Mohammed and his family while they fled through the desert like hunted animals. Finally they were forced to give up.

Total time required: a week instead of a year. Total cost: 77,000 pounds – peanuts compared to what the army had asked for. Churchill was delighted. He persuaded the government to maintain the air force out of purely economic considerations. Then he offered the RAF six million pounds to take over control of the Iraq operation from the army, which had cost eighteen million thus far.[83]

102

1920 Like other colonial powers, the British had already been bombing restless natives in their territories for several years. It began with the Pathans on India's northwestern border in 1915. It didn't help much just to destroy their villages. But if their irrigation ditches were bombed, their water supply would be emptied and the topsoil washed away from the terraces. Then they got the message.[84]

The British bombed revolutionaries in Egypt and the rebellious Sultan of Darfur in 1916. In 1917, bombers put down an uprising in Mashud, on India's border with Afghanistan. During the third Afghan war in 1919, Dacca, Jalalabad, and Kabul were bombed by a British squadron chief named Arthur Harris. In his memoirs he writes that the war was won by a single strike with a ten-kilo bomb on the Afghani king's palace.[85] Harris would spend the rest of his life trying to repeat that strike.

That same year, the Egyptians demanded independence, and the RAF sent in three squadrons of bombers to control the rebellious masses. In 1920, Enzeli in Iran was bombed in an attempt to create a British puppet state, and in Trans-Jordan the British put down an uprising with bombs that killed 200.

This kind of thing was, only ten years after the first bomb, already routine. But in Iraq the assignment was different. It was called "control without occupation." The RAF and its bombers were assigned to replace completely fifty-one battalions of soldiers, which was what the army had needed to control a country that, during the First World War, had freed itself from centuries of Turkish rule and now refused to accept the British as their new masters.[86]

In principle, the inhabitants were supposed to be warned before a raid. In principle, houses, animals, and soldiers were supposed to be targets, and not the elderly, women, or children. In practice, things didn't always go that way. The first report from Baghdad describes an air raid that causes wild confusion among the natives and their families. "Many of them jumped into a lake, making a good target for the machine guns."[87]

Churchill wanted to be spared such reports. "I am extremely shocked at the reference to bombing which I have marked in red. If it were to be published it would be regarded as most dishonouring to the air force... To fire willfully on women and children taking refuge in a lake is a disgraceful act, and I am surprised that you do not order the officers responsible for it to be tried by court martial..."

What did he expect – at that price? It wasn't possible to keep an entire people in check merely with threats of violence. Churchill wanted results, but he didn't want to know how they were achieved. ➤ **106**

103

1921 The first person to step forward and openly acknowledge what the others were hiding was the Italian Giulio Douhet. He arrived as a young cadet in Torino, the capital of the Italian auto industry, and wrote his first book on the military use of motor vehicles (1902). In 1910 he published a book on the problems of the air force, and in 1912 he was appointed chief of the newly formed air squadron in Torino. The next year he and Gianni Caproni constructed the first heavy bomber, a tri-engine monster created to make bombardment from the air the dominant form of attack.

When the World War broke out, Douhet became famous for his criticism of the way the war was conducted and his impassioned pleading for the use of the heavy bomber. The generals were enraged, and Douhet was relieved of his post and court-martialed. But he was justified when the defeat of Italy in 1917 proved that his criticisms had been correct. Several years later the Ministry of War published Douhet's most important work, *Il dominio dell'aria* (*Dominion of the Skies*, 1921). It came out in German in 1935 and in English in 1942, but long before then it had exercised decisive influence on military thought, not least in Great Britain.[88]

104

Douhet's principal argument is that war is transformed by the technical means at its disposal. Barbed wire and rapid-fire arms transformed warfare on land, the submarine transformed war at sea. The air force and poisonous gas will lead to changes just as great. The war of the future will be total war.

In the old days, civilian life could go on relatively undisturbed behind the front. International law even created a legal distinction between "combatants" and "noncombatants." We have now passed this stage, Douhet argues, since air warfare makes it possible to attack the enemy far behind the fortified lines. It erases the distinction between soldiers and civilians.

Air raids can never hope to achieve the same precision as artillery fire. But neither is that necessary – targets for bombs should always be large.

In order to succeed, air raids must be carried out against very large centers of civilian population. Is this forbidden? All international agreements reached during peacetime will be swept away like withered leaves during war. So let's forget false hopes. When you're fighting for your life – and today that's the only way to fight – you have the sacred right to use any available means to avoid going under. To destroy your own people for the sake of a few paragraphs of legalese would be madness. Air warfare offers for the first time the chance to hit the enemy where he's weakest; poisonous gas can make that first blow fatal.

It has been calculated that 80 to 100 tons of poisonous gas would suffice to enclose London, Berlin, or Paris in deadly clouds; they could then be destroyed with strategically placed firebombs, while the gas prevents the fires from being extinguished.

"The thought is of course harrowing," writes Douhet. Especially terrifying is the knowledge that every advantage belongs to the one who strikes first. So it will not be possible to wait for your opponent to take up these so-called inhuman and illegal weapons first for you to obtain the (entirely unnecessary) moral right to make use of these weapons yourself. No, necessity will force every nation to use the most effective weapons available, immediately and with the greatest possible ruthlessness. ➤ **111**

105

The prophets of strategic bombing were advocating war crimes. Among the states that had signed the 1907 Hague Convention, "bombardment, by whatever means, of towns, villages, dwellings or buildings which are undefended, is prohibited."

But the word "undefended" remained ambiguous, argued James Wilford Garner, when he, an expert in international law, summarized the First World War in *International Law and the World War* (1920).

In air attacks on cities, military damages had been insignificant or nonexistent, while noncombatants had been subjected over and over again to illegal destruction of life and property. Air warfare had regularly done what it claimed to avoid while failing to do what it claimed to achieve.

So new rules were necessary. Garner suggests that air attacks should be allowed "within the military zone," while it should be forbidden "to make attacks on cities and villages far behind the lines."[89] ➤ **115**

106

1922 "What are the rules for this kind of cricket?" asked the newly appointed chief for India's Northwest Province, Sir John Maffrey. The air force headquarters for India answered that international law did not apply "against savage tribes who do not conform to codes of civilized warfare."[90] Warning ought to be given before an attack (so that people could take cover), but on the other hand, the attack should be a surprise (since that would increase the death toll). Loss of life was, after all, what made the greatest impact on morale.

Women held little value for the Afghans, reported headquarters, but instead were considered "a piece of property somewhere between a rifle and a cow." So killing Afghani women could not be justly compared with similar losses among European civilians.

In 1922 a RAF memorandum lists a series of available means of terror: timed bombs; phosphorus bombs; "crow's feet," which maimed humans and livestock; whistling arrows; crude oil used to pollute drinking water; and "liquid fire," a forerunner to napalm. "There was no sign of discomfort" regarding such methods in war, writes the English historian Charles Townshend.[91]

107

1922 The pilot found the Hottentots on a little plateau about 3,000 feet above sea level. "There they sat, warming themselves by tiny fires for they can hardly exist at night without their fires," said the Johannesburg newspaper the *Star* in a report from the Bondelzwart uprising in Southwest Africa, 1922. It was at dawn on a Sunday morning, and the plane carried a full load of bombs and ammunition. "These 'little yellow men' were taken completely by surprise. They had often sought refuge from their enemies here – ten men could hold the mountaintop against an army. But now they were completely at the pilot's mercy." "Bombs were dropping from 100 feet. Machine-gun fire was opened. Many of them tumbled into the gorge...scores were killed. Those who could escape fled in all directions... Now their flocks and herds are scattered. Heaps of carcasses are piled up in the reserve. Huts have been burned down to the ground... The Hottentots, if one may judge from the admissions of prisoners, are absolutely dismayed by this new actor in native warfare... The aeroplane, the natives may find, has made war an impossible thing for them."[92]

108

Several days later, the *Star*'s reporter places these events in a larger context. Now the story is seen as a chapter in the natural extinction of the race: The Hottentot is too devoted to his animals. Every animal he has ever owned is burned into his memory. If his herd is taken from him, he loses his will to live. Of the ten Hottentot tribes, three have already died out. The rest are in the process of disappearing. These days, when societies are formed for all kinds of threatened species, it might be time to form one in defense of the Hottentot, the *Star*'s reporter concludes.

South Africa continued to bomb uprisings in Southwest Africa in 1925, 1930, 1932, and so on up to 1989, when Namibia became independent.[93] ➤ **112**

109

1922 For Theodore Savage and his neighbors out in the country, the first bombing raids on London are nothing more than a glowing spectacle against the night sky. But soon the refugees stream in like huge swarms of "human rats." Driven to desperation by fear and hunger, they flood the countryside. "Women, like men, asserted their beast-right to food – when sticks and knives failed them, asserted it with claws and teeth; inhuman creatures, with eyes distended and wide, yelling mouths, went down with their fingers at each others' throats, their nails in each others' flesh..."[94] In Cicely Hamilton's *Theodore Savage* (1922, revised 1928), England has been bombed back into the primitive state depicted by Hobbes, Malthus, Darwin, and their successors.

Timid little Theo does not turn into a true wild beast, but he learns to hunt rabbits and root through garbage like an abandoned dog, always hungry, always afraid, always on his guard against both strangers and neighbors, for everyone is his enemy. When tribes gradually start to take form, it is on the basis of fear, brutality, superstition, and the hatred of strangers. A wild-eyed fanatic preaches the new gospel – salvation through ignorance.

In the end, the old, helpless Savage is the only survivor of the legendary age before the Catastrophe. For his grandchildren his name becomes a symbol of a dead civilization, so entirely erased that no one knows any longer what it was for or how it was lost.

110

1923 Who is it that bombs us back to barbarism? In Anderson Graham's *The Collapse of Homo Sapiens* (1923) the answer is very clear. It is Africans and Asians who, for some reason, have been able to achieve the technological expertise that up to this point has been the basis for the superiority of the West. Before the novel is over, we have learned that the universities must take the blame for their criminal foolishness in teaching students of foreign races.

"They had even discovered a deadlier gas than ours, and explosives of such power that two or three bombs had been enough to wipe London out of existence." And now the dark races are using this advantage to level the civilization they hate.

The bombers fly so low that you can see the dark skin of the soldiers and their foreign uniforms, you can hear their crude laughter as they drop their little bombs.

"They gassed such as made a stand and hunted to death those who ran away. Such children as escaped fled in mad terror to the wastes and the woodland, where they lost the last tatters of civilisation... In winter they died as the flies do because they had not the wit left to store against its rigours... The tree that has taken centuries to grow can be cut down in an hour."[95]

➤ **126**

111

1923 There is no pretense in Douhet. He knows what it's all about and he says it openly, shamelessly, almost with pleasure.

He was followed by a string of lesser prophets, who tried to give terror a more human face.

The good thing about air warfare is that instead of killing people, we can destroy their economy, writes the British military theorist J. F. C. Fuller in *The Reformation of War* (1923). The bombardment of bridges and railways stops the transport of food and ammunition to combatants. It then becomes unnecessary to kill them. "Thus in the extended employment of aircraft, we have the means at hand of compelling a bloodless victory." Gas provides an even greater means of humanizing war. If deadly gas is used, soldiers will at least not have to be shot to pieces. With the use of mustard gas, men will be injured, but only rarely killed. If nerve gas is used, the men simply fall asleep and can be disarmed without even being injured. Air raids are immoral only if they cause greater harm than ground warfare. The war of the future might indeed be harder on the civilian population, but on the other hand, wars will be shorter and less bloody, predicts Fuller.

Five hundred airplanes, each loaded with 500 five-kilo bombs filled with mustard gas can injure 200,000 Londoners in a half-hour, changing the city to a raging madhouse. A landslide of terror would sweep aside the government in Westminster. "Then will the enemy dictate his terms... Thus may a war be won in forty-eight hours and losses of the winning side may be actually nil!"[96]

➤ **124**

112

1923 In Baghdad in February of 1923, the newly arrived staff officer Lionel Charlton visited the local hospital in Diwaniya. He had expected diarrhea and broken bones, but was instead suddenly and surprisingly confronted with the results of a British air raid. The difference between a police baton and a bomb was brutally obvious.

Had it been a question of war or an open rebellion, he as an officer would not have had any complaint, he writes in his memoirs, but this "indiscriminate bombing of a populace... with the liability of killing women and children, was the nearest thing to wanton slaughter." He became more and more doubtful about the methods by which "an appearance of law and order" was maintained in Iraq.[97]

Soon a new sheik had stirred up a rebellion and had to be punished. But from 3,000 feet it was not so easy to target him specifically. When the bombs exploded without warning in the crowded bazaar, innocent and powerless subjects would be killed along with their oppressors.

Was it right for an entire city to suffer for one man's crime? And was he even a criminal himself? Perhaps the informants who had fingered him had personal reasons to go behind his back. To bomb a city on those grounds was a form of tyranny that threatened to make the British even more hated.

Charlton's superior, John Salmond, made no bones in admitting that the bombs struck at the innocent. But the established political line had to be followed. If the air force was to survive as an independent branch of service, it had to prove its efficiency and could not afford sentimentality.

As expected, when the rebellious sheik was bombed, more than twenty women and children lost their lives. Charlton no longer wanted any part of it. He requested to be relieved of his post on grounds of conscience. Headquarters sent him back to England, where he was forced to retire in 1928. ➤ **23**

113

1924 Squadron chief Arthur Harris was Lionel Charlton's exact opposite. Harris took on assignments with enthusiasm and often acted as a bomber himself. He "was very keen on bombing and he was good." He had the idea of converting transport planes into heavy bombers so that more bombs and bigger bombs could be dropped. But his foremost achievement was dropping showers of small incendiary bombs on the thatched straw roofs of villages. In March of 1924 he reported the results:

"Where the Arab and Kurd had just begun to realise that if they could stand a little noise, they could stand bombing..., they now know what real bombing means, in casualties and damage; they now know that within forty-five minutes a full-sized village (*vide* attached photos of Kushan-Al-Ajaza) can be practically wiped out and a third of its inhabitants killed or injured by four or five machines which offer them no real target, no opportunity for glory as warriors, no effective means of escape."

This formulation appears again in a draft of a report, "Notes on the Method of Employment of the Air Arm in Iraq," which the RAF presented to parliament that August. It was expunged from later versions, which instead emphasized that the air force offered a humane means of controlling ungovernable peoples.[98]

114

Why was it Charlton who protested punishment from the air? Why was it Harris who loved to bomb?

We know altogether too little about them as human beings to answer that question. The little we know is ambiguous.

One of them relates that he was often beaten by his father. Once when his father had been even more violent than usual, something happened that had never happened before. Obeying an irresistible impulse, the boy asked for permission to kiss his father's punishing hands, showering his father with proof of his love. Both the punishment and the reason for it were washed away in the wave of feeling that pain had aroused in him. What his father felt he did not know, nor did he care, "so long as he was allowed to caress him lovingly in this utterly strange manner." These episodes (the first was apparently followed by several similar ones) "were put to an end by boarding school at the age of eight."[99]

With these childhood experiences – did he love to bomb? Or did he refuse?

The other boy was sent, as were most of the children of British stationed in India, to a boarding school in England when he was only five. When he saw his parents again after a long time, they were barely-recognizable strangers. Of his time at school he remembers only cold, hunger, and a sense of total abandonment. But that did not break him; on the contrary, he got used to depending on no one but himself. His experiences toughened him so that even as a child he "developed the equanimity and stoicism of one much older than his years."[100]

With such childhood experiences – was he the only man to protest the methods of the air force? Or had he learned to bomb women and children? ➤ **118**

115

1924 As 1922 turned to 1923, a commission on international law met in The Hague to attempt to formulate new military laws for air warfare. The chair of the commission, the American international jurist John Bassett Moore, described their discussions in *International Law and Some Current Illusions* (1924).

There were two major opposing plans. The British wanted to limit bombing to "military objectives," a phrase which, however, remained undefined. The Americans wanted air attacks to be permitted only in "the combat area," which was defined as the area where land troops were engaged.

Even during the First World War, the term "military objectives" had proven to be so flexible that it scarcely provided any shelter anywhere; during the Second World War it would be expanded still further, until after the war the entire globe was considered to be one giant military objective.

The term "combat area" could be more sharply defined, as an area within firing distance of a particular kind of artillery or a specified number of kilometers from the enemy's front lines. If the American plan had become law (and the law had been enforced), London would never have had to experience the Blitz, the British Bomber Command would have had to sit on its hands until after the invasion in 1944, and the Americans would never have been able to drop bombs, let alone atom bombs, on Japan without first invading the country.

The Japanese were among the supporters of the American plan. But the compromise finally agreed upon by the commission grew out of the British notion of "military objectives": "where a military objective is so situated that it cannot be bombarded without the indiscriminate bombardment of the civilian population, it cannot be bombarded at all."

The United States and Japan were prepared to sign that wording, but because of resistance, especially from Great Britain and France, it never became international law. It remained for a long while a commonly respected – though nonobligatory – point of moral orientation.

116

Would it have made any difference, if the law had followed the moral?

The resistance provoked by both the original American proposal and the final compromise indicates that at least the two camps considered the distinction meaningful. The suggested wording was certainly much clearer than that of the 1907 Hague Convention. It would have been difficult for the British to justify development of an entire new service branch that could not be used without committing war crimes.[101]

And the Germans? The conquered Germans had no air force at all. It was scrapped by the 1919 Treaty of Versailles. The victorious powers were sole rulers of the sky. And not even under those circumstances could they agree to strengthen the convention in order to protect civilian populations.

In 1925, the great powers did manage to concur on the total prohibition of gas in war. That prohibition was upheld without exception between so-called civilized states. It is true that the Spaniards and Italians violated it in Africa, and that many then argued that the prohibition had no teeth and so therefore should be repealed. But the fact that criminals break the law is no good reason for "criminal law to be abandoned," comments Moore wryly.[102]

117

1924 But in fact there were lawyers who wanted to ignore criminal law. J. M. Spaight was a leading British expert in international law and at the same time was one of the most enthusiastic prophets for the air force. "We are in face of a new force of almost limitless potentialities," begins his influential book *Air Power and War Rights* (1924). "It can turn the old, crude, hideous, blood-letting business into an almost bloodless surgery of forcible international adjustment."

To slaughter armies and sink navies are not the aims of war, but only its means. The true aim is a psychological one: "Victory or defeat is a state of mind."

For the first time in history, it has now become possible to achieve this goal without first killing soldiers, who are after all only the armed tools of the enemy nation's sovereign people. The air force will devote itself to breaking down the morale of the people, for everything depends on their willingness to continue fighting.

The operations of armies and navies will fade to peripheral importance. "The attacks on the towns will be the war." The side that attacks the enemies' cities with the heaviest hand and greatest success will win.

This is the situation to which the law must adapt, according to Spaight. If lawyers have not yet realized this, they will soon find themselves defeated by reality. "It is necessary that international law should show itself ready to move with the times, to be practical, transient, conciliatory in face of the new conditions, not precise, pedantic, obstructive."[103] ➤ **133**

118

1925 The British were not the only ones to bomb their colonies into submission. The Spaniards were even more brutal in Morocco. On June 29, 1924, twenty Spanish planes dropped 600 bombs on villages near Tetuan, causing large civilian losses. The Moors responded to these "Christian methods of warfare" by torturing and maiming Spanish prisoners of war.[104]

In September, the German consulate in Tetuan reported that the Moroccan rebels were now being "punished in the heart of their country." The air force blew up houses, burned harvests, and attacked villages with mustard gas.

Gas was forbidden by the 1925 Geneva Convention. In the summer of 1925, the Red Cross requested permission to send inspectors to the war zone in order to investigate reports of a gas war. The Spanish refused. But two German military men were invited to serve for a time with a Spanish air corps "in order to get experience, particularly of the use of gas in air warfare." In a secret report from that trip, the Germans wrote that "Spain was primarily dependent on the result of systematic air attacks and the devastating effect of poison gas."[105] ➤ **123**

119

1925 "All warfare is cruel, and those who engage in it must expect to reap cruelty. The Rifis ill treated, and no doubt in some cases deliberately murdered, the Spanish and French prisoners. The French and Spanish dropped hundreds of tons of high-explosive bombs upon the villages of the Rifis and Jibala. The Spaniards used gas. But in my opinion the most cruel, the most wanton and the most unjustifiable act of the whole war was the bombing of the undefended town of Sheshuan in 1925 – when every male inhabitant capable of bearing arms was known to be absent – by a squadron of volunteer American airmen with the French Flying Corps. A number of absolutely defenceless women and children were massacred and many others were maimed and blinded."[106] ➤ **389**

120

France and Spain divided Morocco in 1912, but the Spaniards were only able to hold a strip of coastline, and in 1921 they suffered a blistering defeat at Anual. Their response was to occupy the holy city of Chechaouen, in which only three Europeans had ever set foot up to that time. Chechaouen was intended to be a base for the conquest of the interior, but soon the Spaniards were trapped there and had to endure four years of siege.

By the fall of 1924, they could no longer keep it up. The retreat began on November 17.

On November 19, the winter rains began and the guerrillas struck. The Spaniards were mired in the mud, lost their materiel, and could not bring out their dead. The six-mile retreat lasted more than a month and cost the lives of 17,000 men.[107]

This was the Spanish Dien Bien Phu in Morocco. And it is also, thinks Ali Raisuni, the reason that Chechaouen was reduced to ruins. The air attack was not a military operation, it was an act of revenge.

121

Spain's future dictator, Francisco Franco, was twenty when he came to Africa in 1912. He spent more than ten years there. The colonial war was the great formative experience of his youth.

In 1920 he participated in the founding of the Spanish Foreign Legion, composed of pardoned criminals and misfit veterans of the World War – an international mix of riffraff that liked to parade with their enemies' heads mounted on the points of their bayonets. The discipline was such that a soldier could be shot for the slightest offense, but was allowed to commit whatever outrages he liked in the conquered Moorish villages.

It was these legionnaires that the German air force moved over to Spain at the beginning of its civil war in 1936. They brought with them all the brutality of the colonial war.

To rule Morocco was to terrorize its people. To rule was an expression of inborn superiority. The people were children who needed a father's firm hand. Franco brought these colonial attitudes back home. The occupation of Morocco stood as the model for his forty-year occupation of Spain.[108]

122

Franco was the last to leave Chechaouen in 1924 and the first to return in 1926 when France had won the war for Spain. He never forgot Chechaouen. It was there that the taboo against calling in the air force of a foreign land to bomb one's own territory was first broken – and the taboo against bombing a city full of defenseless civilians, as well. Chechaouen laid the foundation for Guernica.

➤ 390

123

1925 At the same time, a popular rebellion against French domination was underway in Syria. Extensive bombing went on throughout the autumn of 1925 against cities and villages in the Druze region. Massive attacks were directed against Hama and Suwayda, but a particularly controversial case involved the bombardment of the Muslim neighborhoods of Damascus on Sunday, October 18, 1925. More than 1,000 civilian victims were claimed by the attack. Syria protested, referring to the prohibition of bombardment of undefended cities in the laws of war.

The French held that they were dealing with "bandits," and that the law of war could not be applied to a police action.

In analyzing this case, the American professor of international law Quincy Wright finds

The bombing of Chechaouen in 1925, as depicted in Abd el Krim's memoirs.
Guernica, twelve years before Guernica.

that two theories were used to support the French position.

According to the first theory, Syria, like all other non-European societies, stands completely outside international law. This theory claims that there are three kinds of humans: civilized, barbarian, and savage. International law only fully recognizes the civilized. Why? Well, Asians and Africans cannot have the same rights as Europeans for the same reason that certain individuals, for example, criminals, idiots, or the very young, cannot have them.

"The right of undeveloped races, like the right of undeveloped individuals, is a right not to recognition as what they are not, but to guardianship – that is to guidance – in becoming that of which they are capable, in realizing their special ideals."[109]

It was this kind of guardianship that France was practicing in its bombardment of Damascus, according to this theory, which was embraced by a number of leading authorities in international law.

According to a second theory, international law could not be applied to the bombing of Damascus because the French action in Syria was a domestic French concern. While Syria was not part of France, the French in Syria (like the British in Iraq) were there at the behest of the League of Nations. Part of their assignment was to maintain order. How they went about maintaining order was a domestic French concern.

According to Wright, bombing a city and killing hundreds of civilians cannot be called a police action. That much violence means warfare, and the law of war says that undefended cities may not be bombed. The question then becomes "Was Damascus defended?" Only by the French themselves; that is, the city was defended by its attackers. Thus it was not defended and must not be bombed.

Conclusion: "In the present case the bombardment seems to have been illegal, and France, as mandatory and responsible for keeping order, would seem liable."

This was a conclusion that France could easily ignore, since all of Europe was doing the same as France. They just sent out bigger bombers and kept on going. "For several months, always without warning, airplanes and cannons bombarded the villages around Damascus until, in April of 1926, most of them had been laid waste." ➤ **146**

124

1925 The participants in the World War devastated millions of human lives by fighting their enemies' strength. Perhaps the time had come to try to find the Achilles' heel, to attack him where he is weakest. This is the main argument of *Paris or the Future of War* (1925), by the young British military theorist Liddell Hart.

A good way to break the resistance of the enemy is to "dislocate their normal life to such a degree that they will prefer the lesser evil of surrendering."

The same words had often been used to explain the bombardment of British colonies. "Dislocation," in those cases, referred to burning villages and destroying dams, fields, cattle, and stockpiles of food; in short, the people's means of subsistence. These were the methods Liddell Hart now wanted to see applied to Europe.

"Aircraft enables us to jump over the army which shields the enemy government, industry and people, and so strike direct and immediately at the seat of the opposing will and policy."

One can raise moral objections at the apparent brutality of an attack that targets a civilian population. But a sudden and rapid strike from the air causes, on the whole, far less damage than a prolonged war.

Gas is considered a particularly inhumane weapon. But gas could well prove to be the rescue of civilization. Chemists can create panic gas or anaesthetic gas that would allow us "to reap the fruits of victory, but without the lasting evils of mass killing and destruction of property." We therefore ought not to succumb to the unholy alliance between military traditionalists and sentimental pacifists who are now trying to achieve a total prohibition of gas in war and to limit air strikes to strictly military targets, writes Liddell Hart. Ten years later, both Fuller and Liddell Hart had realized that bombs did not produce an immediate victory. It would take many years to reciprocally grind each others' cities to dust. During and after the Second World War, Fuller and Liddell Hart were among the toughest critics of strategic bombing. To bomb civilians, they now said, is not only barbaric, it is stupid.[110]

125

1925 The American prophet of terror bombing was William "Billy" Mitchell. He had gained his military experience in the bloody antiguerrilla war in the Philippines and believed that flight had created a new age in which the fate of all peoples would be determined from the air.[111] "Great Britain leads the world in this conception of air power," he wrote in *Winged Defense* (1925), and referred to the example of Iraq, where the British air force replaced military occupation forces and "put down uprisings quickly."

Air strikes against civilian populations would soften the impact of war by producing rapid and lasting victories. During the new age of the bomb, the question of whether a country should go to war will concern the entire population, since even those who live farthest from the fronts are exposed to the risk of air attack. For that reason, "the air force will become a powerful agent for peace," Billy Mitchell assures us.[112] ➤ **105**

126

1926 Racism reaches a macabre climax in Irish author Desmond Shaw's *Ragnarok* (1926). The French attack London with gas and firebombs. When the city-dwellers attempt to flee through the flames, they find the city surrounded by African troops who, "with their white eyes rolling in their black faces," slit the bellies of the refugees and drive them back into the inferno. The French officers try to keep their soldiers from killing children, but in vain. "The black blood was boiling and within a few minutes they were running amok amongst the women and children, ripping them up one after another and uttering cries of beasts." In this way the blacks use their "ripping knives" to kill a half-million Londoners, and when night has fallen, they have formed a ring of iron around the children. But their campfires offer target indicators for the British avengers from the air, who begin to "pour down their flaming cargo" – clearly some kind of napalm – "upon the black masses."

"The British planes...simply sprayed into and over the black wretches, who began at once to rush about screaming as their bodies took fire... In vain did they try to escape from the incinerating fire which just...left the stench of charred flesh... In vain did they fling themselves into the Thames, already full of the bodies of their victims."

Soon London lies in ruins. A day and a night bombarded with gas, several weeks of starvation and epidemics – and the civilization that took millennia to build is gone. Only a few survivors remain, and hordes of brown rats that swarm the empty streets. "For the people lived on the rats and the rats lived on the people."[113] ➤ **139**

127

1926 The image of aerial bombing offered by the novels about the future changed character with the First World War. Before the war, the bombs ensured Europe's domination of the world, while during the 1920s and 1930s, Europe feared that it would be bombed back to the Stone Age. But in the tales about the superweapon, the dream of conquest lives on. The only fear expressed here is that the superweapon might fall into the wrong hands. This is what happens in Reginald Glossop's *The Orphan of Space, A Tale of Downfall* (1926). When we meet the Communist dictator, the doctors have just told him that his wife will never be able to bear him an heir. She has fallen victim to the side effects caused by experiments that his experts have conducted with radiation from the air. For twelve months the birthrate in the Soviet Union has been falling steadily. Perhaps it wasn't such a good idea to meddle with nature? "But what could we do? We had to wipe out millions quickly, and it was no use prolonging operations."[114]

He paces solemnly up and down the room. "We must finish what we have started," he says. First find something that can halt the process of sterilization. We need millions of workers to build our new world. We will even need the Chinese for now, as mercenaries. But eventually we will have to deal with them, as well. And then the south shall be rayed out of existence! The British can wait. "We can exterminate them all in a twinkling of an eye, once we are ready to sweep the skies."

The red peril has been united with the yellow. On Soviet soil, 500 million Chinese Communist soldiers are waiting to sweep over the face of the earth like an all-consuming tidal wave.

Western civilization is saved by an atomic spaceship that "lets loose a Holocaust" over Moscow. The skies glow like the Northern Lights, and it is only with the greatest of effort that the pilot manages to control his ship. The human tidal wave that was to flood Europe is no more.

The novel ends with the pilot's honeymoon trip to China. He wants to show his beloved what the atom bomb has accomplished, and so they travel via Moscow. Fascinated and amazed, the newlyweds gaze out onto an enormous body of water – where the Soviet Union once was, the Baltic and Black Seas have united.

The red peril has disappeared along with the yellow. There is no longer any threat to the West. Eternal peace reigns, thanks to the superweapon.

128

1926 Should atomic power remain in the hands of the whites? Or should we share our secret with the peoples of the world? This is a central issue in Hans Dominik's *Djinghis Khans spår, En roman från tjugoförsta århundradet* (*The Trail of Ghenghis Khan, A Novel of the 21st Century*, 1926). A world conference is convened to settle the question. The dangers that accompanied the invention may be greater than the immediately visible advantages, warns Professor Isenbrandt, atomic physicist. For that reason, licenses should be issued only to dependable people, and only for economic purposes. But immediately voices are raised, accusing Europe of wanting to use atomic power for imperialistic purposes. The conflicts seem endless.

"They will never stop," says Professor Isenbrandt. "The gulf between the races is too great. No bridge can cross it. This is a question of a categorical either-or."

Quite right: one day some black miners in South Africa gang up on a smaller group of whites and drive them away "for a trifling reason." The recently quelled revolt in Morocco blows up again. In Algeria, in Tunisia, wherever blacks are working for European companies, the flag of revolt is raised. The whites are defeated by overwhelming black masses. Then the message arrives that the Chinese are on the move. All the colored races unite under the leadership of the Chinese against the whites.

Then Isenbrandt explodes his superweapon over the Mongolian masses. "He watched the magnificent spectacle, his work, with the joy of the master. He was the one who had freed the element and bent it to his will. Even now he was filled entirely with the great task of acting as the protector and savior of the threatened colonies."

"It was wrong," he says sharply, "when our prophets of the past promised the same rights to everyone in the world. Now everywhere on earth the black, brown, and yellow races are calling for freedom... Woe betide us if we grant it! Our power and even our existence would soon be at an end."

The superweapon will be the white race's, and thus humanity's, salvation. For "only the pure white race can fulfill the task it has been given." ➤ **132**

129

1926 The difference between the two space pioneers Tsiolkovsky and Goddard was that the American also conducted practical experiments. On March 16, 1926, he launched the first liquid-fuel rocket. It was propelled not by gunpowder, but by liquid oxygen and gasoline. He described it as "almost magical as it rose, without any appreciably greater noise and flame, as if it said: I have been here long enough; I think I may be going somewhere else now if you don't mind."

It didn't go particularly far into space. Just fifteen meters, about as far as the Wright brothers' first flying machine.

130

1927 In Europe there were some people who were not laughing at Goddard. On June 5, 1927, they met at an inn in Breslau (called Wroclaw today) and formed the Association for Space Travel (*Verein für Raumschiffahrt*, VfR). One of those taking this initiative was the German-Hungarian space pioneer Hermann Oberth, an impractical physics teacher in a little town in Transylvania and the author of *Die Rakete zu den Planetenraumen* (*The Rockets to Outer Space*, 1923). Oberth's disciple Max Valier, who popularized the idea of space in his book *Der Verstoss in den Weltenraum* (*The Penetration of Space*, 1924) was also a member of the group.[115]

The first of these German space books to be translated into Swedish was Otto Gail's *With a Rocket through Space* (1928). He predicted that the day was near "when America, with help of Goddard's rockets, will have the power to reduce London, Paris, and Berlin to ruins without needing to put a single soldier into combat or risk a single airplane."[116]

The one who would succeed in this was Wernher von Braun. He was eighteen in 1930 when he became a member of the Association for Space Travel, which began to experiment with rockets that same year. The money came from the German military, which was investing in unconventional weapons since they were forbidden conventional ones by the Versailles Treaty. Soon von Braun had more than eighty coworkers on a big rocket project.

Goddard kept on working alone. There were two problems that preoccupied him: How could he get the rocket to leave the earth's field of gravity? How could he steer it toward its goal? With help from a small grant from the Guggenheim Foundation he moved to Mescalero Ranch, a few miles outside of Roswell, New Mexico, and there he tested the first gyro-steered rocket. Two toys had been rolled into one, once the top took its place inside the incendiary. It would be a winning combination.

But the stock market fell in New York, Guggenheim rescinded the grant, and Goddard was forced to go back to New England. He writes not a word in his journal about his fiftieth birthday on October 5, 1932, but on the October 19 he notes as usual: "Went to the cherry tree." ➤ 136

131

1927 The interwar novels set in the future often told how civilized people bombed one another back to barbarism. But the novels of the superweapon had the opposite tendency, as a rule. The superweapon creates peace and civilization.

The tales of the superweapon sometimes warn against "meddling with the mechanisms of nature," or letting the weapon "fall into the wrong hands." But otherwise their mood is thoroughly triumphant. Only in some rare exceptions does the author realize that the superweapon poses a threat even to the winner.

An early example is Pierrepont B. Noyes's *The Pallid Giant* (1927), which reappeared twenty years later as *Gentlemen, You Are Mad* (1947). There the peacemaking effect of the superweapon is shown to be transient, since it is based on a balance of terror that can be upset at any moment.

"Science has at last devised a force of universal death – [called] Klepton-Holorif! – a force with which we can, if we so will, sweep from the earth whole peoples, every human being, life itself."

Why would anyone want to use such a weapon?

"I fear not [our enemies'] desire to kill. Even they are not so wicked as to crave the death of millions. *I fear their fear.* They dare not let us live, knowing or even fearing that we have a power so terrible, to kill... All is ready. Thirty of the fastest 'air-machines' have been equipped with Klepton-Holorif. Ere the sun goes down a second time their flight can make all the earth outside of Sra a lifeless desert."

"The blow you aim at them will strike down many innocent; yea, more – beyond control, it may strike back and overwhelm us all."[117]

This argument falls on deaf ears. For the new fear, the fear of the others' fear, can take over even the souls of the strongest men and make them into murderers.

"I, Rao, Ramil's son, saw the extinction of humanity, I saw the last human child die a miserable death... I, Rao, Ramil's son, am the last of my kind. When I see the desert that men have made of what was called 'the world,' I am prepared to die."[118] ➤ 137

132

1928 The hero of Philip E. Nowlan's novel *Armageddon 2149 A.D.* (1928, 1962) loses consciousness in a radioactive coal mine in 1927 and comes back to life in a completely new world in 2149.

There the Han people (the Chinese name for themselves) rule. The few remaining Americans are hunted down like quarry in their own country, where deep forests cover the ruins of once-glorious cities. The center of the world is now China, and America lies at the outskirts, where the Chinese lords of the air keep fifteen cities of glittering glass floating in the sky. A little campaign of destruction now and then is enough to show the savages who is in charge.

But there is much that happens in the great forests that the Han people little suspect. The savages have united and are raising a revolt. Soon they have leaping-belts that allow them to move as easily through the air as they do on the ground. They travel in floating spheres that can stand still in the air. They keep up radio contact with the ground and destroy their enemies with rocket-powered atomic weapons.

Like all true battles, this one too must be finished with the bayonet. The Chinese who were so deep underground that they survived the atomic weapons get their throats cut with knives. "Thrust! Cut! Crunch! Slice! Thrust! – I thrust with every ounce of my strength...the blade on the butt of my weapon caught him in the groin – and from the corner of my eye I saw Wilma bury her bayonet in her opponent, screaming in ecstatic joy..."[119]

"Had the Hans been raging tigers, or reptiles, would we have spared them? And when, in their centuries of degradation they had destroyed the souls within themselves, were they in any way superior to tigers and snakes? To have extended mercy would have been suicide."[120]

Wilma traveled later to other countries that had followed the American example and overthrown the rule of the Hans. She showed sympathy and respect for people of all races. "But that monstrosity among the races of men, which originated as a hybrid somewhere in the dark fastness of interior Asia, and spread itself like an inhuman blight over the face of the globe – for that race, like all of us, she felt nothing but horror and the irresistible urge to exterminate."

There was something inhuman or perhaps nonhuman in the Hans that aroused the lust to kill. Perhaps they were not people at all, but hybrids, partially aliens from another planet. However that may be, "the fact remains that they have been exterminated, that a truly human civilization reigns once more..."

In the 1962 edition, the racism is slightly toned down – "the inhuman yellow plague" becomes "the inhuman plague," for instance. ➤ **186**

133

1928 It was not Hitler who inspired Spaight's sense of an ominous future. Hitler was still a zero on the German political scene. Spaight was thinking of the democratic Weimar Republic and democratic England. The British air force commander Hugh Trenchard, who needed strategic bombing in order to rationalize an independent air force, was of course even more convinced that the rules of war were meaningless: "Whatever we may wish or hope," he wrote in 1928, "there is not the slightest doubt that in the next war both sides will send their aircraft out without scruple to bomb those objectives which they consider the most suitable. I would, therefore, urge most strongly that we accept this fact and face it."

The U.S. had voiced a different position in the beginning. But by now they had been bombing revolutionary farmers in Nicaragua for several years, without consideration for civilian victims. It was time to acknowledge the facts. In 1928 the U.S. gave up its attempt to strengthen the Hague Convention's prohibition against air attacks on civilians.[121]

Bombing as popular entertainment. The RAF attacks a "native village" at an aerial show in Hendon near London, 1927. *The Graphic*, 1927:II.

134

1930 On Valentine's Day, 1930, General Douhet quietly passed away while dozing in his rose garden. But first he managed to publish his last will and testament:

"People weep to hear of a few women and children killed in an air raid but [are] unmoved to hear of thousands of soldiers killed in action. All human lives are equally valuable; but...a soldier, a robust young man should be considered to have the maximum individual value in the general economy of humanity."[122]

Here it seems that the general has reversed the old idea that a soldier should sacrifice himself to defend his mother and his sister. In an air war, on the contrary, he sacrifices his mother and his sister so that he himself, with his higher military value, can live on to do the greatest possible harm to his enemies' mothers and sisters.

"War," writes Douhet, "has to be regarded unemotionally as a science, regardless of how terrible a science.

"Any distinction between belligerents and nonbelligerents is no longer admissible today either in fact or theory. Not in theory, because when nations are at war, everyone takes a part in it: the soldier carrying his gun, the woman loading shells in a factory, the farmer growing wheat, the scientist experimenting in his laboratory. Not in fact, because nowadays the offensive may reach anyone; and now it begins to appear that the safest place may be the trenches."

Even inferior forces can mount a defense for a time on the ground. "In the air, fighting forces are as naked as swords." On the ground, defense has become paramount; in the air, defense is worthless. "He who is unprepared is lost." The air war will be short; one of two sides will quickly take the advantage, that is, they will rule the air, and once this rule has been won, it will be permanent.

"A heroic people can endure the most frightful offensives as long as there is hope that they may come to an end; but when the aerial war has been lost there is no hope of ending the conflict... A people who are bombed today as they were bombed yesterday, who know they will be bombed again tomorrow and see no end to their martyrdom, are bound to call for peace at length."

➤ **140**

135

1931 In the final stage, the Arabs were driven from their springs, out into the desert where the Italian air force could finish them off. For years afterward their mummified corpses were found along the paths leading to Egypt. According to official figures, in 1928–1931 the Arab population was reduced by thirty-seven percent.[123] Of those who survived, nearly half were interned in concentration camps. Once again – somewhat prematurely, as time would tell – Italy's 1911 military walkover in Libya was declared at an end.

➤ **80**

136

1932 That same year, 1932, a group of Soviet marine engineers under the leadership of B. V. Bulgakov sought a patent on a system for "inertia navigation," consisting of two accelerometers held horizontal by gyroscopes.

Von Braun and his colleagues demonstrated their rocket to the military for the first time. It never reached out into space, but fell to earth after a little more than a kilometer. But the charming aristocrat von Braun, whose father would soon be a minister in a conservative administration with close ties to the army, made a good impression on the officers.

Soon the army was competing with the air force in pouring money into von Braun's project. No amount was too great. They just needed to find a place where he could test-fire his rockets in peace.

"Why don't you take a look at Peenemünde," asked his mother. "Your grandfather used to go duck hunting up there."[124]

➤ **154**

137

1932 Noyes's "pallid giant" returned five years later in Carl W. Spohr's tale "The Final War" in *Wonder Stories* (1932). Two superpowers of the future divide the world. Peace is based on mutual terror. One of the sides surprises the other with a sudden,

The pilot's gas mask as a symbol for the high-tech inhumanity of air warfare.
The Graphic, August 18, 1928.

devastating attack. After an equally violent counterattack, the war stagnates. Year after year new weapons are invented, all of the great cities are laid to waste, all life is driven underground, where the people fight for space with hordes of rats and cockroaches. Finally a little hunchbacked scientist discovers the ultimate weapon: the atom bomb. He realizes the consequences of his invention and tries to hide it from the military. But a spy takes the secret to the enemy, and his own country's police torture him until he talks. Once both sides have mass-produced the weapon, no one dares to use it, since both are armed to the teeth.

The inevitable happens. An officer on his way to having his little unit wiped out in the conventional war presses the red button that releases the tactical atomic weapon. The enemy responds. Soon the bombing fleets from both sides are in the air and heading for each other. And now no one can stop the mutual suicide. In order to be effective, deterrence demands automatic and absolute reprisal. If deterrence fails, the same automatic action spells unavoidable mutual destruction. So civilization goes under.

"These plans were carried out...after the men, in whose power-mad brains the plans had originated, were crushed in their deep concrete dugouts. There were no staffs, no governments, only these orders, which had to be carried out."[125]

138

1932 Spohr's penetrating analysis of the dilemma of nuclear deterrence was published the same year – 1932 – that Chadwick discovered the neutron and Carl Anderson the positive neutron, called the positron. Cockcroft and Walten split the nucleus of lithium and derived two alpha particles. Lawrence started up the first cyclotron in Berkeley, and at Columbia University, Urey discovered deuterium.

In 1932 (the year of my birth), the world took a big step on the road toward the future Spohr had already portrayed.

➤ **176**

139

1933 The only consolation offered by this plummet into barbarism is that it goes so quickly. The war of attrition in the trenches of the First World War would not be repeated. The pain would be short. In his book *Men and Machines* (1929), Stuart Chase speaks of "the two-hour war" – "the whole business will be over in a couple of hours."[126]

The gas takes effect just that quickly in Ladbroke Black's *The Poison War* (1933). When England is attacked by air, a wave of terrified people streams northward from the south coast and meets another wave of desperate Londoners streaming southward. The two waves break against each other into chaos and are caught by the gas that suddenly spreads the great silence of death over them all.

I read one of these horror stories as a child. It was *Europe at the Abyss* (1933) by the German author Hanns Gobsch. I remember especially one nighttime air raid on Paris:

"Fifty airplanes arrive. A hundred! Five hundred! Three million people, stricken with anguish, can sense the approach of death. It rushes toward them at two hundred kilometers per hour. From the depth of three million hearts the cry rises: flee! flee!... Past overturned cars, over dying horses, over broken human corpses, the shrieking flood of humanity surged... In the rush, hundreds were trampled and turned into a single pulpy mass... Scraps of human bodies, wreckage from cars and bits of asphalt fly like pattering rain over the boulevards. Streams of blood rise in the gutters..."[127]

Many nights I fell asleep with images like those in my head. Certainly the end would be swift. But that was of little comfort to an eight-year-old.

➤ **141**

Before radar: the engine sounds of incoming bombers are picked up and listened to during a French practice maneuver, *Illustrated London News*, September 6, 1930.

140

1933 In February of 1932, the League of Nations convened on disarmament. Now Germany was once again a participant in the discussions of the great powers. At the very opening of the conference, the Germans moved for a total prohibition of bombing: "The release of war materials of any type whatsoever from airships, as well as the preparation for such action, is forbidden without exception." As an alternative measure, the Germans seconded the American plan of 1922, that bombing should be permitted only in combat areas. Switzerland, Holland, and Belgium objected that their immunity under these circumstances would be nothing more than an abstraction, since their countries were so small that they would be entirely consumed by the combat zone. Sweden and the other Nordic countries supported Switzerland. Great Britain was torn between the desire to protect that most vulnerable of Europe's capitals, London, and the need to bomb the Empire's rebellious subjects. The English plan aimed for a total prohibition of bombing "except for police purposes in certain outlying regions."[128]

Germany, which had lost both its air force and its "outlying regions" in the Treaty of Versailles, opposed the exception. The two sides were at a deadlock.

In March of 1933 the conference took up the question of firebombing as a threat to civilian populations. Not only do incendiaries cause damage where they are dropped, but the fire they cause spreads out of control. The conference therefore wanted to prohibit firebombs along with chemical and bacterial weapons, which have the same uncontrollable character. A resolution of that kind seemed to lie within reach, and they were already working out the practical details.[129]

But in January of 1933, Hitler had come to power and had begun to rearm Germany. It was only logical that in October of that same year, he walked out of the conference on disarmament and withdrew from the League of Nations. Without Germany, even this attempt to redefine the laws governing air warfare came to nothing. ➤ **144**

141

1934 The definitive poison gas novel is Neil Bell's *Valiant Clay* (1934). It sold 100,000 copies with its prophecy that the war would begin on September 3, 1940, with an attack by Germany on Poland, developing later into an international gas war with 1.5 billion dead.

The Soviet Union attacks China but the Chinese air force strikes back, turning Russia into a wilderness, from which a handful of survivors flee westward and die in the ditches or are torn to pieces by dogs that have gone wild.

After ten days, there is nothing left in the entire world to destroy. Then the war is over. The President of the United States calls a meeting in Washington, where the leaders of the world meet in a makeshift wooden hut. Meanwhile, in the ruins surrounding them, a hostile crowd puts up barricades and throws a rope around the narrator's neck. His last words: "Unless war is made impossible, there is no future for mankind."

Gas attacks against large cities were recommended by Douhet and a number of other military theoreticians, despite the fact that international law prohibited the use of gas as a weapon. This picture and the following one depict an imagined gas attack on London. Taken from *Illustrated London News*, February 1, 1930; originally created for *Berliner Illustrierte Zeitung*.

U

142

1934 In the barbarism that follows the bombs, the animal kingdom is ruled by rats. This is especially striking in M. Dalton's *The Black Death* (1934). A group of British vacationers emerge from an underground cave to find themselves the only survivors of a German gas attack. A couple of hundred pages later the protagonist looks down into a bomb crater, sees something moving down there, and suddenly realizes that the entire crater is teeming with large, brown rats. They catch sight of him and begin to climb up the steep walls of the crater.

He leaps onto his bicycle and manages to escape. But soon he hears a dull thud of something that has fallen from a roof. It is a gigantic rat. Another one follows. The rats have taken over.

Even the Germans, who have come to inspect the result of their war, are attacked by starving rats. They take off running for their airplane, but find that it, too, has been invaded by the rats. While Carl gets the plane into the air, Mark takes off a shoe and starts to strike out on all sides. He is badly bitten, the blood streams from his hands, reddening the walls and seats. "They could hardly move without treading on the soft squelching mass of dead vermin."

"England has always been a thorn in the side of Europe. It was necessary to perform a radical operation. And nothing irreplaceable has been lost. We have their best poets and writers in excellent translations. The contents of their museums will be transferred to ours. It was a stubborn race, undisciplined, unmanageable. An ugly business stamping them out."[130]

143

1934 According to these novels, a threat existed even worse than that of the rats. This was the threat posed by the basement level of one's own society, the underclass, the "laboring masses," as the socialists had it, "the dangerous classes," according to the bourgeoisie. The workers in these novels are depicted as so primitive that they are the first to be seized with panic, and so disloyal that their panic could lead to an attempt to overthrow the government.

In *Invasion from the Air* (1934), Macilraith and Connolly describe these events. The novel's thesis appears already in its preface: the bombs' primary effect is to demoralize the people and spark rebellion in the workers' districts. The narrative shows how the enemy planes focus their destruction on the workers' neighborhoods, how they drop their phosphorus bombs in patterns designed to produce the greatest possible effect. The whole district is leveled, 20,000 dead lie in the smoking ruins, 40,000 of the injured and dying are laid out on blankets, rugs, old newspapers, or the bare sidewalk, awaiting the medical help that never arrives.

The workers have had enough now. They break into gun shops, arm themselves, and take over storehouses in the harbor. At dawn the police and military arrive, supported by uniformed Nazis. The military attempts to parley and find a solution, but the Nazis, made of stronger stuff, put down the revolt violently.

The reports streaming into the government indicate that the revolutionary spirit has spread throughout the entire country. In order to avoid the total breakdown of bourgeois society, the war must be stopped immediately, "and all efforts concentrated on the suppression of the disruptive elements."[131] In this way, and only in this way, can the plunge into barbarism be halted. In this cause the government has the welcome support of the disciplined and well-organized Nazis, who are already rationing water, distributing food, and maintaining order in large areas of London. ➤ 155

144

1935 But the Hague Conventions of 1907 were still valid international law. In the 1935 edition of the British standard text on international law, without the slightest flexibility or conciliation toward the demands of the time, Hersch Lauterpacht wrote: "There ought, therefore, to be no doubt that International Law protects noncombatants from indiscriminate bombardment from the air, and that recourse to such bombardment constitutes a war crime."[132] The wording was as specific and pedantic as the law allowed; the purpose was precisely to prevent the total war that drew closer by the day.

145

1935 "Total war" was an expression that began to be used in France during the First World War.[133] Douhet called it *la guerra integrale* (integrated war). The most famous use was in *Der totale Krieg* (1935), the title of a book by General Erich Ludendorff.

Modern war is total in the sense that it touches the lives and souls of every single citizen in the warring countries. Air bombardment has intensified the concept, since the entire area of the warring country has become a theater of war. "The total war is a struggle of life or death and therefore has an ethical justification that the limited war of the 19th century lacked," writes Ludendorff.

Colonial wars were total for the tribes and peoples fighting for their lives, but for the enemy who could easily and painlessly crush them, these raids were "immoral acts that do not deserve the exalted name of war."[134]

Ludendorff belonged to a nation without empire. He saw quite clearly the connection between the total war that the peoples of Africa and Asia had endured and the total war that now awaited Europe. The difference between Ludendorff and Oppenheimer was that the same "totality" which according to the lawyer made total war a crime, in the eyes of the general gave it moral justification. ➤ 9

146

1935 The power of the air force to rule without occupation was greatest on open terrain, especially in desert regions with clearly defined, completely visible targets and little possibility of cover.

In contrast, the RAF failed to put down a 1932 uprising in Burma, where the jungle hid the rebels. In May of the same year, the RAF bombed an uprising in northwestern India, but the rebels spread out into the villages and disappeared. The same thing happened over and over again – as soon as the bombers showed up, their targets disappeared. The only thing left to bomb were the villages where the rebels could be presumed to be hiding. If you bombed them, there would be a storm of protest – if you didn't bomb them you revealed your impotence.

The British press began to take an interest in the way the air force was administering justice. In May of 1935, the *Manchester Guardian* cited a Colonel Osburn: "When our troops enter a bombed village the pariah dogs are already at work eating the corpses of the babies and old women who have been killed. Many suffer from ghastly wounds, especially some of the younger children who...are all covered with flies and crying for water."[135]

That same year, Arthur Harris complains in a report that the governors of British East Africa have been seized by an "anti-bombing phobia," and he hopes that they will "come right in time."[136] And the British commander in India writes to the viceroy: "I loathe bombing and never agree to it without a guilty conscience. That, in order that 2,000 or 3,000 young ruffians should be discouraged from their activities, dozens of villages inhabited by many thousand women, children and old men...should be bombed...is to me a revolting method of making war, especially by a great power against tribesmen."[137]

147

1935 The Swedes hardly noticed the British bombing. But the Italian attack on Ethiopia in October of 1935 awakened their indignation. Ethiopia was the only African country that had managed to retain its independence and become a member of the League of Nations. Sweden had long-standing ties to Ethiopia, where Swedish missionaries had preached, Swedish doctors had operated, and Swedish officers had trained the Ethiopian army. So when the bombs fell in Ethiopia, they were much closer to home for Sweden than those that fell in Iraq or Morocco.

I was not yet able to read, but I remember the pictures and the stories, I remember my father's voice when he recited Bo Bergman's "Holy War," which he knew by heart:

We blow it to bits. We civilize with explosions.
Here lie the civilized, in long, quiet rows.

148

1936 On New Year's Day, 1936, the Italians bombed the Swedish Red Cross ambulance in Ethiopia, and *Dagens Nyheter*, one of Stockholm's dailies, wrote: "That was their New Year's greeting to the Swedish people – contempt and destruction of our work of mercy, death to them who had gone out to support the maimed and the suffering."

That year there was a stream of Swedish eyewitness testimonies to the bombing. Håkan Mörner described how he spread out the giant Red Cross flag over the roof of the hospital to protect it from the bombers.

"The bombardment went on with no decrease in intensity. The circling planes discharged several bombs at a time and raised with a little jerk when they were free of that weight. The heavy warheads fell whining to the earth, bored deep into the ground and, with deafening roars, opened wide and deep craters. The incendiary bombs burst into white, seething clouds of flame."

During the course of the afternoon, eighty-five wounded were brought to the hospital. "It was depressing to see these terribly brutalized people sitting on the steps of the polyclinic, waiting for care. There sat a man with half his foot blown away by a piece of shrapnel; his wife was trying to stem the flow of blood with her shawl. A woman bears a bloody bundle in her arms, a child who may already be dead. None of them complains or cries. All of them stare silently into space and wait for their turn to come into the room where Doctor Mahgub and Abdahllah are working, as bloody as butchers."[138]

149

In December the Italians had used tear gas, and in January came the mustard gas. Gunnar Agge saw drops of an oily liquid lying like a veil around the bomb craters. "When the soldiers' bare feet, calves, and hands came into contact with it, great burn blisters erupted on their skin. Their eyes began to burn like fire and could no longer be opened. A stinging, choking vapor seemed to constrict their throats. Blind and half-suffocated, the men staggered away through the undergrowth and remained lying there until their comrades came later and found them. Where the gas had touched grass and leaves, even at a great distance from the craters, they yellowed and withered, and the smell, carried by the wind, could be detected more than a quarter of a mile away."[139]

150

1936 In May of 1936, the Italians took over the capital city, Addis Ababa, and Mussolini declared the end of the war. On June 30, 1936, Haile Selassie, the emperor-in-exile, appeared before the League of Nations to appeal one last time to the conscience of the world:

"It is not against soldiers only that the Italian government has conducted this war. They have concentrated their attacks primarily on people living far from the battlefield, with the intention of terrorizing and exterminating them.

"Vaporizers for mustard gas were attached to their planes, so that they could disperse a fine, deadly poisonous gas over wide areas.

"From the end of January 1936, soldiers, women, children, cattle, rivers, lakes, and fields were drenched with this never-ending rain of death. With the intention of destroying all living things, with the intention of thereby ensuring the destruction of waterways and pastures, the Italian commanders had their airplanes circle ceaselessly back and forth. This was their foremost method of warfare.

"This horrifying tactic was successful. Humans and animals were destroyed. All those touched by the rain of death fled, screaming in pain. All those who drank the poisoned water and ate the contaminated food succumbed to unbearable torture."[140]

151

During the seven months of the war, the 500 planes of the Italian air force flew 7,500 missions and dropped eighty-five tons of bombs.[141] Mussolini's son, Bruno, was one of the pilots: "We had to set fire to the wooded hills, to the fields and little villages... It was all most diverting... The bombs hardly touched the earth before they burst out into white smoke and an enormous flame and the dry grass began to burn. I thought of the animals: God, how they ran... After the bomb racks were emptied I began throwing bombs by hand... It was most amusing... Surrounded by a circle of fire about five thousand Abyssinians came to a sticky end. It was like hell."

It was Bertrand Russell who excerpted this passage and cited it in his book *Power* (1938). Russell is especially interested in the godlike feeling of power that emerges when one can easily and playfully destroy others from an unreachable position on high. He writes: "If one could imagine a government that governed from an aeroplane, staying on the ground as little as today's governments stay in the air, wouldn't such a government get a completely different view of its opposition? Wouldn't it 'exterminate resistance in whatever manner involved the least trouble'?"

Mussolini probably spent considerably less time in the air than he did on the ground, but he ordered a systematic politics of terror and extermination in Ethiopia. Hundreds of villages were burned, and survivors were shot on the mere suspicion of rebellious views. Young intellectuals were killed methodically in order to make the country easier to govern. The first generation of Ethiopian elementary schoolteachers was practically wiped out. The massacres from the air and on the ground followed one after another during the five years that Italian power in Ethiopia lasted.[142]

152

1937 When did the Second World War actually begin? Was it on September 18, 1931, when the Japanese attacked China and turned the northeastern Chinese province into the Japanese vassal state Manchukuo? Or was it in March of 1932, when the Japanese air force suddenly bombed Shanghai and caused several thousand civilian deaths? Or perhaps in January of 1933, when the Japanese occupied northern China all the way down to Beijing and Tientsin?

The Japanese called the war "the China incident." From the European perspective, all of that happened much too far away to be considered a world war. The world was in Europe. But when the Japanese attacked the railway station in Nantao on August 26, 1937, and not only killed hundreds of civilian Chinese, but also wounded the British ambassador, Sir Hughe Knatchbull-Huggesson, it did make an impression.

In its official protest, the British Foreign Office said: "Such events are inseparable from the practice, illegal as it is inhumane, of failing to draw that clear distinction between combatants and noncombatants in the conduct of hostilities, which international law, no less than the conscience of mankind, has always enjoined."[143]

Two young poets by the names of Auden and Isherwood discovered this war. Many years later I found their description of their journey in a used bookshop in Beijing. Here is how they describe the victims of an air attack: "Over by the...gate lay five civilian victims on stretchers, waiting for their coffins to arrive. They were terribly mutilated and very dirty, for the force of the explosion had tattooed their flesh with gravel and sand. Beside one corpse was a brand-new, undamaged straw hat. All the bodies looked very small, very poor, and very dead, but, as we stood beside one old woman, whose brains were soaking obscenely through a little towel, I saw the blood-caked mouth open and shut, and the hand beneath the sack-covering clench and unclench. Such were the Emperor's birthday presents."[144]

153

Even if the actions of the Japanese and the Italians excited indignation, the image of the world as seen in *The Clipper of the Clouds* remained intact. A quarter-century after the first bombing attack, it was still Africans, Arabs, or Chinese who were bombed, while we Europeans could still look up at the airplanes in the sky with the certain knowledge that nothing bad would happen to us. We were already civilized.

But under the surface calm, evil dreams began to rise. The character of our fantasies changed. Before there were airplanes, we had dreamed of triumph through bombing other races, other planets, other solar systems. But now that we really were bombing other races, we had nightmares of being bombed ourselves. ➤ 7

154

In May of 1937, Peenemünde was ready, with 350 employees. The crucial problem was navigation, which also included stabilization. Without a certain primitive navigation capability they could not get the rocket up into the air at all. Von Braun presented the problem to the Kreiselgeräte (Gyroinstrument) Company, which made Anschütz-Kaempfe's compasses for the navy and autopilots for flight. The company invented a steering mechanism called Sg 33, with the sole function of holding the rocket to a vertical course. Where it fell was its own business. Little wagons on rails measured the acceleration. Jet vanes guided the rocket laterally.

In December of 1937, 120 military top brass gathered for another demonstration of the rocket, which was put off day after day because of rain and cold. Meanwhile mice gnawed through the electric cables and caused constant short-circuits. Finally the rocket *Deutschland* could be launched. It crashed after twenty seconds. The same thing happened with the next three. The control system was too weak; the rockets rotated in the air.

The next year New England was devastated by a hurricane that blew down thousands of trees. Goddard's journal: "Cherry tree down. Have to carry on alone." ➤ 195

155

During the 1920s, novels about the future often dealt with a time of barbarism after the conclusion of a war. The novels of the '30s, on the other hand, exhibit a clearly prewar character; they warn of the barbarism that will follow a war that they see in the making. The closer we approach the outbreak of war in 1939, the more frequently the moral question is posed: "Do we have the right to cast ourselves and all of humanity into this abyss?"

In *The Day of Wrath* (1936) by Irishman Joseph O'Neill, firebombs transform the cities of Europe into furnaces where entire populations are cremated at 3,000 degrees centigrade. Nor is Japan spared: "One squadron of poison-bombers will wipe out a million of these Yellow brutes in Tokyo alone inside ten minutes... The destruction of Tokyo would come," thinks the hero, "but the murder of millions of helpless Japanese women and children would not give me back my beloved."[145]

If the destruction of Tokyo was murder, who were the murderers?

Every man who drops a bomb is guilty, answers Captain A. O. Pollard in *Air Reprisal* (1938). Either they are asinine enough to put their fate in another man's hands and let him decide for them, or they really want to kill women and children in order to satisfy some hidden desire. In either case, they must be held responsible for their actions. "If he were able, he would punish every one of them for a ghastly crime against humanity."[146]

What does he mean, "crime against humanity"? According to what law? Applicable to what color of skin? ➤ 8

156

1937 The Germans dropped millions of bombs in Spain during the Civil War in 1936–1939. A few thousand of them fell over Guernica. So why was it these 5,771 bombs that made history?

Perhaps, paradoxically enough, because the city was so little. Most of the German air raids were carried out against large centers like Madrid and Barcelona, which could not be destroyed by twenty-nine tons of bombs. What was the loss of 271 houses to the great Madrid? But when the same number of houses was destroyed in Guernica it meant that the entire center of the city was leveled. The destruction was total.

This is not the entire explanation, for several other small cities were bombed without becoming famous. Several miles from Guernica lies Durango, which had been attacked from the air already in March of 1937 and then again repeatedly attacked at the beginning of April. The number of civilian victims was as great as in Guernica. Why didn't Durango become a symbol?

"Our town was considered a coarse industrial city," say the people of Durango today. "Guernica already had a special position as the capital city of the Basques, where they would convene under the holy oak. The destruction of Guernica became a symbol because Guernica was a symbol already."[147]

157

1937 Another decisive factor was that a number of foreign correspondents happened to be in the vicinity and got to Guernica before Franco's troops. The most influential was George Steer's report in the London *Times*.[148] In order to stress its importance, the newspaper put it on the editorial page.

Steer describes how he arrives at two o'clock in the morning in a city aflame, where the streets are impassable and house after house falls into a fiery wreck. The only military targets – a little armament factory and two barracks – lie outside the city and are untouched.

The only goal of the attack seems to have been to terrorize the civilian population and destroy the cradle of Basque culture. In fact, the Germans were ignorant of the city's cultural significance. For them, Guernica was an unimportant site for an experiment, a place where they were testing a particular blend of incendiary, high-explosive, and splinter bombs.

158

1937 On April 28, the same day on which the report in *The Times* appeared, Stockholm's *Dagens Nyheter* put Guernica in a single column at the bottom of the front page, beaten out by "Deadly Finale to a Jönköping Appendectomy" and "Customs Classifies Camels as Ruminants." Buried inside the newspaper was the destruction of an entire city and the loss of hundreds of lives – Guernica transformed into a smoking ruin. Bolivar, Arbadegue, and Guerricalz are also mentioned. "The civilian population and the government troops have suffered great losses in dead and wounded. Altogether three cities have been laid in ruins." Guernica was as yet only one among several bombed cities.

But when the newspaper returns to the subject a few days later under the headline "The Spanish Tragedy," it is Guernica and only Guernica that takes the spotlight. The air attack is described as "the most gruesome episode in the history of modern warfare."[149]

159

The image of a peaceful little town suddenly surprised by the inferno of war, of an ancient culture desecrated by flying vandals – even those images might soon have been forgotten had the Fascist and Nazi propaganda machines not attempted a coverup. For five days the media were kept out of Guernica while Franco's troops cleared away all traces of the German presence. Then the journalists were served up a new version of what had happened, a version which during the Franco regime reigned as the official story: there never was an air raid; "the Reds" had burned down their own city.

The coverup continued to fan the flames of the Guernica debate. Even as late as the 1960s, Gunnar Unger of *Svenska Dagbladet* was trying to pass off Franco's lies, giving Ulf Brandell, the foreign news editor for *Dagens Nyheter*, good cause to report the latest findings of the Institute for Contemporary History in Munich. Thus lies keep the truth alive.[150]

160

The truth about Chechaouen required no coverup. Bombing natives was considered quite natural. The Italians did it in Libya, the French did it in Morocco, and the British did it throughout the Middle East, in India, and East Africa, while the South Africans did it in Southwest Africa. Will any ambassador ever ask forgiveness for that? Of all these bombed cities and villages, only Guernica went down in history. Because Guernica lies in Europe. In Guernica, *we* were the ones who died.

161

Throughout the interwar years, the fear in Europe grew – the fear of a new kind of war, a war that would suddenly strike like lightning from a clear sky at peaceful, unarmed people.

Guernica gave a name to that fear.

Here is a prophecy from the year of my birth, 1932, uttered by the Tory party leader Stanley Baldwin: "In the next war you will find that any town within reach of an aerodrome can be bombed within the first five minutes of war to an extent inconceivable in the last war... The only defence is in offence, which means that you have to kill more women and children more quickly than the enemy if you want to save yourselves."[151]

Douhet himself could not have put it more succinctly.

A number of military experts were already portraying the notion of sparing civilians as absurd and antiquated. The supposed immunity of civilians was, according to M. W. Royse in *Aerial Bombardment* (1928), quite simply a function of the artillery's limited range. Now that flight had extended that range enormously, there was no reason to limit warfare to those who could defend themselves.

The destruction of Guernica made such a huge impression because it was precisely what everyone was waiting for.

162

1937 In Paris, Pablo Picasso was waiting. Already, in January of 1937, he had taken on the assignment of a large painting for the Spanish pavilion at Expo '37. The date for the opening ceremonies was approaching, and Picasso had not yet put brush to canvas. Guernica gave him his subject. He read a translation in *L'Humanité* of George Speer's reportage in the London *Times*, and on the first of May he began to paint the picture that would, more than anything else, make the name "Guernica" known throughout the world.[152]

The painting was hung in Paris while the air in Guernica was still acrid with smoke.

163

Chechaouen had no Picasso. There was not even a camera there to record the destruction. Among the tens of thousands of documents collected by Ali Raisuni, there is not one single image of Chechaouen after the bombing.

164

1938 During the fall, Picasso's *Guernica* moved on to Oslo and Copenhagen, and in March of 1938, the painting was exhibited in Stockholm. This exhibition was a sufficiently remarkable occurrence that a suburban elementary schoolteacher brought his son (me) along for a trip to the city.

The tragedy of modern art is, wrote a leading Swedish critic, Gotthard Johansson, that it has detached itself so completely from human society, even from the human being. This became especially clear when modern art, like Picasso's *Guernica*, tried for once to grasp a reality beyond art. "By the time the viewer has managed to solve the complex riddle of the image, he has long since forgotten the Spanish Civil War... If Picasso's image of Guernica is capable of exciting any indignation, it will more likely be against modern art than against Franco."[153]

➤ 293

165

1939 The Japanese were hardly innocent victims. On the contrary, they began the Second World War with their unprovoked attack on China. They began the strategic bombing war by dropping incendiary bombs in 1939 on China's provisional capital, Chungking, which lay far from all combat areas. An eyewitness reports to *The Times*:

> "The bombing was the worst exhibition of cold-blooded mass murder that the Japanese have so far been able to perpetrate... The areas infected were raging infernos. I never saw anything like it. Most of the houses which climb the hillsides are made of timber, perched on long piles. They burned like tinder. The phosphorus kept the fires raging and a breeze extended them... Three quarters of a square mile of houses were in flames... The cries and shrieks of the dying and the wounded resounded in the night, muffled only by the incessant roar of the ever-hungry fire. Hundreds tried to escape by climbing the old city wall but were caught by the pursuing flames, and, as if by magic, shrivelled into cinders."[154]

"It is the continuous nature of the terror that has the most killing impact on morale," reported Edgar Snow from Chungking. But air attacks can also have a boomerang effect. "They quite simply ensured that the will to resist hardened among the great mass of people, they made the enemy more tangible and drove people closer together... Extensive and indiscriminate bombing of civilian centers kill relatively few people: the victims of Japanese raids during a period of three years was less than 200,000. But they arouse a completely *personal* hate that no one can really understand who has not huddled in a cellar or burrowed his face into a field to escape dive bombers or seen a mother search for her son's torn-off head or smelled the stench of burned schoolchildren."

This was how it began – many years before a single incendiary bomb had fallen on Japan. And so it continued. Americans who had served in China often were especially eager to give the Japanese a taste of their own medicine. One of them was Curtis E. LeMay.

➤ 223

166

1939 When the Second World War broke out on the first of September in 1939, I was seven years old and had just started school. Suddenly I realized that my father was already an old man. He didn't even know how to put out a firebomb. He wouldn't be able to get out of the cellar of a house that had collapsed, he had no idea how to hide in the forest and dig down into the snow. He was stuck back in the First World War, and if I wanted to survive the second one, the responsibility would be all mine.

167

I had only been going to school for a few days, so it required a concerted effort to work out the war headlines in the newspapers. One of the first books I tackled was *Air Attack! What Should I Do?* I learned to read in order to find an answer to that question. It was a matter of life and death. I remember the picture on the cover: a mother and child in silhouette against bombed-out ruins. And today when I find the little pamphlet in the collections of the Royal Library, I recognize immediately the Rosengren Safe Company's advertisements for steel doors. "Above: Airtight door with rubber seal. Below: Bulletproof door, sold with or without rubber seal."

I nagged at my father, begging for a door like that, mangling the words for the new military terminology. I wanted a door complete with steel flames, rudder seals, air-blocks, and, by special order, a peephole covered with shatterproof glass.

168

We would have to try to survive in the laundry room. The basement laundry room had a huge cast-iron washtub where two enormous women boiled the laundry over a wood fire. These ladies arrived a couple of times a year to do a big wash in a cloud of white steam. The room also had a cement basin where the laundry was soaked the night before the big wash, and later, once it had been boiled, was scrubbed on a board, rinsed, and wrung out.

The laundry room was the basement's innermost chamber, a space that had been blasted out of the mountain and thus offered a certain amount of protection from bombs. But of course the basement windows first had to be secured with sandbags, and of course we had to have an axe and a crowbar in the shelter so that we could get out when the house collapsed on top of us and of course we had to have emergency supplies in case we were trapped for a few weeks, and wet blankets in case the house caught fire, and sand and shovels and a fire-extinguisher, and most important of all – we had to have that door from Rosengrens, preferably an airtight one to protect against gas attacks, but at least a bulletproof one, we just had to have it. But my father didn't understand that.

He thought the war would come marching in, just like in the old days, slowly but surely. He didn't understand that war these days would fall from the skies, without warning, in the middle of the night. I was the one who knew that, and I lay awake nights waiting for it until I fell asleep.

169

1939 A horse and wagon attracted no particular attention on Långbrodals Road. That was the usual means of transport. But if, on the other hand, a car came by, we rushed to the fence for a look. Cars were not fueled by gasoline, but by a gas produced by burning birch wood in a kind of stove fastened to the back of the car. This gas was

Flyganfall!
Hur skall jag handla?
ÅKE KRETZ

I learned to read in order to survive. Here is the cover of the book I used. The typography, language, and message – all of it seemed matter-of-course and inalterable.

extremely poisonous. The fuel commission had a special office, the wood gas office, which ruled on compensation for injury from wood gas. I had my first summer job in that office.

It was almost impossible to imagine that the world would ever be any different from the way it was. It was taken for granted that a crackling, rasping voice would reach us through headphones via a "crystal set." That was the way the world sounded. Only one person at a time could listen to it, and the news was always too important for me to have a turn. Just after the beginning of the war we bought a family radio with a façade like a stained-glass rose window in a church. In the middle of the rose sat a wheel with a knob. That was what we used to tune in to the stations. Everyone had a radio like that. It was taken for granted that radios looked that way. The dark brown finish and the sacred form suited *the stormy times* that unfortunately had cast their influence even as far as *our calm and peaceful nation*, where the task of the air defense was to assist in *times fraught with danger*, to relieve *the horrors of war* and to instill *confidence and trust*, so

This was the kind of door you had to have. It shut the war outside.

that our people, *without being forced to their knees*, could survive the *horrors of an air attack on the homeland.*

That was the language of the times, taken just as much for granted as the radio it came from or the typography that set it on paper. What is currently taken for granted is at any given moment practically impenetrable. It demands an extraordinary force of effort to realize that a thousand other "nows" were once taken just as much for granted, and that yet another thousand "nows" that never were could be.

It is even more difficult to understand that the "now" we happen to be experiencing is just as coincidental and transient as 1939's "now" once was.

170

So there I lay in my "tourist cot," as it was, taken-for-grantedly, called, dressed in my taken-for-granted plaid pullover, my taken-for-granted knickers, and my just-as-taken-for-granted knee socks, laboriously spelling my way, letter by letter, through the first chapter of Police

Commissioner Kretz's handbook.

> Chap-ter 1. WAR AT HOME. Mis-sus Berg-gren toss-es and turns un-eas-i-ly in her bed. Al-though the dawn draws nigh, she has not yet slept a wink. At any mo-ment the si-rens can sound...

Of course I often made mistakes in the beginning, dropped letters or switched them around. In particular, I saw *barn* (Swedish for "child" or "children") everywhere. When it said *bombarna* (the bombers) I read *bombbarna* (the bomb-children) and could see the children before me. When I saw *brandpatrullen* (the fire patrol) or *brandbomber* (fire bombs) I switched the "r" and the "a" so that "fire" became "child," and everything was happening to me, the *barn*, the child.

171

The handbook continues:

> In the doorway of the air shelter stands Air Warden Berg, counting his charges. Berg has become an enormously important man since the beginning of the air war. He has prepared a provisional shelter in the laundry room. In case the house should collapse, he has set up wooden beams here and there, which, with one end set in the basement floor and the other against the ceiling, should be able to support the extra weight. (*Why hadn't we propped up the roof in our laundry room?*) He has bricked up the basement windows to keep shrapnel out. (*Is it safe enough to have sandbags in front of the windows? Or is it safer to brick them up?*) In the doorway, where Berg has taken up his position, there is a large wooden box filled with a floury substance. It is chloride of lime. (*Why didn't we have any chloride of lime?*) People who enter the shelter after the beginning of the attack first have to step in the box and coat their soles. One can never be sure that they might not have unknowingly stepped in mustard gas.
>
> During the air attack, the alarm bell at the entrance to the basement starts ringing. It is the two *brandposterna* (fire spotters; but I read *barndposterna*, of course – child spotters) in the attic who are calling for help. Berg and his boys (*boys*!) grab their steel helmets and gas masks and disappear up the stairs. When they come back they are sooty but satisfied: "We took care of that, all right," says the oldest Johansson boy. The men are stormed from all sides with questions and... (*Men! I guess if you've put out an incendiary bomb in the attic you're not "Berg and the boys" anymore, but one of the "men."*)

The war offered a shortcut to adult status – but only for the child who could overcome his fear. Only for the child who could hear "Bang, you're dead!" and dare to answer "OK, you got me."

172

Those who, like rats, await their fate in the hole of the air shelter, see nothing of the majesty of war – if there is such a thing. Anguished waiting is their lot. The fighting troops are usually spread out and dug in. Air attacks against them have little effect. But big cities, on the other hand, offer fantastic targets. The destruction per dropped bomb on the home front is greater than that on the military front. All right, says the military, let's attack the home front. So are we left exposed to the tender mercies of the enemy? No, it's not quite that bad. It can with confidence be stated that no mass murder from the air is possible, as long as the air defense is well enough organized.

Every home fire guard, in order to be able to battle incoming fire bombs should have ready at least one mechanical pump with foot treadle (*we had one*), a long-handled cement shovel (*we had one of those, too*), plus a long-handled broom (*but where was our broom?*). In the attic there should be three galvanized steel buckets full of water plus a wooden box filled with a cubic meter of sand.

The most dangerous fire bomb is the phosphorus bomb. Phosphorus ignites on contact with air. Its area of impact is extremely large, as burning drops of phosphorus fly off at wide range. These drops cause deep sores that are difficult to heal and ought to be bathed at once with a solution of sodium bicarbonate. (*Did we have sodium bicarbonate? Where was it?*)

The fire corps will not have time to fight all outbreaks of fire during a raid. Therefore a few alert and resourceful individuals in each building should always be prepared to disable or put out fire bombs. A good post for them would be the attic stairs. The members of the fire patrol are heroes. They put themselves at risk for dangers just as great as those experienced by soldiers at the front.

If they are not able to extinguish the bomb, first the block warden should be notified, then the nearest police station. The appropriate police authority will then assess the necessity of assigning fire corps departments from the general air defense unit. It is, on the other hand, forbidden for the general public to summon the fire corps during the raid by means of the emergency system.

The most important thing is to avoid panic. The air defense warden is responsible for ensuring that the residents of his building adopt appropriate air-raid conduct. From the perspective of the national Department of Defense, panic is more dangerous than any other effect produced by air raids. It is not the dead who are in danger of succumbing to the demands of the attacker, but the terrified.

173

So it was, taken for granted. I got up and walked into the kitchen, still dressed in my knickers and knee socks, to get a glass of milk. Not from the refrigerator, because they didn't exist yet, but from the taken-for-granted icebox. And not from a carton, because they didn't exist yet, but from the taken-for-granted pitcher. And not the homogenized skim milk I drink today, because that didn't exist yet, but the taken-for-granted cow's milk from the taken-for-granted barn on Långbro Farm. Of everything that was taken for granted about "getting a glass of milk," something still taken for granted today, only the glass itself is left as a taken-for-granted.

And even the magical 'taken-for-grantedness' of the words I read has vanished. What at that time was an expression of a taken-for-granted consciousness of the severity of the situation now appears as a cynical proof that from the perspective of the national Department of Defense, it is better that women and children die than that they become hysterical and create panic.

Bang, you're dead. It's for the best.

I understood this all too well. It was quite simply not permissible to be as frightened as I was. And especially since already in advance, long before anything had happened, I was so terribly little and afraid. It was a foregone conclusion. I agreed with it. I even liked it. It gave me a sense of sacrifice and dignity that was exuberantly taken for granted. You got me, I'm dead. Better to die than to allow my fear to infect those who had to be heroes. ➤ **2**

174

1939 On the first day of the Second World War, President Roosevelt appealed to the warring powers to "under no circumstances undertake the bombardment from the air of civilian populations or of unfortified cities." Both sides promised. But the British were not happy. With these promises, an "artificial situation" had been created, which was untenable in the long run, since it allowed no bombing beyond the front, wrote Spaight after the war.[155] No bombing outside the combat area – that was the well-known American position from the interwar negotiations. It was a foolproof way of protecting the civilian population behind the lines from air raids, but it did not allow the Poles to bomb Germany, since they could not move the combat area that far. It prohibited England from bombing Germany, as long as they had no army fighting there, but it allowed Germany to bomb Poland in any area where the Germans had turned Poland into a theater of war. So the only rule that really could have contained the bombing war was a rule that gave the advantage to the attacker at the cost of the attacked – and in so doing, opened the door to war crimes other than those committed by the air force.

175

1939 On October 6, 1939, Poland was vanquished and Hitler offered peace.

It is instructive to play with the thought of what would have happened if the British and the French had accepted his offer. Then Hitler would not have been forced to spread out his troops across all of Europe, but instead could have gathered them for an attack on the Soviet Union. It is probable that he would have won that war.

Those who considered Communism an even greater evil than Nazism could have overthrown Communist rule during the 1940s by supporting Hitler, or even just by accepting the terms he demanded in 1939. The combination of Russian natural resources and German technology and organization would have created a superpower far stronger than the Nazi or Communist powers alone. And when the atom bomb arrived? How would the Cold War have played itself out with such an opponent? Would the Third World have been able to achieve liberation? Would there be any world today at all? ➤ 177

176

1939 The year 1939 saw another breakthrough for atomic physics. An exiled Jewish atomic physicist, Lise Meitner, understood the implications of an experiment that Hahn and Strassman had done in Berlin: without realizing what had happened, they had split an atom.

The news sparked feverish activity in the United States, where other Jewish scientists had sought refuge from Nazism. In March, the Hungarian Leo Szilard showed experimentally that a chain reaction (in which each splitting of an atom caused another) was possible. In August, the scientists – with Einstein as their leader – wrote to Roosevelt and warned him that Hitler could make an atom bomb.[156] ➤ 189

177

1940 Chamberlain refused Hitler's offer of peace. At the same time, he rebuked those who wanted to begin bombing Germany. "Whatever be the lengths to which others may go, his Majesty's government will never resort to the deliberate attack on women and children, and other civilians for purposes of mere terrorism."[157]

But in the spring of 1940, the war entered a new phase with a series of rapid German victories over Denmark, Norway, Holland, Belgium, and France. The British army managed to escape by the skin of its teeth at Dunkirk on May 26. On June 14, the Germans marched into Paris and France surrendered. Great Britain stood alone against Hitler's Germany. Air attack had become the only weapon the Britons still could use to get at the Germans.

The decision that had been made voluntarily on May 11 emerged only two months later as a last, desperate way for Great Britain to stay in the war at all. ➤ 181

178

Why was Churchill's decision to begin bombing Germany never made public? In Spaight's opinion,

> "Because we were doubtful of the psychological effect of propagandist distortion of the truth that it was we who started the strategic offensive, we have shrunk from giving our great decision of the eleventh of May, 1940, the publicity which it deserved. That surely was a mistake. It was a splendid decision. It was as heroic, as self-sacrificing, as Russia's decision to adopt her policy of 'scorched earth.' It gave Coventry and Birmingham, Sheffield and Southampton, the right to look Kiev and Kharkov, Stalingrad and Sebastopol in the face."[158]

179

For Spaight in *Bombing Vindicated* (1944), the bombing war was heroic. For F. P. J. Veale in *Advance to Barbarism* (1948, 1953), it was just barbaric.

Veale sees the bombing war as an enormous experiment in the art of psychological engineering. What military significance was there in sending eighteen British bombers to the peaceful countryside in Westphalia in the hope of destroying some railway stations? What was actually intended was something completely different: to incite German reprisals, thus keeping alive the English will to fight. The British public was fooled into blaming the Blitz entirely on the German leaders, who in fact, according to Spaight, were doing all they could to put an end to the bombing.[159]

First and foremost, according to Veale, the bombing war was a defeat for international law. Churchill not only sacrificed London and other British cities, he also sacrificed those conventions for the protection of civilians that it had taken Europe 250 years to evolve. "The splendid decision" reinstated barbarism. Attila and Genghis Khan must be smirking in paradise. Wrote Veale, "To these men, the limitless possibilities of this new method of achieving an ancient purpose would have been clear."[160]

180

The lawlessness that the European states had so far only allowed themselves outside Europe was brought back to Europe by the Bomber Command, writes Veale.

This is an important observation. What Veale misses is that the Bomber Command was not the only or even the first to import the methods of colonial wars.

Hitler began the Second World War with an unprovoked attack on Poland. For him, the Poles stood outside the community of European values and outside the protection of international law, which was one expression of those values. "Poland shall be treated as a colony," he said.[161] "Therefore I have issued the order to my SS troops – for the time being only in the East – to kill mercilessly and without pity men, women, and children of Polish origin and language. Only in this way will we win the *Lebensraum* we need... Poland will be depopulated and colonized by Germans."[162]

Ten thousand intellectuals – the same number of people listed in the Swedish *Who's Who* – had already been killed during the first three months in an effort to deprive the Polish people of its leaders. Two million Jews were crowded into ghettoes. After the "ethnic cleansing" (as we would call it today) the country was divided, and large regions were annexed by Germany and its new ally, the Soviet Union.

In short: the ruthless expansionist policies carried out by Italy in Ethiopia and Libya, Spain in Morocco, the United States in the Philippines, and the Western European democracies of Belgium, Holland, France, and England throughout Asia and Africa for more than 100 years were now brought home to Europe by Hitler and applied in an even more brutal form to the Poles.[163]

It is obvious that this brutality could not be limited to Poland. It spread like a plague, and by means of "the splendid decision" came to characterize the air war as well. ➤ **174**

181

1940 Churchill's decision to begin bombing Germany originally applied only to military targets, which included, however, communication and transportation links; that is, railway stations; that is, targets that often lay in the center of large cities.

On June 20, 1940, the definition of "military targets" was expanded to include industrial targets, which meant that the workers' homes adjacent to those industries also became targets.

On September 6, Hitler responded with the Blitz against English cities that went on for half a year and killed 40,000 British civilians.

On October 16, the British government decided to open what would later, during the war in Vietnam, be called "free fire zones." These were areas where bombing was unrestricted when weather or other conditions made it impossible to find military or industrial targets.[164]

Two weeks later, there was a question as to whether it was worth going to the trouble to find military or industrial targets at all. According to Churchill's statement of October 30, he wanted to maintain the rule that targets should always be military. But at the same time, "the civilian population around the target areas must be made to feel the weight of war."[165] Churchill was most likely not unaware that his wording echoed General Sherman's famous promise that he would let the American South feel "the hard hand of war" by burning their cities.[166]

This was precisely the Bomber Command's new assignment: twenty to thirty German cities were to be attacked with incendiary bombs followed by attacks with high-explosive bombs to prevent the Germans from fighting the fire.

"Thus, the fiction that the bombers were attacking 'military objectives' in towns was officially abandoned," says the official British history of the air war. "This was the technique which was to become known as 'area bombing.' "[167]

Churchill did not want to admit to his administration that this meant an essential change in British policy. It was a matter, he said, of "a somewhat broader interpretation" of principles already applied.

And in a way, he was right. The basic decision had been made on May 11. After that, through its own inner logic, the bombing war produced the most efficient methods to cause the greatest possible damage.

182

1940 On Halloween, the RAF received its orders to firebomb German cities. A week later, the British bombers attacked the birthplace of Nazism, Munich. The week after that, the Germans answered with an attack on Coventry.

Coventry was not only a cathedral city; it was also an important center for the British arms industry, primarily because of two large airplane-engine factories and twenty or so subcontractors that produced engine parts for airplanes. The industries were situated in residential areas, near the extremely flammable medieval city center, which provided kindling for the German incendiary bombs. The civilian injuries (six of every thousand of the city's inhabitants were killed or seriously wounded) were seen as an unavoidable side effect.

Coventry was the most successful German bombing raid up to that time. Hardly any of the famous Coventry industries were left undamaged. But even so, the city's industrial production did not decrease by more than a third, and it took just a little over a month to get back to full production. The Germans calculated that six consecutive raids of similar success would be required to take out the city's industry completely. This would not be feasible.

"Area bombing" means that a military target is destroyed by leveling the entire area in which it lies. This demands huge quantities of bombs and heavy planes, which the Germans did not have. Their standard bomber was a twin-engine Heinkel 111, which clearly did not come up to the requirements for range and cargo capacity.

The Germans could achieve a few individual successes, like Coventry, even with these planes. Did they incite panic? Defeatism? The desire for revenge? None of the above, according to opinion polls and eyewitness reports of the time. Most of Coventry's citizens realized that a raid to avenge a raid that was in its turn revenge for an earlier raid would not prevent new raids, but just make the war even more bitter.[168] ➤ **190**

183

1941 Were Kipling's own political convictions expressed in "As Easy as ABC"? Or was the tale heavily ironic?

It was read differently by different readers. For C. G. Grey it was certainly not ironic. In his book *Bombers* (1941), Grey describes the interwar "colonial bombing" as a model for the future. The French, "with that intellectual honesty and freedom from hypocrisy which is their chief charm," had even invented a special airplane, called *Type colonial*, "where they could sit in the shade with plenty of space for their machine guns and shoot the indigenes in comfort."

The exercise of power from the air was, according to Grey, a new political system, which in the future ought to be used to ensure world peace. In that connection he wants to recommend Kipling's short story as one of the pearls of English literature. The tale, he says, "gives an idea of what civilisation may be like in a hundred or so years hence, when bombing has done its work, and humanity is content to be policed by an International Air Force which works under the orders of ABC."[169] ➤ **89**

184

1941 All the pronouncements about the people's right to self-determination were forgotten after the First World War, but came back rested and ready for the next one. In the Atlantic Charter of August 1941, Churchill (reluctantly) and Roosevelt (eagerly) united in respect of "the right of all peoples to choose the form of government under which they will live...sovereign rights and self-government restored to those who have been forcibly deprived of them."

Upon returning home, Churchill stressed that this was simply a question of general principle. Self-determination in this instance, he said, applied to "people suffering under the Nazi yoke and did not alter the imperial commitments of Britain."

The Empire still ruled a third of the globe, and the notion that any people would wish for liberation from British oppression was utterly strange to Churchill.

The Americans understood the Atlantic Charter more literally. "The age of imperialism is ended," said Assistant Secretary of State Sumner Wells on May 5, 1942. "The principles of the Atlantic Charter must be guaranteed to the world as a whole – in all oceans and in all continents."[170]

These words inspired hopes that the U.S. and its Allies had no intention of fulfilling. ➤ **229**

185

1941 In December of 1941, a group of British scientists led by Solly Zuckerman found that the greatest part of the injuries inflicted on people by bombs is caused by very small fragments of metal that penetrate the body at a high rate of speed. The result is "an internal explosion," which in a fraction of second increases the original size of that part of the body three or four times.[171]

The causative factor in this effect is the amount of energy that is transferred to the body's tissues. If the weight of the fragment is doubled, the energy is also doubled. If the speed is doubled, the energy is quadrupled. If the fragment passes through the body and goes out on the other side, it takes much of its energy with it and kills only if essential organs are hit. If the fragment does not pass through, it transmits all of its energy into the body and the injuries are much more extensive. Zuckerman's research was done originally to try to protect people from the effects of bombs. But once the formula had been figured out, it could also be used to maximize injuries. The bombs used in the Second World War broke up into relatively few pieces upon explosion, each of which was much larger than needed for causing injury. There was an enormous potential to be exploited here, if bombs were developed that broke up into many more fragments that moved at a higher rate of speed. ➤ **334**

186

1941 The superweapon is aimed, as we see, at people of other races. In the beginning it was a humane instrument, which spared human beings and only destroyed their weapons. In the beginning its power was demonstrated before it was actually used, and often the mere demonstration sufficed. But gradually the superweapon's effects began to resemble mass destruction. It became an instrument of extermination. Sometimes the blacks were wiped out, sometimes the red, but the yellow peoples always received the harshest treatment. They are exterminated in nearly all of the tales:

The climax is achieved in Robert A. Heinlein's first novel, *Sixth Column* (1941), which in a single phrase – "the Ledbetter effect" – conveys the main idea of countless superweapon tales:[172]

The pan-Asian hordes have flooded America. The problem is to kill 400 million "yellow apes" without having to injure real people. The best minds of America hide out in the Rocky Mountains and create a ray that destroys "Mongolian blood," but leaves all other blood untouched. This is the Ledbetter effect.

The weapon looks like a water pistol and is used in the same way. When the trigger is pressed, the weapon emits a ray that is deadly for Chinese and Japanese but harmless for everyone else. An infant can use it – it is completely foolproof, since it really cannot hurt a fly, much less a real person. For Asians on the other hand, it means instant death.

This racist wish-dream was written a year before the attack on Pearl Harbor. In the book version there were some small changes. "Yellow apes" is changed simply to "apes," for example. ➤ 131

187

1941 The policy makers were probably not reading tales of the future. Otherwise they could have learned something from Steven Krane in Alfred Bester's novella "Adam and No Eve" (1941), where he crawls across the scorched shell of the earth in search of the sea.

He is the only survivor of an earth that has been burned to cinders by a nuclear chain reaction. By mistake he discovers a catalyst that causes iron atoms to disintegrate, giving off enormous quantities of energy. Experienced scientists warn him, but he does not listen to their advice. And now he has destroyed the earth. All of its people are dead, all of its life extinguished. He eats his last provisions and throws away the can. "The last living thing on Earth eats its last meal. Metabolism begins the last act."

His only hope is to reach the sea, where his decaying body can give nourishment to the microorganisms that can carry on the cycle of life. "They would live on his rotting remains. They would feed on each other. They would adapt themselves... They would grow, burgeon, evolve."[173] Fertilized by his decomposing body, the sea, mother of life, would bear life once more.

188

1941 In Robert A. Heinlein's novella "Solution Unsatisfactory," of the same year (1941), Germany is winning the war. Then the United States provides Great Britain with a dose of the ultimate weapon, a radioactive dust, enough to wipe out the entire population of Berlin.

Before the U.S. gives its permission to use the weapon, the German ambassador is fully informed. Leaflets are dropped on Berlin with photographs of the weapon's effects and warnings to leave the city.

"We were calling 'Halt!' three times before firing. I do not think that...the President expected it to work, but we were morally obligated to try."[174] And then the dust-bombs fall. Berlin's population is obliterated. The narrator sees films that show how they die. "I left what soul I had in that projection room and I have not had one since."

After Germany's defeat, the question is what to do with a weapon capable of destroying all of humankind? Should it be entrusted to a democratically formed international organization?

No, that would hand the weapon over to 400 million Chinese and 300 million Hindus "with no more concept of voting and civic responsibility than a flea," says Heinlein.[175] Even with a less racist conception of the political abilities of Asians, a democratic system that automatically granted Asia power over the rest of the world might be daunting.

If democracy has to be limited, where do you draw the line? To give the power over life and death to one or more of the rival superpowers would be all too uncertain, in Heinlein's view. Atomic weapons require an international military dictatorship under the leadership of a wise and benevolent American.

Heinlein, one of the most widely read authors in the world today, often expressed his conviction that ordinary people are too stupid to participate in the governance of a country. The irrational and emotional masses must be controlled by an elite. Democracy is an antiquated system of government that should be replaced by other, more effective forms, he believed.

But even this antidemocrat depicted the dictatorship under atomic weapons as a clearly unsatisfactory "solution," not only in the novel's title but also in its creed:

> For myself, I can't be happy in a world where any man, or group of men, has the power of death over you and me, our neighbors, every human, every animal, every living thing. I don't like anyone to have that kind of power.

➤ 199

189

1941 In March of 1940, Albert Einstein once again wrote to President Roosevelt about the possibility of an atom bomb. The American Defense Department then invested a total of $6,000 on the development of a superweapon that no military man believed in.

In March of 1941, a group of young physicists in California managed to change uranium to plutonium. When they had produced a half-microgram, they began to bombard it with slow neutrons and found that it could be split. A British-American team was formed, and on December 6, 1941, the day before the bombing of Pearl Harbor, the United States decided to back the atom bomb.

➤ 187

190

1942 In 1940, the English dropped 5,000 tons of bombs on Germany. In 1941 they dropped almost five times as many: 23,000 tons. But the panic and defeatism that the theorists of air warfare had counted on and innumerable authors had fantasized about still failed to materialize.[176] In August of 1941, a report showed that only a third of those planes that claimed to have hit their targets really had done so. The British bombing campaign guzzled enormous resources. But was it really effective?

In February of 1942, this question was raised in the House of Commons, and the Cambridge professor A. V. Hill sharply criticized the Bomber Command: "The loss of production in the worst months of the Blitz was about equal to that due to Easter holidays... Everyone now knows that the idea of bombing a well-defended enemy into submission...is an illusion... We know that most of the bombs we drop hit nothing of importance... The disaster of this policy is not only that it is futile but that it is extremely wasteful... "[177] We now know that it took on the average three tons of British bombs to kill a single German civilian. Each bomber killed three Germans per attack. Of those three, maybe one produced war materiel.[178]

A Member of Parliament by the name of Garro Jones pointed out that a bomber cost ten times as many work hours as a fighter plane, so the Germans could afford to lose nine planes for every bomber they shot down. And as far as accuracy was concerned, Jones said: "We know that these heavy bombers cannot operate except from extreme altitudes or by night. In the former case they cannot hit their targets; in the latter case they cannot find their targets and have not found them..." Sir Stafford Cripps answered on behalf of the Government that the bombing of Germany had been decided upon at the time when Britain stood alone against the Germans. Bombs, whether they were wasteful or not, were the only means of fighting back. Now the situation had changed and the Government would, as soon as possible, consider a change in the appropriation of resources.

191

The situation had already changed by June of 1941, when the Germans suddenly attacked their ally, the Soviet Union. It changed once again in December of 1941, when the Japanese attacked the U.S. naval base at Pearl Harbor. Both of these surprise attacks were at first very successful. But in December of 1941, the German advance was stopped outside Moscow. And when the United States, with its tremendous production capacity, entered the war, the outcome could hardly be doubted.

The emergency situation that had been used to justify British terror bombing of civilians no longer existed. Nor were there any German attacks that demanded response – the German air force was fully engaged on the eastern front and had long since stopped bombing England. The American bombers, like the Japanese when they attacked Pearl Harbor, were oriented toward precision bombing of strictly military targets. The time was ripe for the change in priorities promised by Sir Stafford Cripps to the House of Commons.[179]

192

1942 Now it was no longer the British who were in direst need. During the first year after the attack on the Soviet Union, the Germans did away with two million Russian prisoners of war. Jews and Communists were particularly vulnerable. German *Sonderkommandos* (special detachments) behind the front murdered about 100,000 Jews a month during the second half of 1941.[180] In only two days in August, 23,600 Jews were murdered in the Ukraine. In September, 33,771 Kiev Jews were murdered at Babi Yar, and in Auschwitz the poisonous gas Zyklon B was tested on Soviet prisoners of war, with the aim of "a total solution to the Jewish question in the area of German influence in Europe," as Göring wrote in his order to Heydrich.

British intelligence had broken the SS radio code and kept its government well informed both of planned murders and the ones already committed.[181]

When the British parliament debated the Bomber Command's contributions to the war effort in February of 1942, between seventy-five and eighty percent of the Jews who would be killed in the Holocaust were still alive. A year later the proportions had reversed – in February of 1943, seventy-five to eighty percent of the Jews who would die in the Holocaust had already been killed.[182]

Could this crime have been prevented? Was there anything that someone could have done to stop this death machine?

The only imaginable actor was the Bomber Command. But the heavy bombers could only reach Berlin in a pinch. Their range did not extend any farther east. It was physically impossible to bomb the gas chambers in Poland.

But bombing was only one of the possible ways for the Bomber Command to act. The other way would have been – to stop bombing.

193

When Cripps's promised reappraisal of war priorities was taking place, the British might have remembered why they had created a force of heavy bombers in the first place. The intention had been to deter the enemy from bombing Britain or from committing other crimes. Now more than ever there was a crime to prevent. The threat to commence bombing had already been used, but the promise to stop bombing remained an option.

The bombing of cities was not yet particularly effective, but the Germans feared an escalation of the bombing war. The British knew that. They had something to offer, something the Germans would very much like to have. They could have offered to stop bombing German women and children in exchange for a halt in the German murder of Jewish women and children. Maybe the Germans could even have been forced to apply the international convention on the treatment of prisoners of war – in the east as they had already done in the west.

Had it been six million Britons who were on their way to the gas chambers in February of 1942; had it been two million British prisoners of war who were about to be murdered by the Germans – then the British government surely would not have hesitated for a moment. But there is no hint that the alternative of a halt in the bombing war was even discussed and then discarded.

194

1942 Instead, a new and secret splendid decision had been made: the Bomber Command was to continue and intensify bombing of German cities, especially residential areas. Backing this decision were analyses that showed that during its lifetime, an average bomber could destroy the homes of 4,000 to 8,000 Germans. "People don't like to have their homes destroyed. [They] seem to mind it more than having their friends or even their relatives killed... On the above figures we should be able to do ten times as much harm to each of the fifty-eight principal German towns. There seems little doubt that this would break the spirit of the people."[183] And there would be a certain amount of damage to industry and communications into the bargain.

On Valentine's Day of 1942, this policy was expressly formulated in Directive 22 to the

Bomber Command. The attacks should focus "on morale of enemy civil population, in particular industrial workers," and "[the] aiming points [were] to be built-up areas, not, for instance, the dockyards or aircraft factories... This must be made quite clear if it is not already understood."

Shortly thereafter the man for the job was appointed: Arthur "Bomber" Harris. No hobbies. Never read a book. Didn't like music. Lived for his job. His closest colleague was an old pal from the bombing of Iraq. His closest superior was an old pal from the bombing of Aden. The gang was together again and ready for another go.[184] ➤ **196**

195

1942 After the first British night raids against German cities in March of 1942, work on a German missile intensified. One of the leading rocket officers, Walter Dornberger, recommended a month-long night-and-day campaign against British cities – by creating chaos and panic it would contribute in a decisive way to the end of the war, he believed.[185]

Von Braun constructed a laboratory dedicated to navigational control in Peenemünde, and equipped his new rocket with a third gyro that prevented it from rotating in the air. After several unsuccessful attempts, he finally got the rocket that would become the V-2 to rise eighty kilometers up into space. When it fell to earth it had traveled 190 kilometers from the launch site. "The spaceship is born," said Dornberger in his speech at the officers' mess that evening. He compared the V-2 to the wheel, the steam engine, the airplane, and the Paris cannon. ➤ **212**

196

1942 On March 27, 1942, Goebbels noted in his diary:

> Beginning with Lublin, the Jews in the general government are now being evacuated eastward. The procedure is a pretty barbaric one and not to be described here more definitely. Not much will remain of the Jews. On the whole it can be said that about sixty percent of them will have to be liquidated, whereas only about forty percent can be used for forced labor...in such cases, sentimentality is unsuitable.

The "final solution" had begun.[186]

The following evening, on March 28 (my tenth birthday), Harris launched his offensive against German residential areas. He ran a night raid on Lübeck with incendiary bombs, leaving 15,000 people homeless. On April 18, he burned down Rostock. On May 30, for the first time he sent 1,000 bombers at the same time to the same target, Cologne, destroying the homes of 45,000 Germans and killing many of them in the process. The real bombing offensive had begun.[187] ➤ **11**

197

For Fieser the chemist, the sticky incendiary bomb was a purely scientific problem. He first investigated the status of the research and found that the American air force had no incendiary bombs at all. There were only two specialists working on the problem. They recommended a two-kilo bomb that created a pool of melted iron. But no attempt had been made to measure the effects of this bomb scientifically.

Fieser began from scratch. He analyzed the factors that determined the effectiveness of an incendiary bomb. He defined the term and devised an apparatus for comparing the effects of different bombs. He defined a goal he could work toward and a method to test whether he was approaching his goal.

Then he began to look for an appropriate material to use for the lumps of burning gel. It turned out that a mixture of rubber and gasoline produced the desired stickiness combined with easy ignition. Fieser chose a shell, the M-47, which had originally been intended to carry mustard gas. The shell was filled with gel in the laboratory at Harvard and was set off behind the university's stadium.

The result exceeded his expectations. Fieser traveled to the Edgewood Arsenal with the experimental bomb in his sleeping compartment. The porter who carried it in laid it on the lower bunk and said, "It feels heavy enough to be a bomb."

Even in 1964, when Fieser smugly tells this story in his memoirs, he is quite obviously proud of himself and of the imaginative yet strictly scientific way he solved his problem.[188]

198

1942 It was no coincidence that the American air force had no incendiary bombs. The Americans were confirmed precision bombers.

Technologically they took Carl Norden's bombsight as a point of departure. By the 1930s, this invention made it possible to calculate when a bomb should leave the airplane in order to hit a given target on the ground. Their strategy was based on the observation that an entire transport system might depend on a particular type of lubricant. It was not necessary to destroy railways in order to cripple them; bombing the lubricant factory would suffice.

Mass destruction was unintelligent. The point was to find and hit the most vulnerable points of the opponent's industry. In this kind of strategy the incendiary bomb, with its uncontrollable effects, had no place.[189]

When the Americans began to bomb Germany in August of 1942 together with the British, incendiary bombs were pitted against high-explosive bombs, night bombing against day bombing, and area bombing against precision bombing.

American commanders of middle rank came under a great deal of pressure, not only from their British colleagues but also from their superiors, who demanded results, and from their men, who did not want to die.

The process can be studied down to the last detail, since all of the decisions and the logic behind them have been preserved for each day and every squadron. The historian Conrad C. Crane has gone over the material. He finds that despite the pressure, American commanders stubbornly and without compromise held fast to precision bombing as their primary strategy – all the way up to the last months of the war. The difference between operations in Europe and Japan is striking.[190] ➤ 219

199

1942 In August of 1942, when Germany was at the height of its conquests, the Manhattan Project was initiated in the United States. In November, Westinghouse delivered three tons of pure uranium. Enrico Fermi and Leo Szilard began to build a reactor. On December 2, 1942, at 3:30 A.M., the reactor achieved the first chain reaction. Szilard: "I shook hands with Fermi and I said I thought this day would go down as a black day in the history of mankind."[191]

Still, he and his colleagues kept on working – afraid that Hitler's scientists would beat them to the goal. Once the breakup of Germany approached and it was clear that Hitler had no superweapon, the situation changed. Szilard wrote to Roosevelt and warned of the mutual terror that would ensue if he used the atom bomb.

Roosevelt died before the letter could reach him. ➤ 232

200

1943 Even today there is no hint in any British museum of the systematic attacks on German civilians in their homes, no hint that these attacks constituted crimes under international humanitarian law for the protection of civilians.

In 1942, 37,000 tons of bombs were dropped on Germany, primarily at night and in residential areas. According to a document dated October 5, 1942, Charles Portal, commander of the air force, planned to increase the quantity of bombs to 1,250,000 tons for the following two years. This was calculated to kill almost 1,000,000 civilians, seriously injure another 1,000,000, and leave 25,000,000 homeless.[192] The Air Ministry asked to be spared such calculations: "It is unnecessary and undesirable in any document about our bombing policy to emphasize this aspect, which is contrary to the principles of international law, such as they are, and also contrary to the statement made some time ago by the PM, that we should not direct our bombing to terrorize the civilian population, even in retaliation."

It was, in other words, unnecessary to tell the truth. It was not desirable, even in an internal document. And if the House of Commons were to exert pressure, as they did on Harold Balfour on March 11, 1943, one could always toss out a little word like "wantonly": "I can give the assurance that we are not bombing the women and children of Germany wantonly."[193] In my Swedish dictionary, synonyms offered up for "wantonly" are informative. The British, for example, did not bomb the Germans "arbitrarily," not "thoughtlessly," not "for pleasure," or "mischievously" – that much Balfour felt he could assure. What he did not deny was that they did it intentionally.

201

Longtime Labour Party MP Richard Stokes was not satisfied with that answer. On March 31, he made the question more specific, asking whether "on any occasion instructions

According to the British, it was the "Nazi key industries" that were hit by the blows of the RAF hammer. This and the following image were taken from Paret's *Persuasive Images* (1992)

In the German image, it was residential areas and churches that were being bombed. Ludwig Hohlwein designed this poster in 1942.

have been given to British airmen to engage in area bombing rather than limit their attention to purely military targets?"

The government answered: "The targets of the Bomber Command are always military, but night bombing of military objectives necessarily involves bombing of the area in which they are situated."

Stokes responded with an even more specific question: "Was it true that now the objectives of the Bomber Command are not specific military targets but large areas, and would it be true to say that probably the minimum area of target now is 16 square miles?"

The government answered only that its policy had not changed.

Stokes repeated his question.

The government's spokesman called him "incorrigible," but still refrained from answering the question.[194] This was of course only a parody of keeping Parliament informed in a democratic society. In a dictatorship like Hitler's, no government spokesmen whatsoever were available for questioning.

202

1943 Three years after the end of the war, my host family in St. Albans still knew nothing. And they did not want to know. They had not even heard of the bombing of Hamburg.[195]

British air attacks on Hamburg killed more people than all German air attacks against English cities put together. About 50,000 died in a single night, the night of July 27, 1943. The majority of them were women, children, and old people.

This raid was the most successful so far in the history of the Bomber Command. Everything went according to plan. The British managed to block out enemy radar with aluminum foil, so that the bombers could act almost undisturbed. The pathfinder planes dropped their markers on the proper positions. Twelve hundred tons of incendiaries fell in tight clusters on the marked residential areas.

Several days of high temperatures and low humidity had left the houses unusually flammable.

The firefighters were still trying to put out the blaze from an earlier raid in a part of the city far from the current target area. Thousands of small fires joined together in one enormous inferno that sucked great masses of air into its center, where all the oxygen was consumed. The firestorm reached hurricane levels.

"It was as if I was looking into what I imagine an active volcano to be," remembers one of the airmen.

Another one heard his captain sigh into the intercom, "Those poor bastards."[196]

203

Those poor bastards sat in the air-raid shelters of 16,000 apartment buildings that burned down. Those who followed instructions and dutifully sat there, as I myself would have done, were all killed. They were suffocated when the shelter filled with smoke or when the firestorm had consumed all the oxygen. Only their bodies could testify as to how they had died.

The corpses often lay crowded into heaps near the barricaded exits. Other bodies were stuck in the hardened black mass of their own fat, which had melted and run out onto the floor.

The infants lay in rows like grilled chickens. Other corpses had vanished completely; nothing was left but a fine layer of ash on the tables and chairs.

Most of those who left the shelters burned to death out on the street instead. Many lay face down, with one arm over their heads, as if to shield themselves. Many had shrunk to the size of dwarves; others had blown up like balloons. Some seemed completely unharmed but were naked – all of their clothes except for their shoes had disappeared. Others lay with outstretched arms and blank faces, like mannequins. Still others were totally charred. Their skulls had burst at the temples where the brain pushed out, and their intestines bulged out under their ribs.[197]

204

A few managed to save themselves through the storm of flames, "a snowstorm of burning flakes."

Traute Koch, 15: "Mother wrapped me in wet sheets, kissed me and said: 'Run!' "

Herbert Brecht, 15, wound up in a flooded bomb crater: "Above there was this terrible heat but I was lying safely in the water... Eventually there were about forty people lying in the crater... The screams of the burning and dying people are unforgettable. When a human being dies, he screams and whimpers and then there is the death rattle in his throat. Not at all bravely and not as beautiful as in a film."

Käte Hoffmeister: "We came to the door which was burning just like a ring in a circus through which a lion has to jump. Someone in front of me hesitated. I pushed her out with my foot; I realized it was no use staying in that place... We got to the Löschplatz all right but couldn't go on across the Reiffestrasse because the asphalt had melted. There were people on the roadway, some already dead, some lying alive but stuck in the asphalt. They must have rushed on to the roadway without thinking. Their feet had got stuck and they had put out their hands to get out again. They were on their hands and knees, screaming."[198]

205

1943 The raid on Hamburg was exceptional only in terms of its singular success, asserts the British historian Martin Middlebrook. In Hamburg, the Bomber Command succeeded in doing what the heavy bombers tried to do every night when they took off for Germany.

Arthur Harris was proud of their results. He asked his department to say clearly and plainly that the aim of the bombing offensive was "the obliteration of German cities and their inhabitants as such."[199] A bizarre correspondence ensued, in which the Ministry flatly denied to Harris that Harris was doing what they both knew he was trying his utmost to do.

Harris was proud; others felt sick. Freeman Dyson, who became one of the 20th century's leading nuclear physicists, was hired in his youth as a civilian employee by Harris's office. He served as an operations analyst at the time of the firestorm in Hamburg. He had access to all the information on this raid and on the other residential bombings that were so carefully kept from the British people. This knowledge gnawed at his conscience. He felt a constant need to shout it aloud in the streets, but he didn't dare: "I sat in my office until the end, carefully calculating how to murder most economically another hundred thousand people." After the war he compared himself to the bureaucrat-murderers working in Eichmann's death machine: "They had sat in their offices, writing memoranda and calculating how to murder people efficiently, just like me. The main difference was that they were sent to jail or hanged as war criminals, while I went free."[200]

206

In both cases it was a question of the well-organized mass murder of innocent people, sanctioned at the highest level but contrary to international law. The similarities were quite concrete, as well. When the rescue teams made their way into Hamburg's shelters, they were faced with scenes reminiscent of those encountered at the same time by Jews forced to clear the bodies of other Jews out of the gas chambers – "intertwined piles of people, killed by fumes and pressed against the vents and the barricaded doors," writes Peter Englund in his convincing analysis of both events.[201]

But the difference between the German and the British war crimes is, he stresses, also very clear.

In the first place, the order of magnitude in the two cases is completely different. The Germans murdered about 6,000,000 Jews and about 5,000,000 other "*Untermenschen*" – gypsies and Jehovah's Witnesses, the handicapped and the homosexual, Communists and Social Democrats, Poles, Ukrainians, and Russians. The allied bombing offensive against Germany claimed about half a million civilian lives. That is less than the margin of error surrounding the Germans' crime.

In the second place, the victims of the Germans were almost completely defenseless. There were, to be sure, uprisings in the ghettos and camps, but these were exceptions and were all put down with the harshest brutality. The Bomber Command's greatest victories – Hamburg and Dresden, for example – were won over cities that either were or had been made totally defenseless. But that was an exception. Up to the conclusion of the war, Germany's cities defended themselves energetically; the graves of 56,000 British airmen testify to that fact. Perhaps the most important contribution made by the Bomber Command to the war was forcing the Germans to assign so many resources to the defense of their cities.

And in the third place, the British had no plans for a conquest that would require the killing of Germans in order to make room for British settlement. Even though Harris claimed that the object was to level "German cities and their inhabitants as such," the aim of the British was never to exterminate the Germans, but only to force their surrender. The air attacks against Germany stopped as soon as the German armed forces had surrendered.

The German war crimes, on the other hand, were committed for the most part after the surrender of their opponents. More than 2,000,000 Soviet prisoners of war were murdered after they had surrendered. Millions of Russians were left to starve once the German occupying forces had appropriated their food and sent it to Germany. The German bureaucracy planned to starve another 20,000,000 people in order to make room for German settlement in Poland and the Ukraine after the war.

As a part of this process, the Jewish people, the primary objects of Nazi hate, were to be completely wiped out. Hundreds of thousands of Jews from areas where no German settlement was planned at all were driven into Poland to be murdered. "All of them were doomed. All of them had to go," writes Peter Englund.[202]

207

After Hamburg, the German leadership knew what the Bomber Command could and would do. Hitler knew what Germany could expect.

For the Allied leadership it had been equally clear for more than a year what the Germans were doing with the Jews. In fact, we know today that Allied intelligence had a clear picture of the planned genocide as early as the summer of 1941.[203]

Hitler seems never to have even considered offering to stop the murder of the Jews in exchange for a halt of British bombing of German cities.

Churchill and Roosevelt promised again and again to punish the German leadership for the murder of the Jews – after the war. But it appears that they, in their turn, never considered an offer to stop bombing German cities in exchange for the lives of the Jews. On the contrary: the British Foreign Minister shuddered at the thought of such an offer from Hitler.[204]

An end to the bombing in exchange for closing the death factories – it might even have been a smart move in the propaganda war. If Hitler had said no, the British could have washed their hands of the guilt for every subsequent bombing raid: "That's what you Germans get for murdering the Jews."

But the offer was never made. Why?

In the summer of 1943 there were still more than two million Jews left to rescue. That is why, according to historian David Wyman, the foreign offices of both England and the United States tried to delay and block the spread of facts about the Holocaust. They were afraid that if the truth were known, demands would be made for rescue operations, which in their turn could lead to mass immigration of Eastern European Jews – something that both England and the United States wanted to avoid at any cost.

They feared immigration more than extermination. "There is a possibility," wrote the British Foreign Secretary, "that the Germans or their satellites may change over from the policy of extermination to one of extrusion, and aim as they did before the war at embarrassing other countries by flooding them with alien immigrants."[205] Europe seems to have continued sliding into the abyss for two reasons – one side was more concerned about preventing immigration than genocide, while the other side was more concerned about being able to murder Jews than stopping the murder of its own civilians.

208

1943 People got used even to the unthinkable. Hamburg, like Coventry before it, refuted all of the prewar speculations about how people would react to the bombs. As it turned out, people did not become lunatics or savage beasts. On the contrary, they closed ranks. They went to work as usual.

By the end of the year, eighty percent of Hamburg's industrial productivity was restored. The people were living in cellars, where everybody was a *Kumpel* (chum). "We shared everything. People helped each other. Anyone could go alone in the streets and not be robbed or molested... Today it is risky even to go to the U-Bahn."[206]

But Harris still believed that he could win the war all on his own. The Allies dropped a total of 180,000 tons of bombs on Germany in 1943. On December 7, Harris reported that he had completed the destruction of a quarter of the thirty-eight most important German cities. During the first four months of 1944 he hoped to destroy another quarter of them, which would force the enemy to surrender and make invasion unnecessary.

The air staff responded that only eleven percent of Germany's population lived in the thirty-

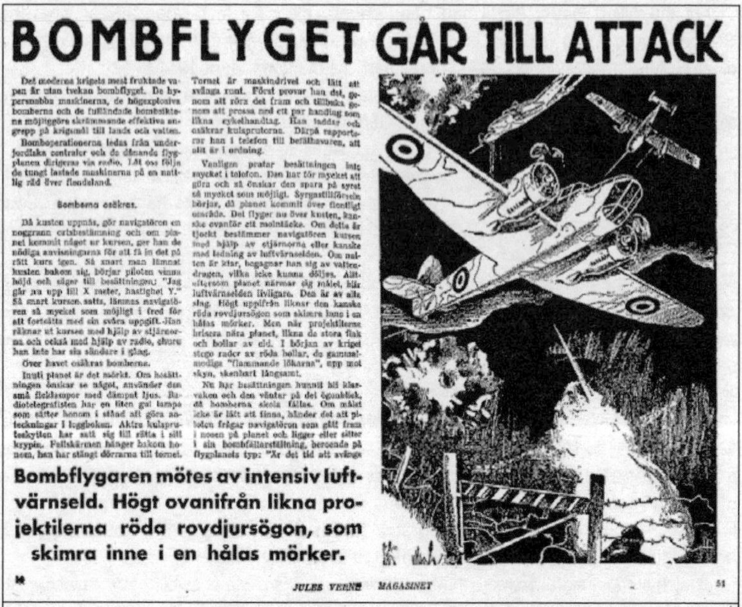

BOMBFLYGET GÅR TILL ATTACK

Det moderna krigets mest fruktade vapen är utan tvekan bombflyget. De hypersnabba maskinerna, de högexplosiva bomberna och de fulländade bombsiktena möjliggöra skrämmande effektiva angrepp på krigsmål till lands och vatten.

Bomboperationerna ledas från underjordiska centraler och de dånande flygplanen dirigeras via radio. Låt oss följa de tungt lastade maskinerna på en nattlig räd över fiendeland.

Bomberna osäkras.

Då kusten uppnås, gör navigatören en noggrann ortsbestämning och om planet kommit något ur kursen, ger han de nödiga anvisningarna för att få in det på rätt kurs igen. Så snart man lämnat kusten bakom sig, börjar piloten vinna höjd och säger till besättningen: "Jag går nu upp till X meter, hastighet Y." Så snart kursen satts, lämnas navigatören så mycket som möjligt i fred för att fortsätta med sin svåra uppgift. Han räknar ut kursen med hjälp av stjärnorna och också med hjälp av radio, ehuru han inte har sin sändare i gång.

Över havet osäkras bomberna.

Inuti planet är det mörkt. Om besättningen önskar se något, använder den små ficklampor med dämpat ljus. Radiotelegrafisten har en liten gul lampa som sätter honom i stånd att göra anteckningar i loggboken. Aktre kulsprutesskytten har satt sig till rätta i sitt krypin. Fallskärmen hänger bakom honom, han har stängt dörrarna till tornet.

Tornet är maskindrivet och lätt att svänga runt. Först provar han det, genom att röra det fram och tillbaka genom att pressa med ett par handtag som likna cykelhandtag. Han laddar och osäkrar kulsprutorna. Därpå rapporterar han i telefon till befälhavaren, att allt är i ordning.

Vanligen pratar besättningen inte mycket i telefon. Den har för mycket att göra och så önskar den spara på syret så mycket som möjligt. Syrgastillförseln börjar, då planet kommit över fientligt område. Det flyger nu över kusten, kanske ovanför ett molntäcke. Om detta är tjockt bestämmer navigatören kursen med hjälp av stjärnorna eller kanske med ledning av luftvärnselden. Om natten är klar, begagnar han sig av vattendragen, vilka icke kunna döljas. Allteftersom planet närmar sig målet, blir luftvärnselden livligare. Den är av alla slag. Högt uppifrån liknar den kanske röda rovdjursögon som skimra inne i en hålas mörker. Men när projektilerna krevera nära planet, likna de stora flak och bollar av eld. I början av kriget stego rader av röda bollar, de gammalmodiga "flammande lökarna", upp mot skyn, skenbart långsamt.

Nu har besättningen hunnit bli klarvaken och den väntar på det ögonblick, då bomberna skola fällas. Om målet icke är lätt att finna, händer det att piloten frågar navigatören som gått fram i nosen på planet och ligger eller sitter i sin bombfällarställning, beroende på flygplanets typ: "Är det tid att svänga

Bombflygaren mötes av intensiv luftvärnseld. Högt ovanifrån likna projektilerna röda rovdjursögon, som skimra inne i en hålas mörker.

JULES VERNE MAGASINET 51

As a young reader of *Jules Verne Magazine*, I learned to think of bomber pilots as heroes.

eight most important cities. The Gestapo could probably maintain German morale; what Hitler feared most was precision bombing of industry essential to the war. They asked Harris to attack the strategically important industrial cities of Schweinfurt and Leipzig. Instead he went on, night after night, setting fire to the working-class neighborhoods of Berlin.

209

1944 On February 9, 1944, Bishop George Bell asked for the floor in the House of Lords and began to enumerate, one by one, all of the libraries and works of art destroyed by British bombers in Lübeck, Hamburg, and Berlin.[207]

He referred to a report in the London *Times* that stated that the British bombed even when the ground was completely invisible. "The whole town, area by area, is plotted carefully out. This area is singled out and plastered on one night, that area is singled out and plastered the next night..." Disgusted, the Bishop quoted a boastful marshal who promised that the towns of Germany would be "pull[ed] out like teeth," one after another. He concluded, "How can the War Cabinet fail to see that this progressive devastation of cities is threatening the roots of civilisation? The Allies stand for something greater than power. The chief name inscribed on our banner is 'law.' It is of supreme importance that we, who with our allies are the liberators of Europe, should so use power that it is always under the control of law."

The government's spokesman responded without a blush that the RAF had never carried out any terror raids. This was at the same time that Harris was secretly ordered to stop the terror and start bombing German war industry.

Why didn't Harris follow orders? Why did he continue as before?

210

In his memoirs, published in 1947, Harris still maintained that he would have won the war on his own if he had only been allowed to keep on bombing residential areas without the distraction of other assignments.

It seems that he was convinced each night that these particular burning houses would be the ones to incite rebellion among the German working class against Nazism and the war, just as the generals in the First World War had believed with each new offensive that this was the one that would break through the enemy lines. The one time they were successful would prove that all of the earlier, apparently meaningless attacks had been legitimate.

In the same way, Harris was forced to commit crime after crime in pursuit of the one success that would justify every crime that had gone before.

211

1944 In April of 1944, the Nazis began to assemble the Hungarian Jews for transport to Auschwitz. At about the same time, the American air force came within striking distance of Auschwitz from its newly won bases in Italy.

One of the central notions of German propaganda was that Jews were running England and America. According to Goebbels, it was the Jews who were ordering the bombing raids on German cities. In his internal instructions to the German press, Goebbels depicted the extermination of the Jews as revenge for the bombings.[208]

In the spring of 1944, these supposedly all-powerful Jews were begging the War Department to stop the killing by bombing the railroads around Auschwitz.

The Operations Division answered on June 26: the suggestion was not feasible, since "it could be executed only by diversion of considerable air support essential to the success of our forces now engaged in decisive operation." This was the standard response given automatically to every suggestion. It meant that the responsible parties had not even considered the question. On the same day, seventy-one Flying Fortresses flew over the railroad to Auschwitz on their way to more distant objectives.

On July 7, 1944, oil refineries near Auschwitz were bombed.

On August 20, 127 Flying Fortresses bombed the factories at Auschwitz.

A few miles away, the gas chambers continued their operations without interruption.

On September 13, the factories at Auschwitz were bombed yet again. One of the ninety-six heavy bombers managed to drop its bombs on a railroad leading to the gas chambers – by mistake.

The industries at Auschwitz were attacked for the last times on December 18 and 26. At that time the transport of Jews was still going on. On January 18, 1945, Auschwitz was evacuated, and on January 27, Russian troops burst into the emptied camp.

If the War Department had reacted immediately, half a million Jews could have been saved by bombers, writes historian David Wyman. If the gas chambers had been bombed at the same time as the factories, at least 100,000 could have been rescued, he asserts.

Another historian, William D. Rubenstein, objects that the Jewish organizations' request for the bombing of the railroads around Auschwitz came too late. Even if the bombing had been approved, the attacks could not have been planned and carried out in time; that is, before the deportation of the Jews of Hungary was finished.

In answer it must be said that when targets were important to the War Department it did not wait for formal requests from the public to begin planning attacks. Besides, transports of Jews were still arriving at Auschwitz six months after the War Department had turned down the request from the Jewish organizations. The American air force did not normally require that much lead-time.

➤ **213**

212

1944 The Paris cannon was the First World War's most famous artillery weapon, an almost unmovable monster that fired on Paris with ten-kilo shells from a distance of nearly 80 miles. What Dornberger wanted from Von Braun was a missile that could reach London from twice as far with projectiles of an explosive strength 100 times that of the Paris cannon. He got it. But how useful was it? The creators of the Paris cannon had been blinded by the technical wonder of their invention – but they were never quite clear on what they wanted to do with it. This mistake was now repeated with the V-2. The Germans had thought that London would collapse when the missiles began to fall from the sky in the summer of 1944. In comparison with their hopes, the result was pathetic. The total explosive power of all the V-2s launched at England was no greater than what was usually dropped by the heavy bombers in one big RAF raid.

The V-2 killed 5,000 people in total – a single British bombing raid often claimed more victims. The costs were enormous – for the resources poured into the missile, Germany could have had 24,000 fighter planes. Above all, it was impossible to know in advance where a V-2 would fall. It had a hard time hitting even a gigantic target like London.[209]

➤ **253**

213

1944 On April Fools' Day in 1944, Harris was forced to place his heavy bombers at Eisenhower's disposal in preparation for the invasion of Normandy. The civilian population there consisted of Frenchmen, who suddenly had to be spared at all costs. This proved to be not quite as impossible as had been claimed. British bombers, when given the proper orders, were fully capable of distinguishing between civilian and military targets.

Half a year later, Harris got his planes back. Everyone realized that the end of the war was near. But as the end approached, the war intensified. The adaptation of British industry for the production of heavy bombers, which Churchill had ordered in May of 1940, now began to bear fruit in earnest. Eighty percent of all of the bombs of the war were dropped during the last ten months.[210]

The question was which targets to choose.

Should the bombing of residential areas continue?

The reasons that had motivated the "splendid decision" and the series of consequent decisions no longer applied. Great Britain now had allies engaged in combat. The Germans could be beaten on the ground. It was not technically impossible to limit bombing to military targets. The hopes that had been pinned on the destruction of cities had proven to be false. With victory within reach, it was time to begin planning for the postwar period. Did the victors want Germany's harbors to be inoperable? asked Richard D. Hughes in his criticism of the bombing policy. How did they think they were going to support occupation forces, in that case? "Do we want a Germany virtually de-housed, lacking all public utility services, whose population is little better than a drifting horde of nomads ripe for any political philosophy of despair and almost impossible to administer and reeducate?"[211]

Those who wanted to continue residential bombing answered that if the bombing could shorten the war even by a single day or save a single Allied soldier's life, it was worth it. Arthur Harris accepted without complaint order after order to concentrate on the oil industry, where the German war machine might be brought to a halt. But in his thinking, conditioned by decades of colonial warfare, there was no room for the oil industry. It was the towns that must burn.

Dutifully he submitted plans for the bombing of oil plants. But these were "diversions from the main offensive," which was still aimed against residential areas, that is, against "morale," that is, against women, children, and old people.

214

1945 Dresden was the Florence of Germany – an old cultural capital, full of art treasures and architectural masterpieces that the bombing had left untouched throughout five years of war. So the city was full of refugees and practically undefended when the British attacked on February 13, 1945.[212]

The stated intent behind the attack was to stop German troop transport to the wavering Eastern Front. This could have been accomplished in Dresden – if they had destroyed the railway bridge over the Elbe. But in the end, the bridge remained intact. In fact, it was not even cited as a target for the British attack.[213]

The other stated purpose was to "show the Russians what the Bomber Command can accomplish."[214] They succeeded in this. Dresden was to be the Bomber Command's greatest victory of the entire war. The firestorm in Hamburg, which they had tried in vain time and again to repeat, returned here in an even more horrifying form. The temperature rose above 1,800 degrees Fahrenheit. Approximately 100,000 civilians were killed – the precise number is impossible to determine, since so many bodies could never be identified or even separated from one another once they had passed into "the semi-liquid way that dust actually returns to dust."[215] These are the words of Kurt Vonnegut. As a prisoner of war in Dresden he survived the raid and helped to dig out the corpses.

215

Margret Freyer walked around looking for her fiancé:

> Dead, dead, dead everywhere. Some completely black, like charcoal. Others completely untouched, lying as if they were asleep. Women in aprons, women with children sitting in the trams as if they had just nodded off. From some of the debris poked arms, heads, legs, shattered skulls. Most people looked as if they had been inflated, with large yellow and brown stains on their bodies. People whose clothes were still glowing... I asked for a mirror and did not recognize myself any more. My face was a mass of blisters...my eyes were narrow slits...[216]

Eva Beyer was looking for her mother:

> Nothing but parts of bodies, arms, legs, heads, hands and torsos, being shoveled up into a big heap...Then petrol was poured over it and the whole heap was burnt. Lorries came all the time and brought more of these dismembered people. I became incapable of walking away. The only thing I could think of was, could it be that Mother is among these mutilated things? Mesmerized I stared at the heaps of human remains... Mentally, I started to put together these parts of bodies in order to see whether they could be any of my family...[217]

216

Five years earlier the British had charged the Germans with bombing hospitals in England. Now the RAF had destroyed or seriously damaged nineteen permanent and almost all of the temporary hospitals in Dresden. In the city's largest children's hospital, forty-five expectant mothers had been killed when the building was hit by a blockbuster bomb in the first attack, hit by a number of explosive and incendiary bombs in the second attack, and finally machine-gunned by American Mustangs in the third attack.

Annemarie Wähmann, a twenty-year-old nurse's aide, flung herself to the ground as wave after wave of airplanes at low altitude fired on her defenseless patients with their machine guns. Thousands of bombed-out Dresdeners who had sought the cooling shores of the Elbe were subjected to the same massacre. "Who gave such an order?" she asked. But at that point, probably no order was needed. After killing 100,000 civilians, the pilots had understood the basic principle and were acting on their own initiative.

217

1945 On March 6, Dresden came under discussion in the House of Commons. Once again it was Richard Stokes, of Labour, who brought up the subject. He cited a German description of the raid that had been published the day before in the *Manchester Guardian.* "Tens of thousands who lived in Dresden are now burned under its ruins. Even an attempt at identification of the victims is hopeless." Stokes commented: "Leaving aside strategic bombing, which I question very much, and tactical bombing, with which I agree, if it is done with a reasonable degree of accuracy, there is no case whatever under any conditions, in my view, for terror bombing..."[218]

An undistinguished Junior Minister was sent forth to respond: "We are not wasting bombers or time on purely terror tactics. It does not do the Honourable Member justice to...suggest that there are a lot of Air Marshals or pilots...sitting in a room thinking how many German women and children they can kill."

That was of course precisely what they were doing.

The truth began to filter out, and Churchill perceived that it would do him no good. Up to then he had supported Harris, but on March 28 (my thirteenth birthday), he wrote to his chiefs of staff: "I feel the need for more precise concentration upon military objectives, such as oil and communications behind the immediate battle-zone, rather than on mere acts of terror and wanton destruction, however impressive."

Pressured by his chiefs of staff, Churchill changed his letter and wrote the following instead: "It seems to me that the moment [has come] when the question of the so-called 'area-bombing' of German cities should be reviewed from the point of view of our own interests. If we come into control of an entirely ruined land, there will be a great shortage of accommodation for ourselves and our allies."[219]

When Churchill finally assumed political responsibility and stopped the bombing of residential areas, it was the comfort of the future occupying forces he had in mind.

218

1945 While this discussion was going on, the dead were still arriving in a steady stream at St. John's Cemetery and other burial grounds in Dresden.

It was often impossible to determine from the corpse if the dead person had been a man, woman, or child. If there were identifying papers on the body, a yellow card was filled out and the name was put up on a list. Whenever possible, rings and other objects were collected in a bag and were taken to the police station at Königsufer in Dresden, where relatives could come and get them.

The unidentifiable dead were assigned a red card. Women were especially problematic, since they did not carry their papers on their persons, but in their handbags. And whose handbags were these? Day after day new streams of dead. First they were outside in the rain, snow, and cold. Then in March and April they were left out in the rising temperatures and began to decay. There were not enough rubber gloves, there was not even any water to wash up in. "Eight sanitation workers had to eat out of the same tin. Wash up? Impossible! There was no water."

It became harder and harder to identify the victims. Now they arrived in bathtubs or wooden tubs. On the top of one tub a note read: "Thirty-two dead from the X bomb shelter, number X, X Street."

"My God! Thirty-two dead! They could all fit in a bathtub. And the tub wasn't even full."[220]

On April 16, they stopped trying to bury the bodies. It was no longer possible. The remaining shelters were cleaned out with flamethrowers. ➤ 12

219

Before Fieser's sticky incendiary got into mass production, the Japanese struck at Pearl Harbor and had soon taken control of all of the known sources of one of the two raw materials needed for bombs: rubber.

Fieser now made a series of attempts to replace rubber with various soft soaps, and in February of 1942 he had completed a new recipe:

	gasoline
	5% aluminum naphthene
	5% aluminum palmitate
+	.5% carbon black
=	napalm

It soon emerged that coconut oil could replace aluminum palmitate with no complications, but by then the name of the new substance had already stuck. Everybody continued to call it napalm.

The production of napalm was first entrusted to Nuodex Products, and by the middle of April they had conjured up a brown, dry powder that was not sticky by itself, but when it was mixed with gasoline in a twelve percent solution it turned into an extremely sticky and flammable substance.

One remaining problem was that the portion of napalm that remained in the shell after the explosion just lay there to no purpose. One of Fieser's colleagues came up with the idea of combining napalm with white phosphor, which catches fire upon contact with the air. That way napalm's broad but shallow effects could be combined with phosphor's ability to penetrate, point by point, deeply into the musculature, where it would continue to burn day after day. The first test was carried out on the football field next to the Harvard Business School on July 4, 1942. "The performance from the start was most impressive. Pieces of phosphorus are driven into the gel and large, burning globs are distributed evenly over a circular area about fifty yards in diameter."[221]

220

The next step was to create a life-sized model of a Japanese village, complete with paper walls and tatami mats. It was situated in Utah, where the napalm bomb was tested successfully during the summer of 1943.

Meantime the planners were looking for appropriate targets in Japan. In the beginning only military targets were considered, but in May 1944 the order came to plan napalm attacks against cities as well. It was a definitive break with earlier policy. For safety's sake, the decision-makers wanted to leave a back door open for their own escape: "It is desired that the areas selected include, or be in the immediate vicinity of, legitimate military targets."[222]

221

1945 Obviously it was against Japan that the Americans planned to use napalm.

Why not against the Germans? During the last desperate European counteroffensive in January 1945, General Quesada did in fact work out a plan for mass-bombing Germany with napalm. One of his analysts, David Griggs, maintained that the Quesada plan would save hundreds of thousands of American soldiers' lives. But it was never tried.[223]

It was considered more legitimate to use napalm on the Japanese.

Why?

Perhaps for the same reason that the United States had forbidden Japanese immigration but welcomed Germans. Germans made up the largest group of immigrants, while the Japanese were one of the smallest. The Commander in Chief of the air force, General Hap Arnold, and many other leading American military men were of German heritage. It did not occur to anyone to question their loyalty to the United States, despite their hesitation to use napalm against Germany.[224]

Japanese-Americans, on the other hand, were interned in concentration camps at the outbreak of the war. "A viper is nonetheless a viper wherever the egg is hatched," commented the *Los Angeles Times*. The governor of Idaho added, "They live like rats, breed like rats, and act like rats." Many marines wrote the words "rat exterminator" on their helmets. The Pacific war had clearly racist characteristics on both sides of the conflict, writes American historian John Dower, who has made this a special subject of study. The German atrocities were described as "Nazi" and were not attributed to the Germans as a people, while Japanese atrocities were imagined as arising from the cultural and genetic inheritance of the Japanese people.[225]

"You know that we have to exterminate this vermin if we and our families are to live," said General Blamey to his soldiers in 1943. "We must exterminate the Japanese." In an interview on the front page of the *New York Times* the General explained what he meant: "We are not dealing with humans as we knew them. We are dealing with something primitive. Our troops have the right view of the Japs. They regard them as vermin."[226]

222

The idea of burning down Tokyo preceded the Second World War. It had come up already after the earthquake of 1923, which caused the greatest fire in the history of the world up to that time. A city that inflammable was an almost irresistible target in military eyes.[227] "These towns, built largely of wood and paper, form the greatest aerial targets the world has ever seen," wrote the American prophet of the bombing war, Billy Mitchell, in 1932. Japan was not a case for humanitarian precision bombing. "Destruction should be total, not selective."

Ten years later his successor, De Seversky, echoed Mitchell's message in his bestseller *Victory through Air Power* (1942). The war against the Japanese ought to be aimed at "total destruction," "extermination," "elimination."

When the skies over a nation are captured, everything below lies at the mercy of the enemies' air force. There is no reason why the job of annihilation should at that point be turned over to the mechanized infantry, when it can be carried out more efficiently and without opposition from overhead.

Only when the master of the skies wishes to conserve the property of the manpower below for his own use or for some other reason will he, normally, need to take possession of the surface through the employment of armies...

The conduct of war will be determined by whether the purpose is to destroy the enemy or to capture him.

For the colonial powers the idea was to capture the prey alive and exploit him as labor, but the American strategy lacked all colonial ambition and therefore ought to be aimed at a war of elimination, a task for which bombing from the air was especially suitable.[228] De Seversky's book inspired a Disney film that climaxed with the jubilant destroying of Tokyo.[229]

➤ **165**

223

1945 On November 1, 1944, the American bombers under the command of General Hansell had Japan within range and began a series of planned precision attacks against the air industry. But the results were slow in coming. The commander, Hap Arnold, became more and more impatient. On January 17, he had his fourth heart attack, and three days later Hansell was replaced by LeMay, known for his iron fist.

LeMay had arrived in Europe a few weeks before the firestorm in Hamburg. He arrived in the Pacific Theater a few weeks before the firestorm in Dresden. Hamburg and Dresden showed him what could be accomplished. LeMay was practical, decisive, and heartless. He had a new bomb that would make fire stick. He had a new target, a big city built of wood and paper. Since he knew that the city for the time being was almost without defense, he tore 1.5 tons of guns and ammunition out of every bomber in order to raise the carrying capacity for bombs. He ordered the planes to fly in low over their targets and drop the bombs on residential areas that had been marked in advance, as the RAF usually did. He called it "'precision bombing' designed for a specific purpose."

On the night of March 9, 1945, he dropped 1,665 tons of incendiary bombs into the sea of fire that had been created already by the first wave of bombing.[230]

224

In Tokyo the winter of 1944–1945 was the clearest and coldest in decades. For forty-five days in a row it was below freezing, and it was still snowing at the end of February, remembered Robert Guillain many years later.[231]

But on March 9, spring suddenly arrived. The wind blew hard all day long, and by evening it was almost storming. Around eleven o'clock the air sirens sounded. Soon the Christmas trees dropped by the pathfinder planes shone over the city, which suddenly changed color. It seemed to glow. It turned into a cauldron of flame that boiled over and ran out in every direction.[232]

For the first time, the planes flew in at low altitude. Their long, glittering wings, sharp as the edges of knives, could be glimpsed through the pillars of smoke, and they threw out sudden reflections of the blast furnace beneath.

The order was that every family must stay and defend its own home. But how? The air shelters were nothing more than pits in the ground, covered with boards and a thin layer of earth. The bombs rained down in the thousands; a house could be hit by ten or more at the same time. This was a new kind of bomb; it spread a flaming liquid that ran along the roofs and set fire to anything it touched. The violent wind caught up the burning drops, and soon a rain of fire was falling that stuck to everything.

According to plan, the neighbors formed bucket brigades. After a few seconds, they were surrounded by fire. The fire-extinguishers' hand-pumped streams of water were pathetically insufficient. The fragile houses immediately went up in flames, and screaming families fled their homes, babies on their backs, only to find the street blocked by a wall of fire. They caught flame in the firestorm, turned into living torches, and disappeared.[233] People threw themselves into the canals and submerged themselves until only their mouths were above the surface. They suffocated by the thousands from the smoke and lack of oxygen. In other canals the water got so hot that people were boiled alive.[234]

225

Saki Hiratsuka had, along with his father and about sixty others, sought shelter under the headquarters of the Yasuda Bank. The building's pipes were crushed, and the cellar slowly filled with water. By now most of the people were dead and their bodies floating around the cellar. The heat was horrendous, but the worst thing was that the water kept on rising. Saki made a last vain attempt to open the red-hot steel door. When he had already given up hope, the door suddenly opened from outside and the water rushed out, carrying with it the living and the dead. The firestorm was over and those who stood there among the smoking ruins were saved.

At dawn Masuko Hariono began to work her way back to the youth hostel on bare, skinless feet. Where the Meiji Theater once stood was a mountain of blackened bodies, suffocated, crushed, burned. It was impossible to say if they had been men or women; now they were just burned flesh, swollen, disfigured, and twisted.

Chiyoku Sakamoto's neighbor was pregnant. She went into labor as she fled the fire. She began to die as her baby was born. Both she and the newborn were badly burned. The father put the baby inside his overcoat and went on running. The child survived.

Once they had bandaged Masatke Obata's wounds, only his eyes, which he could not open, and his mouth, which could not speak, were visible. The doctor shook his head and sent him to the morgue in the cellar. There he lay for three days and nights without food or water. He was angered at the thought that his children would be left without an inheritance because he had not had the time to put his affairs in order. His rage kept him alive. On the third day his mother came to the hospital, but she didn't find his name on the lists because the doctor had written the wrong characters. His mother did not give up. She went around calling for him. When she shouted at the cellar door, she heard an odd sound. She brought him home on her bicycle cart. He survived, but his four children were gone forever.[235]

226

The Japanese mass media were silent. Only rumors reached the Emperor. He risked all of his prestige by asking to be taken to the river. There he got out of his car. On the shores of the river lay thousands of corpses, piled up with almost mechanical precision. The tidewater had come in and gone out, leaving the charred corpses like driftwood. He said nothing. There was nothing to say. He suddenly realized that Japan had lost the war.[236]

227

Many of Japan's leaders were struck by that same insight. A quarter of the capital in ashes, a million people homeless, 100,000 horrifying deaths – the first mass attack against Tokyo put the city into a state of shock. With a minimum amount of coordination between their military and diplomatic actions, the Allies could have used this state of shock to offer concrete terms for peace. The only condition that they already knew the Japanese would never negotiate – keeping their emperor – would also serve Allied interests. There was no reason for either side to want to prolong the war.[237]

But the Americans were too busy patting each other on the back. Telegrams of congratulation poured in to LeMay. Air force headquarters in Washington, D.C., was ecstatic. Arnold was jubilant. Not only was Tokyo the greatest victory of the American air force ever, they said, but the Japanese had been served up the biggest military catastrophe in the history of war.[238]

But nobody bothered to take political advantage of the situation.

The American press described the military destruction, not the human cost. There were no figures for the number of civilian victims. The Secretary of Defense, Henry Stimson, who had the numbers, was the only one who seemed troubled. Arnold assured him that they had done everything in their power to keep civilian losses down, and Stimson believed him – or pretended to.[239]

228

1945 Meanwhile, LeMay hurried on without harvesting the political fruits of his victory. Nagoya, Osaka, Kobe, and Nagoya once again – in ten days nearly half of the destruction that the whole bombing war had caused in Germany was visited on Japan.[240]

Then there was a forced break in bombing, because the napalm had run out. This pause was not used to forward a peace initiative, either.

The firebombing started up again in the middle of April when the napalm production had caught up. Germany's surrender on May 8 came and went without an Allied peace offer to Japan. The bombing continued. At the end of May, 3,258 tons of napalm were dropped on the undamaged parts of Tokyo, causing greater damage than any other single air attack in history. LeMay: "We knew we were going to kill a lot of women and kids when we burned that town. Had to be done."[241] No one counted the human cost anymore; damage was measured in surface area, square miles. In all of Germany, seventy-nine square miles had been destroyed in five years – in Japan, 178 square miles in a half-year.[242]

Without anyone questioning the methods.
Without ensuing demands for political followup.[243]
Killing seemed to have become an end in itself. ➤ 231

229

1945 The European countries impoverished by the Second World War could not afford to conduct expensive colonial conflicts. But nor could they afford to lose Malaya and other colonies with large export surpluses that brought in dollars.

The solution was a bombing war. This had worked well between the World Wars, after all. Since then, both bombs and airplanes had undergone enormous improvement. It should be quite possible to keep rebellious peoples in check from the air. The French began on the very first day of peace. On May 8, 1945, while exuberant crowds celebrated the peace throughout Europe, the people of the Algerian city Sétif demanded the right of self-determination they had heard so much about during the war.

When the police couldn't handle the situation, the French military came in with bombers and tanks. A few days later the revolt was crushed, and forty-odd Algerian villages had been leveled. Seventy Europeans and fifty times as many Algerians had been killed. Or perhaps it was 100 times as many – they weren't counted very carefully. The event was hushed up, and the little that did come out drowned in the celebration of peace.[244]

230

1945 A few weeks later, the French landed in the former French mandate of Syria and wanted to regain power. The Syrians, who had declared independence in 1944, resisted. The French General Oliva-Rouget has received harsh criticism, but he only did what the French had done with instant success in Sétif – he engaged bombers and artillery against cities like Aleppo, Damascus, Hama, and Homs.

The difference was that this happened before the public eye. The British helped the Syrians to dig out their dead and carry away the wounded. "For God's sake do something about this beastly mess without delay!" telegraphed the British consul. His American colleague forwarded a question from Syria's President Quwatli: "Where now is the Atlantic Charter and the Four Freedoms?"[245]

It turned out that the power of the bomb could not stand up to the public gaze. Domination from the air could only be practiced when the victims were anonymous, invisible, and speechless. In 1925 the French had bombed Damascus successfully. In 1945 the bombing led to the expulsion of the French from the city, and they were forced to acknowledge Syria's independence. ➤ 243

231

In July, when their sixty-six largest cities had been burned down, the Japanese diplomats desperately sought someone on the Allied side who would discuss terms of surrender. On July 18, the Emperor telegraphed Truman and once again asked for peace. No one seemed interested.[246]

For lack of bigger game, the United States now bombed cities with only 100,000 inhabitants, scarcely worth the cost of the bombs. By the beginning of August they were down in the 50,000 range.

There were only four reserved targets left. One of them was called Hiroshima, another Nagasaki. ➤ 13

232

1945 Roosevelt's successor, Harry Truman, took no notice of the scientists' warnings. Germany was defeated, so the atom bomb would end the war with Japan and "impress Russia," as Secretary of State Byrnes said to Szilard.[247]

The Chicago scientists refused to give up. On June 11, 1945, the so-called Franck Group Report came out, which argued powerfully against the use of the bomb: "If the United States were to be the first to release this new weapon of indiscriminate destruction upon mankind she would sacrifice public support throughout the world, precipitate the race for armaments and prejudice the possibility of reaching an international agreement on the future control of such weapons."[248]

Truman referred the question of how the bomb should be used to a committee chaired by Secretary of Defense Stimson. The committee recommended that the Japanese not be warned, that the attack should not be directed against a civilian area, but that the objective ought to be "a vital war plant employing a large number of workers and closely surrounded by workers' houses."

The recommendation was self-contradictory (a residential area is by definition a civilian area) and unrealistic (the effects of the bomb could not be limited to any particular part of the city). In reality it was the civilian core of the city that was the center of the target.

233

1945 In countless tales of the future, the superweapon had destroyed the enemy and ensured peace. That this would be the case in reality as well seems never to have been seriously questioned. But just as in the fictional accounts, there were many who suggested that the weapon ought to be demonstrated or at least explained before use, that "HALT!" ought to be called before the shot was fired. On June 27, 1945, Ralph A. Bard, Undersecretary of the Navy, appealed to the government that the United States should inform the Japanese of the type of weapon that was about to be used against them and give assurances at the same time about the future role of the Emperor. Only in that way would the U.S. be able to preserve its position as "a great humanitarian nation." His plea went unheard, and Bard left the administration.[249]

On July 16, the first test of the atom bomb was carried out in New Mexico. The next day, Leo Szilard and sixty-nine of the scientists who had made the bomb possible sent a petition in which they asked Truman not to use the bomb without first warning the opponent. The military took care of the letter and saw to it that it never reached Truman.

On July 26 came the Potsdam Declaration, in which the United States and Great Britain threatened Japan with "prompt and utter destruction" if the country did not surrender unconditionally. Nothing was said of the Emperor's role, nothing of the atomic weapon.

On July 28, the Japanese rejected the Allied ultimatum as expected – while at the same time continuing their fruitless attempts of the last several months to get the Allies to the negotiation table.[250]

234

1945 On the morning of August 6, 1945, at 8:16 and two seconds, the dream of the superweapon became reality. The first atom bomb exploded without warning over Hiroshima with the force of 12,500 tons of trotyl. A new kind of war had begun. The events of the first second of this new war unfolded like this:

> 0.0
> The bomb was detonated at approximately 600 meters above the Shima Hospital in central Hiroshima, during the peak of the morning rush hour. The temperature at the point of detonation rose to several million degrees in a millionth part of a second.
>
> 0.1
> A fireball fifteen meters in diameter with a temperature of about 300,000 degrees was formed. At the same time, neutrons and gamma rays reached the ground and caused direct radioactive injuries to living organisms.
>
> 0.15
> The fireball expanded, and the blast wave expanded even more rapidly; the air was heated until it glowed.
> 0.2-0.3
> Enormous amounts of infrared energy were produced and caused most of the direct burn injuries to people.
>
> 1.0
> The fireball reached its maximum dimensions, about 200–300 meters in diameter. The blast wave, which spread the fire, advanced at the speed of sound.

When the rescue teams managed to get into the area later in the day, they did not find many to rescue. Their task consisted primarily in gathering and removing tens of thousands of corpses. Those who had died immediately were left in the ruins. Those who had lived a few minutes or a few hours longer lay in heaps on bridges and the shores of the river or floated in the water, where they had tried to save themselves from the firestorm.[251]

About 100,000 people (95,000 of them civilians), were killed instantly. Another 100,000, most of these civilians as well, died long, drawn-out deaths from the effects of radiation.

➤ 14

235

And that's how it always had been.

The first the Americans heard of the atomic weapon exploding in Hiroshima on August 6, 1945, forty-four months to the day after Pearl Harbor, was President Truman's announcement: "Sixteen hours ago an American airplane dropped one bomb on Hiroshima, an important Japanese Army base."[252]

He forgot to mention that Hiroshima was not only a military base, but a city of more than 400,000 civilians, and that the bomb was aimed not at the base but at the heart of the city.

The following day, Truman expanded on the explanation. A military base had been selected for the attack, he said, "because we wished in the first attack to avoid, as much as possible, the killing of civilians." But if "the Japs," as he called them, did not surrender, this consideration would soon have to be set aside, and "unfortunately thousands of civilian lives would be lost."[253]

This left the impression that thousands of civilian lives had not been lost in Hiroshima. As Truman well knew, that was a lie.

236

1945 Two days later, on August 8, the Soviet Union entered the war against Japan at the request of the United States.

The next day, the U.S. dropped an atom bomb on Nagasaki.

On August 14, Japan surrendered.

The American leadership saw this as cause and effect. The superweapon had brought peace.

The next day, the military censorship that had been in effect throughout the war was lifted – with one exception. Nothing could be reported about the effects of the atom bomb.[254]

➤ 241

237

One of the preconditions of the Korean War was that the Soviet Union attack Japan at the conclusion of the Second World War. That had not been a matter of course. If the Soviet Union had not entered the Pacific War, the U.S. could have occupied all of Korea by itself and ruled the country as it pleased. But in the spring of 1945, the Japanese troops in China and Korea still seemed like formidable adversaries. The Pentagon wanted to see the Soviets share the burden of risks and losses, and did not consider Korea strategically important for the United States.[255]

If the United States had not insisted that the Soviet Union enter the war with Japan when Japan was already defeated, there would not have been two Koreas to reunify. There would have been no Korean War.

238

The opposite alternative was just as possible: the Soviet Union could have occupied all of Korea. As it turned out, the Russian Army swept all the way south without encountering any serious resistance. The Russians were well into Korea before the U.S. had managed to land a single soldier there.

But Stalin, too, thought the country unimportant. When the U.S. wanted a cut of the booty, he agreed to stop at the 38th parallel. Had he gone on, not much could have been done to stop him.[256] Korea would never have been divided. And there would have been no Korean War. ➤ **244**

239

1945 On August 8, 1945, two days after Hiroshima and the day before Nagasaki, the U.S., the Soviet Union, Great Britain, and France signed the so-called London Agreement, which made war crimes and crimes against humanity actions punishable in international court.[257]

That sounded good. But there was a catch. How could they prevent the condemnation of their own systematic bombing of civilian residential areas in Germany and Japan, according to the rules that had been accepted before the war as valid international law, even by the Allies themselves? What would they say when German generals, brought to court for destroying entire villages in actions against partisans, responded that they had done precisely what the Allied bombers had done to German cities and villages?[258]

In his concluding report, prosecutor Telford Taylor declared both German and Allied bombing innocent, since "the air bombardment of cities and factories has become a recognized part of modern warfare, as practiced by all nations."[259] The bombing of civilians had, according to the court, become customary law. The fourth Hague Convention of 1907, which forbids air bombardment of civilians, was not applied during the Second World War and thereby, according to the court, had lost its validity.

So rather than establishing that the Allies, too – in fact, especially the Allies – had committed this kind of war crime, the American prosecutor declared that the law had been rendered invalid by the actions of the Allies. What's sauce for the goose is apparently not sauce for the gander.

240

The new position protected the Allies from criticism for what they had already done. At the same time, it did away with the legal hindrances for the future use of nuclear weapons. No one should be able to argue that Moscow or Leningrad had a legal international right of protection from atomic war, if the Soviet Union rolled its tanks over Europe. ➤ **252**

241

1945 Only one journalist, the Australian Wilfred Burchett, broke the rules and managed to get out an uncensored report from Hiroshima. His reportage made the front page of the *London Daily Press* on September 6 with later reprints in papers all over the world: "In Hiroshima, 30 days after the first atomic bomb destroyed the city and shook the world, people are still dying, mysteriously and horribly – people who were uninjured in the cataclysm – from an unknown something which I can only describe as the atomic plague..."[260]

In the city's only remaining hospital, Burchett saw hundreds of patients lying on the floor in various stages of physical deterioration. Their bodies were emaciated and gave off a repellent stench. Many had terrible burns. Burchett quotes a Dr. Katsuba, who was working in the hospital then:

> At first we treated burns as we would any others, but patients just wasted away and died. Then people...not even here when the bomb exploded, fell sick and died. For no apparent reason their health began to fail. They lost their appetite, head hair began to fall out, bluish spots appeared on their bodies, and bleeding started from the nose, mouth and eyes.
>
> We started giving vitamin injections, but the flesh rotted away from the puncture caused by the needle. And in every case the patient dies. We now know that something is killing off the white corpuscles, and there is nothing we can do about it. There is no known way of replacing white corpuscles. Every person carried in here as a patient is carried out as a corpse.

The Japanese scientists who performed autopsies of the corpses in the hospital's cellar confirmed that nothing that had ever been seen could explain the cause of the sickness or how it should be treated.

"I can't understand it," said Dr. Katsuba. "I was trained in the United States; I believed in Western civilization. I am a Christian. But how can Christians do what you have done here? Send, at least, some of your scientists who know what it is, so that we can stop this terrible sickness."

242

The American authorities knew that Burchett's report was coming out, and the same day they published a story that had been kept in reserve for just such an occasion. Their report described 200 Japanese atrocities against prisoners of war, including cannibalism and live burial. This was intended to inspire the thought that the Japanese had got no better than they deserved.

Also on the same day another report saved for the same purpose was published, this one written by the government journalist William Laurence, about how wonderful it had been to bomb Nagasaki. He wrote of the atom bomb: "Being close to it and watching it as it was being fashioned into a living thing so exquisitely shaped that any sculptor would be proud to have created it, one somehow crossed the borderline between reality and non-reality and felt oneself in the presence of the supernatural."[261]

As an additional precaution, General Farrell flew eleven docile scientists into Hiroshima and had them confirm that the bomb had left no trace whatsoever of radioactive contamination.

General Groves assured Congress that radiation caused no "undue suffering" to its victims, that "in fact, they say it is a very pleasant way to die."[262]

But the Americans were spared concrete images of this pleasant death. Photographs of the victims were not allowed to be shown. Three hours of Japanese documentary film of Hiroshima after the bomb were confiscated and not released until more than twenty years later. After another five years, they formed the core of the first documentary film on the victims of the bomb – Erik Barnouw's legendary *Hiroshima/Nagasaki* (1970).[263] ➤ **249**

243

1945 On October 24, 1945, the United Nations statute was signed, the first legal document that – even in passing – asserts "the principle of equal rights and self-determination of peoples."[264] Even the European colonial powers signed the statute. They saw it as rhetorical fanfare, not a legally binding treaty. In practice, they continued to uphold the right of the conqueror anywhere their bombers could maintain European rule.

➤ **256**

244

1945 Even as late as December 1945, events in Korea could have taken a different turn.

Within a few months, the American occupation forces had managed to inspire hearty dislike in southern Korea. The Americans knew nothing of the country, none of them could speak the language. They treated the Koreans like enemies and their defeated enemies, the Japanese, like comrades-in-arms. They selected an eleven-man Korean council with just one seat for the country's majority political movement and ten places for conservative landowners and right-wing officials who had collaborated with the Japanese colonial government and were therefore considered traitors by their countrymen.[265]

On December 16, 1945, the American commander, General Hodge, wrote to MacArthur in Tokyo and suggested that the United States should give up its attempt to control political developments in south Korea. The U.S. was not welcome there, he wrote; the Koreans wanted nothing but reunification and independence – this was the dominant ambition of all the political groups:

> I would go so far as to recommend we give serious consideration to an agreement with Russia that both the U.S. and Russia withdraw forces from Korea simultaneously and leave Korea to its own devices and an inevitable internal upheaval for its self-purification."[266]

General Hodge was a conservative and rather narrow man. He feared that self-determination would lead to revolution and civil war. But it is also in the realm of possibility that the Koreans, left to their own devices, would have solved their problems peacefully. There would not, in any case, have been any Korean War.

245

Nobody listened to General Hodge, despite the fact that he stressed the seriousness of his suggestion by requesting relief from his post. Instead, a separate Korea was created. Resistance was put down with the help of prominent torturers and henchmen from the earlier Japanese colonial government, which now, under American occupation, was given extraordinary powers to hunt nationalists and communists. In free elections, the left would almost certainly have won. Now the right won, at the cost of 589 dead and 10,000 arrested.[267]

In 1949, the last American troops left the country. The dictator of North Korea, Kim Il Sung, was convinced that the regime in the south lacked the support of the people and would fall like a house of cards at the least little blow.

Stalin had the last word.[268] Had Stalin said no, there would never have been any Korean War. Had Stalin known that the U.S. would intervene, he would have said no. Now he was just not interested, and he assumed that the Americans were equally uninterested. He let Kim try to realize his idea of reunification.[269] Both of them thought that it would be a short, local war that would be over before anybody had time to react. ➤ **268**

246

1946 The United Nations General Assembly unanimously passed its first resolution on January 24, 1946. It created an Atomic Energy Commission with the task of forwarding suggestions for the "elimination from national armaments of atomic weapons and of all other major weapons adaptable to mass destruction."

The Commission's work resulted in the so-called Baruch Plan, which was presented on June 14. The plan was predicated on the existent monopoly on atomic weapons held by the United States. According to the plan, the only nation that could have excluded the atom bomb from its arsenal would not be obliged to do so. Instead the idea was to prevent other nations from pursuing nuclear technology. An international organization, dominated by the U.S., would not only have the right of inspection, but also "managerial control" over all raw materials and activities that could result in chain reactions. No nation would have the right to develop nuclear energy, even for peaceful purposes, without permission from this organization. Transgressions would lead to "automatic punishment" – not clearly defined – and members of the Security Council could not exercise their right to veto. Before the plan was fully realized, the U.S. would keep its atomic weapons and have the sole right to produce new ones.[270]

If some nation other than the U.S. had enjoyed a monopoly of atomic weapons, would the United States have accepted the Baruch Plan? Surely not. It was quite a presumption that all of the world's people should trustingly place the power over life and death in the hands of the nation responsible for what had happened in Hiroshima and Nagasaki just a year before.

247

1946 But in fact, that nation already had the power.

The Strategic Air Command became an independent branch of the United States military services in March of 1946. In May of that same year, SAC was appointed the task of preparing atomic attacks aimed at targets all over the globe. On the anniversary of the bombing of Hiroshima, they flew the first intercontinental bomber, the B-36. Now the U.S. had not only a monopoly on the bomb, but also had a plan that could deliver one anywhere in the world. And the next generation of weapon transport was already on the drawing board: the intercontinental missile, later called the Atlas missile.[271]

248

1946 As usual, the futuristic novel was a few steps ahead. In *The Murder of the U.S.A.* (1946) by Will Jenkins, the intercontinental missile is already a reality. The U.S. has lost its monopoly, and seventy million unprepared Americans have been killed in a nuclear ambush. When deterrence has failed, all that is left is reprisal.

Lieutenant Sam Burton is appointed to wreak "the terrible and adequate revenge." But whom is he to attack? When the cities disappeared, so did the communications systems. It takes ten chapters to figure out who should be punished.

Then the question remains: How guilty are children and the elderly in the attacking country, really? How guilty are men and women who have not been able to choose or influence their government? Should slaves be punished for the crimes of their master?

Before Sam drops his missiles, he delivers a little speech in his defense:

> If war is a crime, it must be punished. And human beings are certainly responsible for their governments. They submit to them, if they do not support them. A man who lets himself be enslaved, so that his leaders may plan war, commits a crime against humanity. Ultimately his crime is murder.
>
> We Americans are not sending bombs merely to kill our enemies. We are sending bombs also to save the lives of the hundreds and millions who will be murdered if men ever dare to become slaves again, or nations dare to be anything but free.
>
> I demand the destruction of every city, every hamlet, every cross-road. I demand that the enemy country be turned into a waste of bomb-craters so that for ten thousand years to come any man who thinks of war will look at it and have his blood turn to ice within him.[272]

➤ 251

249

1946 One year after the bomb, John Hersey's piece "Hiroshima" appeared in the *New Yorker*. Here for the first time, the world could encounter six of the survivors of Hiroshima and hear them tell of their experiences.

Dr. Sasaki, the only uninjured doctor at the Red Cross Hospital in Hiroshima, is besieged by tens of thousands of badly wounded patients, most of them with horrifying burns – and he has nothing but saline solution to treat them with. Hour after hour Sasaki walks numbly through the ill-smelling corridors and binds the wounded in the gleam of the still-raging fires in the city. The ceiling and inner walls have caved in, the floors are sticky with blood and vomit. By three in the morning, Dr. Sasaki and his coworkers have been at their gruesome work for nineteen hours straight, and they hide behind the hospital building to get a little sleep. After an hour they are discovered and surrounded by a lamenting circle of patients: "Doctors! Help us! How can you sleep!"

But by far the majority of people never make it to the hospital. Pastor Tanimoto acts as a ferryman taking the wounded from the burning side of the river to the one that is not yet burning. He takes a woman's hands to help her onboard – her skin slips off "in huge, glove-like pieces." Though he is small in stature, he manages to lift some people onto the boat. Their skin is slimy on the chest and back, and he thinks with a shudder of all of the burn injuries he has seen in the course of the day – "... yellow at first, then red and swollen, with the skin sloughed off, and finally, in the evening, suppurated and smelly." On the other side of the river there is an elevated sandbank, and he lifts the living, slimy bodies up there, away from the tidewater. Again and again he has to remind himself: "These are human beings."

Many Americans who had seen the mushroom cloud as a new version of the Statue of Liberty had second thoughts when they read Hersey's report. Albert Einstein bought a thousand copies of the magazine. But the decision to drop the bomb was still too sensitive a subject for discussion.[273]

250

1946 A month earlier, at the beginning of July, 1946, the U.S. Strategic Bombing Survey came to the following conclusion in its official report of the result of the American air war against Japan:

> Japan would have surrendered even if atomic bombs had not been dropped, even if Russia had not entered the war, and even if no invasion had been planned or contemplated.
>
> The Hiroshima and Nagasaki bombs did not defeat Japan, nor by the testimony of the enemy leaders who ended the war did they persuade Japan to accept unconditional surrender.[274]

How could you keep the lid on this kind of news? First, you have it pushed aside with something bigger. The same day the report on the air war against Japan was released, the Bikini bomb was exploded. That took over the headlines.

In the long run, however, an intellectual counteroffensive would be required. Former Secretary of State Henry Stimson had put his name to an authoritative article, intended to give the definitive description of how the decision to drop the first atom bomb was made. The bomb was dropped, wrote Stimson, not to kill but to save lives – the lives of the 1,000,000 to 1,500,000 Americans that it would have cost to invade Japan.

A million American lives? How had Stimson's ghostwriter come up with that number? No answer. The chiefs of staff had estimated the expected losses at between 25,000 and

50,000 at the highest. And why invade Japan at all, when the Japanese had already offered to surrender?[275] ➤ 326

251

1947 The response to Sam Burton's speech arrived the next year in Theodore Sturgeon's tale "Thunder and Roses" (1947).[276] Here, too, the U.S. has been attacked with atomic weapons; most Americans are already dead, the rest have radiation sickness. Here, too, the reprisal has been delayed, but now the hero finally has his finger on the button.

In Jenkins's novel, the surviving Americans cry out in one voice for revenge. In Sturgeon's story, too, there is an eager avenger, but the hero realizes that if he pushes that button he will wipe out not only the murderers, but the rest of humanity, and probably every living thing on earth.

Jenkins wants the slave to pay for his master's crime. Sturgeon asks whether dogs, too, must be punished – and apes, birds, fish, lizards? Should all of creation be eliminated so that those who destroyed the U.S. will not take over the earth?

"We must die," says the female protagonist, Star, in a passage that parallels Sam Burton's speech in Jenkins's novel.

> We must die – without striking back. That would sterilize the planet so that not a microbe, not a blade of grass could escape, and nothing new would grow.
>
> Let us die with the knowledge that we have done the one noble thing left to us. The spark of humanity can still live and grow on this planet. It will be blown and drenched, shaken and all but extinguished, but it will live...if we are human enough to discount the fact that the spark is in the custody of our temporary enemy...

The avenger dashes to the button to launch revenge. The hero kills him and destroys the switch. ➤ 254

252

1947 Not everyone was convinced that it was legal to destroy humankind. J. M. Spaight, the English expert in international law cited above, who before, during, and after the Second World War was one of the most ardent advocates of aerial bombing, had his doubts about the atom bomb. In the third (1947) edition of his book *Air Power and War Rights* he disposes of the arguments put forward for the legality of nuclear weapons.[277]

They shorten wars, say their defenders. This argument, Spaight returns, can also be used for chemical or biological warfare. Not all means of shortening wars are permissible. If it is true that the aftereffects of the atom bomb doom everyone within a large area to death, then nuclear weapons would be impermissible according to law established as early as 1868. The Petersburg Declaration of that year prohibited weapons that "uselessly aggravate the sufferings of disabled men or render their death inevitable."

Precisely because the effects of the atom bomb are so terrible, it is argued, they will create a deterrent to war. But history unfortunately offers no certain guarantee for such hopes, replies Spaight. When dynamite and many other means of destruction were discovered, it was thought they were so horrifying that war would be impossible. Even so, sooner or later people once again took up arms.

Spaight's problem is that he wants to condemn the atom bomb while continuing his defense of area bombing, a practice which led historically to the atom bomb and made its use possible. He finds a solution in a requirement governing the proportion of destruction between the military objective and the area surrounding it. "In atom bombing the disproportion is immense," he writes. Thus he can declare nuclear weapons illegal without condemning the British bombings that he had so ardently supported. ➤ **294**

253

1947 During the Second World War, the Russians had no heavy bombers to speak of, so they invested in missiles. The Russians had potential enemies at close quarters. Even a rather modest increase in the missiles' precision would make them usable against Berlin, Tokyo, or Peking. A hundred-odd engineers were taken from Peenemünde to the Soviet Union, where they continued to develop the V-2. The Russians also took over the Kreiselgeräte Company, which was working on a gyro with a gas bearing, rather than a ball bearing, to give the V-2 increased precision.

On October 30, 1947, the Soviet fired its first missile, a slightly improved V-2. Ten years later, the Russians surprised the world with the first intercontinental rocket and, a few months later, the first satellite, Sputnik, which circled around the earth in an orbit and was wholly visible to the naked eye.[278]

An old Russian aristocrat named Father Nikon had lived for decades as a monk on Mount Athos in northern Greece. After one of his rare returns to modern civilization, I was asked to help him back to his hermit's hut out at the end of the Athos peninsula. We climbed the last 100 meters up an almost vertical mountain wall with the help of chains. That night I had trouble sleeping and went out to get a breath of fresh air. There I saw for the first time the first satellite wandering across the sky between Europe and Africa, on its way from Asia to America, like a Columbus of space. ➤ **257**

254

1949 As yet, weapons capable of destroying all life on earth existed only in tales of the future. But reality was well on its way to catching up with fiction.

In 1947, the first American atomic war plan, called "Broiler," was drawn up. In the case of a Soviet invasion of Western Europe, twenty-four Soviet cities were to be destroyed with thirty-four atom bombs.

In 1948, the new intercontinental bombers, B-36 and B-50, went into service at the Strategic Air Command (SAC), which also had access to bases in England and the Far East. For the first time, American atomic weapons could reach the Soviet Union on a large scale. A new atomic war plan, "Operation Trojan," was adopted – seventy cities were to be destroyed with 113 atom bombs. Tens of millions of people would be killed instantly, and even more shortly thereafter.

The battle plan for 1949 was called "Dropshot." In this one, the SAC was to drop 300 atom bombs on 100 Soviet cities. The bombs had also become more effective, so that the cumulative explosive effect of American's atomic weapons now corresponded to ten megatons, or more than 800 Hiroshima bombs.[279]

Four years after Hiroshima, where new injuries from radiation were still being discovered every day; four years after the firestorms in Japanese cities, which still lay in ashes – four years later, 800 new Hiroshimas had already been planned.

The Soviet cities targeted by the U.S. atomic bombs had already been destroyed by the Germans and had scarcely managed to rebuild. The German cities defended by the U.S. were still in ruins after the British bombings only four years earlier. Back then, the Americans had thought themselves too good to bomb civilians, at least in Europe. Now hundreds of Soviet cities were to be destroyed.

The plans were secret, of course, but even at that time enough leaked out to incite vigorous protests. The churches were among the first to speak, along with the scientists.[280] Even military commanders reacted. "Must the Italian Douhet continue as our prophet, because certain zealots grasped his false doctrines many years ago and refuse to relinquish this discredited theory in the face of vast costly experience?" wrote the admirals of the navy in 1949. "Must we translate the historical mistake of the Second World War into a permanent concept merely to avoid clouding the prestige of those who led us down the wrong road in the past?"[281]

This was blistering criticism. The air force responded that it was simply a sign of the envy felt by an obsolete service branch. And true enough – when submarines later proved to be unassailable carriers of atomic weapons, the admirals overcame their moral scruples and enthusiastically accepted their new role in the planned mass destruction.[282]

255

1949 Never had the United States been more powerful. And never had the powerlessness of power been more evident.

The atom bomb didn't keep Stalin from building an empire of iron-hard police states in the part of Europe where his troops had driven out the Nazis.

The atom bomb didn't stop Mao Zedong from overthrowing the corrupt Kuomintang dictatorship and replacing it with a much more effective dictatorship of his own. In American eyes, the yellow and red perils had now been united, and a half-billion people had suddenly become America's enemies.

The atom bomb could not preserve America's monopoly of atomic weapons. It took only four years for Stalin to explode his first nuclear weapon – a few days before the People's Republic of China was declared in Tiananmen Square on October 1, 1949. The Russians did not yet have any means to reach the U.S. with their bombs, but everyone realized that it was only a question of time before the two superpowers would be able to destroy each other completely – and the rest of us, too. ➤ 262

256

1949 And they tried to ensure that no new laws were passed that might hold them back.

During the final moments of the war, the International Committee of the Red Cross in Geneva had already proposed a review of humanitarian international law. Their work began in 1946, continued with a 1948 conference in Stockholm, and by 1949 had led to four Geneva Conventions on the protection of the wounded on land and at sea, the protection of prisoners of war, and protection of civilians.

Protection of civilians was especially controversial. The Americans pushed through a clause that would make an exception for atomic weapons. The British opposed rules that "restrict[ed] freedom to carry out operations, particularly bombing."[283] Those who had suffered most from bombs, the Germans and Japanese, were not invited to the discussion.

The victorious powers could hardly forbid bombing of civilians without incriminating themselves for what they had already done and planned to continue doing.

The definition of "military objectives" had proved to be quite malleable. The Red Cross now tried to solve the problem. They suggested that any objective could be considered "military," but that certain predetermined zones, demilitarized and under international control, should be established where civilians could seek protection. For the British, even this proved to be an unacceptable limitation on the operative freedom of bombers.[284]

The British also worked hard to eliminate the term "war crime," and any other wording that implied that breaks with the convention were criminal and could lead to legal prosecution.

But even the few conventions that remained (once the British had eliminated everything suggested by their experts on humanitarian international law) caused big headaches for the colonial powers in the coming years. For even if the word "crime" was no longer used, everyone knew that crimes were being committed.[285] ➤ **259**

257

1950 The U.S. also helped itself to the supply of scientists in Peenemünde. With von Braun at their head, 118 German rocket scientists were taken to America and received a billion-dollar budget of a kind Robert Goddard would never have been able to imagine. (He had just died of cancer of the throat. His dream below the cherry tree would not be realized until thirty years later, when Viking I voyaged to Mars.)

The U.S. had a large fleet of heavy bombers. Why then did they want to focus on an unproven, imprecise, and expensive weapon like the missile? Their only imaginable enemy lay on the other side of the Atlantic and Pacific Oceans. How would a weapon that could scarcely hit a target the size of London after an hour in the air be made to hit a target precisely after ten hours in space?

In 1950 the SAC was given responsibility for all intercontinental war. The organization was dominated by pilots with a personal relationship to flying and airplanes, and often to bombing as well. No wonder these men were skeptical about missiles.

In the 1951 contract for the first "ballistic missile" (as the rocket now began to be called), the SAC demanded that a majority of the missiles would be able to strike at the most 500 meters from their target. That figure was probably based on what a bomber was supposed to achieve in "blind bombing," that, is when the pilot is flying on instruments. Implicit in this unreasonable requirement was the desire for the project to fail.[286]

258

The army held a different view. They wanted to fire on enemy areas of deployment and concentrations of troops from a relatively close range, where a reasonable amount of precision was easier to achieve. With the help of von Braun a short- and intermediate-range ballistic missile by the name of Jupiter was developed, equipped with three acceleration regulators, one for each dimension. These were fastened to a platform that, with the help of a gyroscope, was held in a consistent relation to the stars.

The navy piggy-backed for a while on the Jupiter program, but soon began creating its own ballistic missile, Polaris. Its chief feature was not precision but unassailability. While ballistic missiles and airplanes destroyed one another on the ground and in the air, the submarine-based Polaris missiles would sit safely in unknown positions at the bottom of the sea, posing the final threat that would always be there when the other threats had been eliminated.[287]

The competition between the branches of service forced the SAC to accept the guided missile. Massive reprisal with the hydrogen bomb made the 500-meter requirement for precision absurd – you don't need precision to destroy the entire world. ➤ 347

259

By 1947 the British had already given up India, Pakistan, Burma, and Sri Lanka, and were concentrating on defending their power in three types of colonies: (1) those of particular military importance (for example, Aden, Suez, Cyprus, and Gibraltar), (2) those of particular economic significance (Malaya), and (3) those in which British immigrants had settled (Kenya).

Aden was an important British naval base on the route to the Persian Gulf's oil. The peoples around that base had been kept in check from the air since the interwar period. In 1947 the large-scale bombing raids began once again. No negotiations – just fire away. It seemed cost-effective. To force the Quitebi people into submission had taken the army sixty-one days in 1934 and 127 days in 1940. Now in 1948 it took the air force less than three days.

That was the RAF's boast. But the victory proved illusory. The next year, a new people revolted and more villages had to be leveled. The rebellion continued and incited more and more brutality, while at the same time bridges and schools were built to win the hearts of the inhabitants. In the long run it wasn't even cheap.

The last attempt by the British to master the situation was Operation Nutcracker in January of 1964. As usual, the military success was short-lived, and soon the entire country was in open rebellion. Great Britain then declared its intention to leave Aden, which became independent in 1967.[288]

260

In February of 1948, the Communist Party of Malaya introduced a series of strikes and demonstrations for land reform, national independence, and civil rights for the Chinese immigrants who made up nearly half of Malaya's population. The British put down these demonstrations, thereby starting a war that lasted for twelve years.

In the beginning, there were high hopes that the British forces would be able to find and destroy guerrilla camps from the air. But the Malayan Races Liberation Army consisted in large part of battle-tried and well-armed veterans of the jungle war against the Japanese occupation army several years earlier. It didn't take many days for them to split up into smaller groups and make their camps invisible from the air.

In 1949 the British began to use a new tactic. For four years, airplanes were used to flush out the opponent – carpet-bombing was applied to large areas in order to drive the terrorists (as the guerrillas were consistently called) toward the British troops, who waited in ambush.

Their third tactic was to use airplanes to spread defoliant over the fields that were supposed to belong to the guerrillas. The difficulty with this was that they looked precisely like the other farmers' fields. Many innocent people's crops were destroyed and large areas of land were left barren.

In total, 35,000 tons of defoliant and bombs were dropped in more than 4,000 air attacks. But the expected result failed to materialize. The RAF was forced to conclude that "offensive air strikes were almost wholly unsuccessful in Malaya; they probably did more harm than good."[289]

The British were much more successful in playing the two dominant ethnic groups off against each other, and controlling the guerrillas' recruitment bases in the Chinese slums surrounding Malayan cities and villages. A half-million Chinese were moved into camps, where they were held under observation by Malayan police. The British won the military victory, but they were forced to accept the guerrillas' demands for land reform, civil rights for Chinese, and national independence. Malaya declared independence in 1963.[290]

261

In Madagascar, a little clique of Frenchmen, fewer than one percent of the population, had ruled 4,000,000 resistant and rebellious Madagascans for fifty years.

On March 29, 1948, a new revolt broke out, led by demobilized soldiers. It is doubtful that the rebels ever had more than 150 guns of any kind; the rest were armed with spears. The French used bombers, ship artillery and all of their traditional methods: burning villages, mass arrests, torture, rape, and arbitrary executions.

The fighting went on for two years but excited very little interest in Europe. According to a secret French army report, 89,000 Madagascans were killed. A new French governor rounded up the number to 100,000. No Frenchman was called to justice. The leaders of the rebellion who survived the war were sentenced to death but were then pardoned in 1954.

Six years later, they took their places in the first government of independent Madagascar.[291]

➤ 282

262

1950–1955 The powerlessness of power shocked the U.S. The immediate reaction was: We Need an Even Bigger Bomb. Truman gave the go-ahead for work on the hydrogen bomb.[292] The goal was a single B-52 that should be able to carry 3,000 Hiroshimas.

Another reaction was the hunt for supposed traitors within the ranks. This has been linked to the name McCarthy, but it began before him and continued even when he had gone too far and been denounced.

It was in February of 1950 that the then-unknown Senator Joe McCarthy suddenly became world-famous with his statement that there were 205 (or maybe 207 or even just fifty-seven – different newspapers gave different figures) Soviet spies among the highest officials of the U.S. The figure was grabbed out of the air, but his bluff paid off. Frustrated by the powerlessness of power, the Americans let McCarthy run a series of witch-hunt trials against their liberal compatriots. For more than five years, the "Red Scare" held America in an iron grip and violated, with the willing support of the media, most civil rights.

The Soviet Union offered no alternative. Under Stalin, civil rights were not only violated, they simply did not exist.

263

The battle against nonexistent American Communism was carried out in the name of democracy. But the most ardent anti-Communists had long since left democracy behind, especially in tales of the future. It might have been possible in days gone by, they wrote, to let policy be determined through referendum by confused and ignorant voters. Now decisions would have to be made on the basis of real knowledge of atomic physics, ecology, and genetics – if the human race was to survive at all. Ordinary people couldn't do it. "They aren't up to it, Joe," concludes Robert Heinlein in his short novel *Gulf* (1949).

Heinlein dismisses the dignity and freedom of the human being as "monkey prejudice." Believing in democracy is like believing in Santa Claus. Hope now has to be pinned on a new elite, which will not only make up the ruling class, but also a new species, clearly distinguishable from *homo sapiens* biologically. A secret organization has already begun to select the best of the genetic pool in order to isolate it biologically until the two races are permanently divided.

The New Humanity rises above morality and makes its own rules. It calmly dispatches anyone who, in its opinion, does not have the right to live. "We keep a Better Dead list: when a man is clearly morally bankrupt we close his account at the first opportunity."[293]

Heinlein does not seem to realize how closely his "solution" approaches the one already tried by the Nazis.

264

1950 There is no doubt that Spender would have been on Heinlein's dead list. But instead he is executed by his fellow astronauts in Ray Bradbury's *The Martian Chronicles* (1950).

Spender comes to Mars in 2001 with a group of men who are assigned to build a nuclear-arms base. The rocket lands near a city that only a few days earlier had been inhabited by Martians. Spender is fascinated by their architecture, learns their language and culture, and becomes more and more critical of his own civilization.

The extermination of the Martians is, as Spender sees it, a direct continuation of the fate that met the American Indians in the 18th and 19th centuries and has since been the fate of countless other peoples who got in the way of European expansion. They were destroyed almost in passing, sometimes without the conquerors even noticing, and then were forgotten.[294]

Spender fears that this series of genocides will now be completed with the help of nuclear weapons in a final, mutual, and total destruction. He turns into more and more of a stranger to the others at the atomic station. They hunt him down, surround him, and kill him. But when he is dead, they see his worst suspicions confirmed. Far out in space, the earth suddenly bursts into flame: "Part of it seemed to come apart in a million pieces, as if a gigantic jigsaw had exploded. It burned with an unholy gripping glare for a moment, three times normal size, then dwindled."

265

1950 In Bradbury's book, we stand on Mars and watch the world expire. In Judith Merril's first novel, *Shadow on the Hearth* (1950) we are right in the thick of things, with a child in each arm, experiencing the catastrophe from a woman's perspective. The sirens wail while a voice on the radio mechanically repeats those calming reassurances that are so unsettling: "The Army is fully mobilized, and there is nothing further to fear. There will be no more attacks. A screen of radar shields every inch of our borders, from below sea level to the far reaches of the stratosphere. Nothing can get through. We are living inside a great dome of safety."[295]

Gladys recognizes the voice of the governor – a tired old man who tries to mask his confusion with words. What "dome of safety" – when the cities are already lying in ruins? Now the important thing is to protect the children from radiation, to get food and water, to survive without electricity and all the other necessities of modern society.

"The sores look terrible," says the doctor. "But you have taken care of infected sores before, haven't you? This is just many more of those at the same time. Happens unavoidably with the loss of white blood cells."[296]

While looters and madmen shoot one another on the street outside, Gladys washes the pus-filled radiation sores on her daughter's body. The first chapter's scatterbrained, helpless housewife has transformed through the course of the tale into a very experienced woman.

When a hoarse voice on the radio announces in the end that the victory has been won, she screams with laughter. Victory! What "victory"? Whose "victory"?

266

To look at the atomic catastrophe through the eyes of a mother was exceptionally rare. It was by far more common to see it as a possibility for masculine self-realization.

People between the wars had been afraid to be bombed back to barbarism – to filth, starvation, and the rats. But during the postwar period, especially for American men, barbarism began to look promising. The threat of destruction opened the door for male fantasies with roots in the old dreams of the Wild West.

In many masculine tales of the future, nuclear attack becomes the half-longed-for excuse to break the rules of modern urban life.

"The city – envisioned as a hopeless morass of pollution, overcrowding, decadence, and enfeebling interdependence – is obliterated, thus freeing the would-be frontiersman to live out his yearnings for primitive, manly self-reliance in a restored wilderness," writes Bruce Franklin.

Here there are no lost white blood cells, no hint of washing children's radiation sores – no, sir. As soon as the little wife has died in the blast, the husband is free to be Tarzan, hunting in the great luxuriant forests that soon grow up in the ruins of Manhattan. When he happens to catch a glimpse of himself in the mirror, this is what he sees:

"I was as straight as I had always been, but I was much wider than I had thought possible. My arms were as big as my thighs; my chest was immense. My hair was long, reaching halfway down my back..."[297]

Paradoxically, a military technology that had divorced destruction from every personal characteristic of the individual created dreams of a future where the courage, manliness, and physical strength of an already-vanished world were still decisive. ➤ **16**

267

1950 The Korean peninsula is about half as big as Sweden, but the population is five times Sweden's. The Korean people are united by language, culture, and a common history that goes back at least as far as the 4th century A.D. Around 1870, the Japanese began to push into the country. Korea tried to preserve its independence by playing the Russians and the Japanese against each other, and it sought help from the United States and Great Britain, but in vain – Japan annexed Korea in 1910.[298]

Thirty-five years of merciless Japanese colonial rule ensued, opposed by scattered, often communist-inspired resistance groups. When Japan's defeat at the end of the Second World War approached, the resistance movement grew, and when the Japanese surrendered, the movement declared Korea independent.[299]

The resistance movement had a Western orientation but was not acknowledged by the Western powers. Instead, the Soviet Union established a communist dictatorship in the North and the U.S. set up a right-wing dictatorship in the South. Both of the dictators promised to reunify the country and threatened each other constantly with war. Skirmishes and feigned attacks took place on a daily basis along the border. When the real attack came at four in the morning on June 25, 1950, it proved that the South's army was totally unprepared to defend the country, as the North had expected.

What the North had not expected was that on that same day, the U.N. Security

Council would condemn the invasion as an unprovoked act of aggression. Several days later the U.N. authorized its member states (in practice that meant the U.S., primarily) to support South Korea by any means necessary. ➤ 269

268

Normally the Soviet representative to the Security Council would have made sure that no one could react. The Soviet Union would have used its veto against the condemnation of North Korea's war of aggression and against any imaginable countermeasures from the U.N. If the United States had wanted to intervene they would have had to do so on their own, with a Congressional vote and declaration of war. The formalities demanded by the Constitution would, as intended by those who shaped it, have given time for deliberation, for arguments and counter-arguments, which might have even resulted in a decision not to declare war.

It is true that President Truman had strong domestic pressure to intervene. McCarthy was at the height of his rampage. Truman's administration was accused daily of being soft on Communism. The Korean War was a god-sent opportunity for him to show his determination in the war against Communism.[300]

But it is not entirely certain that the U.S. Congress, after careful consideration, would have wanted to send their constituents' sons to defend one Korean dictatorship against the other, especially since both of them wanted nothing more than reunification.

But instead everything went frighteningly fast. For at the decisive meeting of the Security Council (as I heard from my seat in the gallery), Moscow's man was not present. He was boycotting the Security Council in protest at the fact that Taiwan was representing China. Thanks to his absence, the Council was able to make its startling decision. The Korean War was no longer a local war, but a huge international conflict. ➤ 273

269

1950 The very next day, June 28, the Strategic Air Command initiated that support. The U.S. had absolute domination of the airspace over Korea, and the heavy bombers met with no resistance in the beginning. They shuttled back and forth between base and target with as little disturbance as a trip on the Staten Island Ferry. The crews' tours of duty lasted six months. For six months at a time, they rained down death and destruction on the Koreans without having ever met a Korean in real life.[301]

For the American navy, too, it was an unreal war. The great aircraft carriers circled around and around in a routine that involved hard work and intense boredom – but no risk whatsoever of enemy attack. It took three months to destroy the North Korean cities. For want of something better to bomb, the Americans started to level villages as well. After another month, there was nothing left worth the bomb it would take to blow it up.[302]

In the meantime, the North Koreans won a series of victories. They conquered almost the entire peninsula, thereby opening up South Korea to American bombing. Now everything could be destroyed. The Chief Justice of the U.S. Supreme Court, William O.

Douglas, gave the following summary of his impressions after a visit to Korea in the summer of 1952:

> "I had seen the war-battered cities of Europe; but I had not seen devastation until I had seen Korea. Cities like Seoul are badly mangled; but a host of towns and villages, like Chorwon on the base of the Iron Triangle, are completely obliterated. Bridges, railroads, dams are blasted... Misery, disease, pain and suffering, starvation – these are all compounded beyond comprehension."[303]

270

All of this was done in the name of the United Nations. Why didn't the U.N. demand that the laws of war regarding the protection of civilians be obeyed?

In the first place, the state of the laws was unclear. The 1949 Geneva Conventions did not protect civilians from air attack – the Western powers had made sure of that.[304]

And the laws of war that had forbidden bombing of civilian targets before the Second World War – should they still be considered valid, even though all of the warring countries, especially the victors, had systematically broken them during and after the war? In the second place, the U.N. was made up of U.N. member states. If any of them had complained about violations of international law committed by the U.S. in the name of the U.N., the answer naturally would have been "Be our guest, deploy your own troops, so you can decide how to support them from the air. Go ahead and show us how to stop the North Korean invasion – without committing crimes against humanity."

271

If I myself had been sent to fight in Korea, I would certainly have demanded that the war carry as little risk as possible for me personally. Even if it had meant that hundreds of thousands of civilian Koreans would have to be sacrificed, I would have wanted to get out of there alive. Many Americans were of the same opinion.

Of the Korean War's million (and more) air raids, the great majority were tactical missions in support of American ground troops. Whenever the Americans were fired on, they called in air support that leveled the place where the shots had come from. The British journalist Reginald Thompson described how it was done for the readers of the *Daily Telegraph.*

> I have described this in some detail because it was typical... Every enemy shot released a deluge of destruction. Every village and township in the path of war was blotted out. Civilians died in the rubble and ashes of their homes. Soldiers usually escaped. The odd bursts of fire. The halt. The air strike. The artillery. Tanks forward... Namchonjon was an appalling ruin, a scene of almost absolute desolation. There was nothing left of it. It had been a considerable town of at least 10,000 souls, perhaps more, in Korea. None now.

After the Americans had retaken Seoul, about 50,000 corpses were counted, just as many as after the firestorm in Hamburg seven years earlier. Thompson wrote:

> It is inescapable that the terrible fate of the South Korean capital and many villages is the outcome of a new technique of machine warfare. The slightest resistance brought down a deluge of destruction, blotting out the area. Dive bombers, tanks, and artillery blasted strong points, large or small, in town and hamlet, while the troops waited at the roadside as spectators until the way was cleared for them. Few people can have suffered so terrible a liberation.[305]

272

1950 The Korean people were "liberated" again and again while the front rolled like a steamroller back and forth over the peninsula.

In the beginning of September 1950, the North Koreans had taken almost all of South Korea and the Americans were holding on by the skin of their teeth at the southernmost end of the peninsula. Two months later, the Americans had taken almost all of North Korea up to the Chinese border. Another two months later, Chinese "volunteers" had pushed the Americans back to South Korea and retaken Seoul. All of this caused terrible loss of human life. Was it necessary?

In retrospect, the course of history easily acquires the semblance of inevitability. In retrospect, nothing can be changed, and therefore events are depicted as if they had been unchangeable from the beginning. But while history was unfolding, it could have been changed. Other decisions could have been made, which would have turned the course in another direction. So let's take a few steps back. ➤ **237**

273

1950 This was the decisive turning point, but it was not the last one. A new one arrived in October of 1950, when the Americans had retaken South Korea and reached the border of North Korea.

At that point, both the U.N. Security Council and the U.S. government had achieved the goal they had established at the beginning of the war. Again and again they had said that their only intention was to drive the North Koreans back to the border and reinstate the situation that had preceded the invasion.

But now that this goal had been achieved, it seemed insufficient. "The aggressor's forces should not be permitted to take refuge behind an imaginary line," said the U.S. in the Security Council, "because that would recreate the threat to peace."[306]

A few months earlier, the North Korean move across the border had been described, with justification, as a threat to peace. The same border had now become "an imaginary line," and the peace was threatened if the U.S did not cross it. The Americans believed that they had won, and this changed their goals. Their new objective, approved by the Security Council, was to reunify Korea by force and replace the dictator in the North with the dictator in the South. And so the war continued.

274

1951 The new objectives were not acceptable to Peking. The Chinese government attempted to convey this even before the decision had been made. But the U.N. did not acknowledge Peking, because the U.S., which dominated the U.N. at the time, did not acknowledge Peking.

For several decades, the U.S. considered the Chinese government a temporary criminal regime on the verge of collapse. American troops at China's border with Korea would, Peking feared, try to destabilize northeastern China (which the Japanese had successfully done only a few decades earlier) and do everything they could to hasten the fall of the Peking government, a fall which the U.S. considered imminent and highly desirable.

And so China sent its "volunteers" to Korea.

The American air force, despite its domination of the sky, had difficulty stopping them, in part because they were so economical. During the Second World War, German divisions fought on a quarter of what American divisions used in ammunition and supplies. A Chinese division needed only a twelfth of what the Americans required. It sufficed if only a little trickle of transports could make their way between the massive American bombing attacks.

At the beginning of 1951, the Americans had been thrown out of North Korea. Now it was the Chinese who stood at the 38th parallel. Now it was the Chinese who had to show their true colors: Did they want to reinstate the prewar conditions, or did they want to reunify Korea by force?

The Chinese believed that they had won. They continued on over the border in order to replace the dictator in the South with the dictator in the North. And so the war continued.

275

1951–1952 On the anniversary of the outbreak of the war, it was finally clear to both sides that neither could defeat the other. Negotiations for a cease-fire began. Heavy bombers were used as a means of persuasion, for example on the second anniversary of the outbreak of war, when the power plants and dams on the Yalu river were destroyed, or on August 29, 1952, when Pyonyang was hit with the war's worst bombing raid.

The bombs continued to cause "civilian casualties." For the people on the ground, these were very concrete. BBC correspondent René Cutforth described them for the *Manchester Guardian*:

> In front of us a curious figure was standing a little crouched, legs straddled, arms held out from his sides. He had no eyes, and the whole of his body, nearly all of which was visible through the tatters of burned rags, was covered with a hard black crust speckled by yellow pus... He had to stand because he was no longer covered with a skin, but with a crust-like crackling which broke easily... I thought of the hundreds of villages reduced to ash that I personally had seen and realised the sort of casualty list that must be mounting up along the Korean front."[307]

➤ 366

276

1953 While the Korean War was going on, I was supposed to be doing my military service. Strongly influenced by the events of the war, I refused and was instead allowed to complete an extended defense service as a worker in the creosote industry, without weapons.

Three years after the beginning of the war, a cease-fire was finally signed. Everything was back to where it had been in the beginning, with almost the same borders as before the war and the same unfulfilled dream of reunification. No one had won. Everyone had lost. The war is calculated to have cost the lives of 5,000,000 people, by far the majority of them civilians.[308] ➤ 18

277

Probably no one living during the 1950s intentionally and consciously wanted to destroy the world. But now it had become easier to do it than to avoid it. And perhaps lives could even be saved by threatening to do it.

Why did the U.S. allow more than 20,000 young Americans to die in Korea, often after defeats in desperate ground combat against a technologically inferior enemy – even though the U.S. had access to a weapon which, had it been used, would have brought immediate victory?

This question was asked more frequently as the war dragged on. The more Americans died, the more civilian victims piled up on the side they purported to defend, the more the enemy had to be demonized in order to justify what was happening. And the more demonic the enemy became, the more incomprehensible the reticence became that kept the U.S. from destroying evil once and for all.

278

The military was yanking on its leash. In a speech on August 25, 1950, five years after the bomb was dropped on Hiroshima, Secretary of the Navy Francis P. Matthews depicted the war of aggression as a necessary requirement for peace.

"To have peace we should be willing, and declare our intention, to pay any price, even the price of instituting a war to compel cooperation for peace."[309] According to Matthews, Americans could not avoid their duty as "aggressors for peace."

Several days later, Air Force General Orvil Anderson picked up on the theme. During the First World War, England and France had lost the best of their youth in ground conflicts, he said. During the Second World War, attacks against civilian populations had helped to keep military casualties down. Now the question was: "Which is the greater immorality – preventive war as a means to keep the USSR from becoming a nuclear power; or to allow a totalitarian dictatorial system to develop a means whereby the free world could be intimidated, blackmailed and possibly destroyed?"

The general was sure of the answer: "Just say the word, and I will destroy Russia's five atomic nests in a week. And when I stand before Christ, I believe I can explain to him why I wanted to do it – now, before it's too late. I think I could explain to him that I had saved civilization."[309]

279

1953 Matthews was given a reprimand. Anderson was relieved of his post. But two years later, Eisenhower won the presidential election by promising to get tough against Communism. And on October 30, 1953 he approved a new defense strategy, NSC-162/2, which stated that the U.S. would no longer allow itself (as in the case of Korea) to be drawn into limited conflicts using conventional weapons. Potential localized aggressors would instead be deterred by the threat of "massive retaliation" with atomic weapons.[310]

The new policy was announced by Secretary of State John Foster Dulles in January of 1954. Its justification was primarily economic – "more basic security at less cost." It was a way of holding the Soviet Union back without ruinous expense. At base it was the same idea as what the British called "air control" when they used bombers to dominate the Middle East between the wars and to put down postwar uprisings in Aden, Malaya, Kenya, and so on. Power cost too much on the ground. Bombs balanced the budget.

In concrete terms "massive reprisal" meant that the military could plan to deploy atomic weapons whenever and wherever the generals considered it desirable. They were counting on a short war. The NATO forces in Europe only had supplies enough to last for two weeks. Thus, in practical terms, a big Soviet offensive would have to be countered with immediate use of atomic weapons.[311]

General LeMay kept the Strategic Air Command's plans to himself. Actually, he should have been handing them over to the chiefs of staff on a regular basis, but LeMay was the man who had burned down Tokyo. He felt that he had the right to refuse cooperation. The politicians could of course have forced him, and finally they did. But for five decisive years (1951–1955), the U.S. planned for an atomic war with no political oversight whatsoever.[312]

280

1954 "I shall be brief," begins the new President of the United States in Philip Wylie's novel of the future, *Tomorrow!* (1954). He goes on:

> As you know, panic reigns from coast to coast. Four great cities were totally obliterated... Washington met the same fate later. Some twenty millions of us were killed or injured in the attack. Untold numbers, hundreds of thousands, are dying in the progressively worsening riots.
>
> The enemy offers peace. The condition is that we turn over all of our atomic weapons and tear down all of the facilities where such weapons are produced. Once we have satisfied that requirement, we will then be completely at the mercy of our enemy. A second possibility is to continue the war. Perhaps we can defeat the enemy, but it might take a month and during that month the enemy will continue his attacks against us. In the end there might remain in both nations that utter wreckage of civilization which the few predicted for so long, and the many refused to believe.

That is the second possibility. "And the third?" a woman's voice is heard to ask.

One of our submarines is a single, gigantic hydrogen bomb. It could move into the Baltic, dive to the ocean floor, and blow itself up. It would devastate the enemy's country, destroy perhaps two-thirds of his people, and make hundreds of thousands of square kilometers radioactive, so that the vegetation would die as well. That is the only alternative I have to offer to a surrender that would soon be unconditional; or to continue the ongoing destruction with the weapons we have been using thus far...

Naturally the big bang wins out.

Finland was not. Lithuania, Latvia, Estonia, they were not. [Probably neutral Sweden, too, was not, just incidentally.] Kronstad melted, Leningrad...they perished. The radiation-emitting particles filled their lungs, they contaminated their food, they polluted their water and could not be filtered out. Men swallowed, ate, breathed, sickened and perished in a day, a week, two weeks – men and women and children, all of them, dogs and cats and cattle and sheep, all of them.

And so the last war was at an end.

The last great obstacle to freedom had been removed from the human path.

281

In countless fictional futures, we have seen superweapons come and go. Humankind, particularly Western humankind, has come close to going under many times, but has always triumphed in the end – thanks to the superweapon.

Earlier it was the superweapon itself that seemed unbelievable. Now it was all too easy to imagine a weapon that could level entire countries. The happy ending, however, seemed all the more unbelievable.

Wylie paints the happy future in broad strokes. Two and a half years after the big bang in the Baltic, new cities have grown up, more beautiful and magnificent than the ones that were destroyed. "The bombing had proved an ultimate blessing by furnishing a brand-new chance to build a world brand-new – and infinitely better."

Really? What happened to all that radioactivity? Where were all the people dying of radiation sickness? Who was comforting the orphans and making men and women of them? There was already a bomb on the drawing table that could kill a hundred million people – but an "infinitely better world" built on a hundred million corpses was an illusory pipe dream.

➤ 287

282

In Kenya, 40,000 whites, less than one percent of the population, ruled five million blacks. The highest authority was in the hands of the Colonial Office in London.

The first wave of British immigration at the end of the 19th century coincided luckily enough with a smallpox epidemic that decimated and in some regions almost eliminated the Kenyan black population. The land seemed "uninhabited." Those who offered resistance were killed and their villages burned. Like so many other colonists of this period, the British governor, Sir Charles Eliot, believed that the natives were dying out. "There can be no doubt that the Masai and many other tribes must go under. It is a prospect which I view with equanimity and a clear conscience."[313]

After the First World War came a new wave of immigration: thousands of demobilized British officers arrived from Europe, bringing with them – luckily enough – an influenza epidemic that killed more than 100,000 Kikuyu. Five million acres of African land could then be confiscated and made available for British settlement. The blacks became landless farmworkers on ground that had belonged to their fathers.

During the Second World War, 100,000 Africans from Kenya participated as volunteers. They returned home hopeful, inspired by the promises of freedom offered by the Atlantic Charter – and were bitterly disappointed. At the same time, a new wave of demobilized British officers and former colonial officials from British India arrived, firmly determined to uphold white rule in Kenya. The Kenyan response was the Mau Mau Rebellion in 1952–1960. Throughout the 1950s, the British managed to convince world opinion that they were not fighting landless and disenfranchised rebels, but putting down "bestial murderers," primitive natives who, crazed with drugs, rituals, and sex orgies, were cutting the throats of white women and children.[314]

In fact only ninety-five whites were killed in the war, thirty-two of them civilians. During that period, more whites were killed in traffic accidents in Nairobi alone.

According to their own estimates, the British security forces killed 11,500 Mau Mau. For every wounded and captured man, there were seven dead. The number of civilian deaths was never reported. 80,000 Africans were imprisoned in concentration camps, where many died. A strip forty-eight miles long filled with barbed wire and mines was built by forced labor in order to cut the guerrillas off from the Kikuyu reservation. Other forced laborers built 800 fortified villages, into which the Kikuyu people were forced to move, as had been done in Malaya.[315] The Kikuyu were not used to living at such close quarters. Diseases spread, and the mortality in the "model villages" was startlingly high.

283

In 1953 the RAF began to attack Mau Mau from the air. During a typical week in July, there were fifty-six air assaults, 232 fragmentation bombs were dropped, and 19,000 shots were fired by the planes' machine guns. No results could be verified.[316]

The heavy bombers that were sent in the next year had a larger psychological impact. One of the survivors relates:

> The airplane noise came nearer. I turned my head and saw four bombs floating like big eagles under the airplane and a little behind. I pressed my chin to the ground, closed my eyes and ears and prayed God to forgive all my sins: "God, let thy mighty arms be my armor. You are our General; deliver us from evil and from our enemies' slavery! (Poooof! Poooof! Poooof!) God, Thy will be done on earth as in heaven..." – Once more my heart came into my mouth and I could pray no more...

The airplane left after unloading twenty-four bombs each weighing 1,000 pounds. When Jeriko called all the fighters together, we found that a few had bruises caused by the lumps of soil but none was serious. Some *itungati* were still trembling when I started singing: "Listen and hear this story of Nyandarua Hill; so you may realize that God is with us, and will never abandon our cause..." When we finished singing many of us had gained courage and confidence, but we realized that two fighters who were still trembling were suffering shock and couldn't use their voices. We tried to soothe them but all in vain. They later recovered at dinner time about midnight.[317]

284

The bombs forced the guerrillas to split up into small groups, and waves of carpet-bombing drove them, as in Malaya, toward waiting ground troops. The largest of these operations was given the code name "Hammer." For more than a month, an entire division hunted down 2,000 guerrillas, and with the bombers' help managed to kill or capture 160 of them.

Large areas around Mount Kenya were declared off-limits – there the planes could bomb anything that moved. White plantation owners who had their own planes went out and hunted the blacks from the air. The bombings reached their height in September of 1954, when the RAF dropped 500 tons of bombs.[318]

But by then people at home started voicing their opinions. Some protested against the bombing as a kind of class punishment for entire villages – even an entire people. Others thought that it was getting much too expensive – on average, it cost 28,000 pounds to kill one rebel. That didn't bring much glory. In May of 1955, the heavy bombers were withdrawn from Kenya on the RAF's own initiative, after having dropped 50,000 tons of bombs.[319]

Even stronger protests were excited by accusations of murder and torture by the police in Kenya. Black women and men testified that broken beer bottles had been shoved into their vaginas or anuses, that they were whipped, burned, knifed, dragged by cars, or had their testicles crushed with tongs. The accused policemen were sometimes given minimal fines, but most of them went unpunished.[320]

It was clear that the British committed grave violations of the 1949 Geneva Convention. But they themselves had made sure that their crimes could not be punished according to the convention.[321]

In 1960 victory was declared over the "terrorists." But the violence that the victory had cost had buried the colonial administration. Kenya declared its independence in 1963.

285

During the Second World War, France, even after its defeat, continued to administer Indochina, along with the Japanese occupation forces. The only ones fighting the Japanese were Ho Chi Minh's Vietnamese guerrillas, who were armed and equipped by the U.S. When the Japanese surrendered, Vietnam declared its independence.

But the French did not want to loosen their grip. They came back in the fall of 1945 and began to negotiate with Ho about a division of power. After one year, the negotiations broke down, and on December 14, 1946, the first war in Indochina began.

In February of 1947, the victorious French marched into Hanoi. They held the cities and could use the larger roads under cover from the air. But all of the countryside was in Vietnamese hands.

The French troops were stationed at a series of fortified points. They conducted an air offensive. A particularly successful method was to bait a trap. First the air force dropped sacks of rice, and then they bombed the Vietnamese who came to get it.

286

1954 Dien Bien Phu was a gigantic rat-trap of that kind, where the French garrison would put out bait. The plan depended on a serious overestimation of the air force, which was supposed to both supply the French base and destroy with bombs and napalm the Vietnamese who besieged it.

It didn't work. 200 planes flew around the clock to supply Dien Bien Phu with 170 tons of ammunition and thirty-two tons of food per day. More than half of it fell into Vietnamese hands. Fifty-odd planes were shot down, thirty were destroyed on the ground (by guerrilla troops who crept into the base through the sewer system), fourteen crash-landed, and 167 were damaged. The bombing of the deep and well-camouflaged Vietnamese positions around Dien Bien Phu was fruitless.[322]

The rat-trap that had been set for the Vietnamese caught the French occupying forces instead. Dien Bien Phu surrendered on May 26, 1954.

The peace negotiations in Geneva gave Ho Chi Minh control over northern Vietnam, while the French retained the southern part of the country until the results of a general election under international supervision were obtained.

As election day approached, the French turned power over to a Vietnamese puppet administration, which had not signed the treaty and was not planning to make good the promises that the French had made. The French explained with the most innocent mien in the world that they would of course be faithful to the terms of the treaty, but they could not force an independent Vietnamese government to do the same.[323] ➤ **305**

287

1954 On March 1, 1954, the American hydrogen bomb "Bravo" was detonated. It unexpectedly released fifteen megatons, that is, the same explosive energy as fifteen million tons of trotyl. "Bravo" had the strength of 1,200 Hiroshima bombs.[324]

Two weeks later, the air force informed the other branches of service how they intended to use the new weapon. The Soviet Bloc would be attacked with 735 planes armed with nuclear weapons. The targets remained unspecified – LeMay himself would choose them at the decisive moment depending on the existing conditions.

The overall impression was that "virtually all of Russia would be nothing but a smoking, radiating ruin at the end of two hours," reported one participant, Captain William Moore, to his superiors.[325]

It seemed apparent from General LeMay's answer that he is firmly convinced that thirty days is long enough to conclude World War Three.

The SAC is...dominated by a forceful and dedicated commander who has complete confidence in the SAC's ability to crush Russia quickly by massive atomic bombing attacks. No aspect of the morals or long-range effect of such attacks were discussed, and no questions on it were asked.

288

Fortunately, Eisenhower had a better idea of what using the hydrogen bomb would mean. When the South Korean dictator Syngman Rhee suggested a new crusade against Communism aimed at reuniting Korea, he answered:

> When you say that we should deliberately plunge into war, let me tell you that... war today is unthinkable with the weapons that we have at our command. If the Kremlin and Washington ever lock up in a war, the results are too horrible to contemplate. I can't even imagine them.[326]

So atomic war was unimaginable. At the same time, threats of atomic war were supposed to replace conventional warfare and render ground troops unnecessary. It didn't quite mesh.

Immediately after the explosion of "Bravo," Kurchatov and other Soviet physicists completed a study that revealed that soon there would be enough nuclear weapons to "create conditions under which the existence of life over the whole globe would be impossible." A hundred bombs like "Bravo" would suffice to ensure "the termination of all life on earth." The Russian leaders, too, were well informed.[327]

Even so, Khrushchev, almost to the same degree as Eisenhower, continued to build his country's defense on these unusable weapons. Both of them felt that their security rested on an unshakeable determination to use a weapon that would mean mutual suicide.

"Given the utter disproportion between the effects thermonuclear bombs would have produced and any conceivable purpose that might have inspired a war fought with them, it is a wonder anyone took this argument seriously," writes the American historian John L. Gaddis (1997).[328] "Massive reprisal" was supposed to be a cheaper way to keep the Russians in check – but was it reasonable to risk all life on earth to keep the budget balanced?

289

1955 The spring of 1955 was an ecstatic time for me. I had my debut as an author with a long essay called *A Suggestion*. I proposed a new life, lived with greater seriousness. I proposed a new form of writing, directed to a reader "threatened by great danger." A reader who "hears the radio say that the new war has broken out."[329]

My youth gave me love, happiness, success – but always in the shadow of an impending catastrophe, a catastrophe it seemed I could do nothing to stop.

When Barbro Alving and Per Anders Fogelström called a meeting to start up a campaign against a Swedish nuclear weapon, I smiled knowingly at their starry-eyed optimism. They didn't stand a chance against the mass media, the military, the political parties, and the corporations – the entire establishment that was agitating professionally for a Swedish atom bomb. My friends were throwing away their lives, I thought, traveling around the country talking to housewives' clubs and unions, while the editorial page of *Dagens Nyheter* reached a half-million readers a day. What good would it do?

290

1955 The strange thing was that anyone could believe in the idea of a Swedish atom bomb, when not even the huge stockpile of atomic weapons controlled by the United States offered any sense of security. A Soviet attack could only be stopped if the U.S. struck first, maintained air force General Samuel E. Anderson on April 6, 1955, in a talk given to the chiefs of staff. He estimated the combined number of dead for the two opponents in a pair of initial nuclear offensives at seventy-seven million, with sixty million on the Soviet side. Of 134 larger Soviet cities, 118 would be completely destroyed.

How would this impact the Soviet will to continue the war? This question was asked of nine leading American social scientists, but their answer unfortunately could not be quantified. Clearly it was "a matter of judgment rather than of deduction." That was the only assurance to be had.[330]

291

1955 The very absurdity of the situation by the spring of 1955 created "a moment of hope," according to the grand old man of disarmament, Philip Noel-Baker.[331] In Britain, a Committee for the Abolition of Nuclear Weapons Tests was formed, and was later to develop into a Campaign for Nuclear Disarmament with thousands of protestors marching to the nuclear arms factory at Aldermaston. The Korean War was over, the French were preparing to leave Vietnam, Stalin was dead. Both the Soviet Union and the U.S. had new leaders. Both had hydrogen bombs and both knew what that meant.

In 1954, France and Great Britain had crafted a suggestion for mutual disarmament that required great concessions from the Soviet Union. Surprisingly, Khrushchev accepted. In March of 1955, the U.S. offered reciprocal concessions. On May 10, the Soviets came forward with a detailed plan for disarmament based on the agreed-upon principles. Everything indicated that the Russians were serious. In July, the superpowers' heads of state were to meet personally for the first time after the Second World War, in Geneva. It seemed that an agreement was imminent.[332]

A door can be opened, wrote my friend Arne Sand, only where it is most closed. As for me, I called myself "the hopeful wanderer of the blind alley." Why not on the tenth anniversary of Hiroshima? Ten years later, people in Hiroshima were still dying painful deaths from that little bomb that was not even a thousandth as powerful as the ones now being built and tested. Wasn't it time to quit? The air was full of expectation.

The moment drew near. It arrived. And it passed, before we really could understand that it was gone.

292

1956 The next year it was too late. In 1956, France and Great Britain invaded the Suez Canal while the Soviets crushed the uprising in Hungary. The international climate grew colder than ever. The Russians began building their answer to the U.S. fleet of intercontinental jet bombers, and four years later, in 1960, the Soviet Union announced its counterpart to "massive reprisal."

The Soviet Union, declared Khrushchev, had achieved a nuclear capability that would make ground forces archaic, expensive, and unnecessary. They would be cut by a third and replaced by yet more nuclear weapons. Both superpowers had now based their defense entirely on their ability simultaneously to promise and avoid total destruction. ➤ **296**

293

1956 In Sweden, *Guernica* was shown for the first time by an association that wanted to create a modern museum of art in Stockholm. The painting became thoroughly bound up with that plan and with the concept of "modern art" itself. When the Stockholm Museum of Modern Art finally did become a reality in the fall of 1956, it opened with an exhibit of Picasso's *Guernica* and his sketches for the painting. Nineteen years had passed. Since the burning of Guernica, Hamburg had burned, and Dresden and Tokyo and Hiroshima. *Guernica* no longer appeared as a puzzling image, but as "a monument to our time, to an epoch of horror and destruction," as Torsten Bergmark wrote in *Dagens Nyheter* on October 20 of that year. He saw the picture as a 1937 prophecy of what had already occurred by 1956, and at the same time as a merciless prediction of what was then yet to come. ➤ **399**

294

1956 The lack of proportion between military effect and civilian injuries continued to grow, and became grotesque with the hydrogen bomb.

The commander of the U.S. strategic forces, General LeMay, declared in April of 1956 that in event of a war, "between sunset tonight and sunrise tomorrow morning the Soviet Union would likely cease to be a major military power or even a major nation... Dawn might break over a nation infinitely poorer than China – less populated than the U.S. and condemned to an agrarian existence perhaps for generations to come."[333]

Considering the war crimes LeMay had already committed in Japan without having received anything other than fame and promotion, it is natural that he didn't give a thought to the laws of war before making his threat.

295

1956 In the mid-1950s, the International Red Cross began to put together the fragments of international law in an attempt to reinstate the legal protection of civilian populations.

In 1956 the organization presented a draft of rules, which in paragraph 14a forbade the use of any "weapon whose harmful effects...could spread to an unforeseen degree, either in space or in time, from the control of those who employ them, thus endangering the civilian population."[334]

That is a modest description of what LeMay had threatened to do. But the Red Cross's suggestion was not even discussed by the leading powers, all of whom either had or were trying to get nuclear weapons.

The American army's *Field Manual 1956* maintained that nuclear weapons "as such" were legal since there was no international law or convention that limited their use.[335]

➤ **300**

296

1956 Stanley B. Hough brings this problem to its crisis point in his novel of the future *Extinction Bomber* (1956). In the midst of peace, an airplane crew is ordered suddenly to drop an atom bomb on a target in the Soviet Union. The pilot returns without dropping the bomb and is accused of high treason.

His wife explains that her husband had flown bombers for the same reason the politicians had deployed them: as a deterrent to war. At the same time he, like the politicians, was determined never to use nuclear weapons. And in retrospect it turns out that the Russians had a possibility for "massive retaliation" that the pilot's superiors knew nothing about. His refusal to follow orders has saved the world from destruction.

But should a soldier be allowed to refuse orders? Should he be allowed to think for himself? Or has he given up his responsibility to others for good? The military wants to condemn him as a traitor in a secret trial for failing to carry out an attack that the same military publicly denies having ordered and which, had it been carried out, would have led to the destruction of everyone.

"When someone pressed the button, the machine did not operate as it should," says his wife. "It wasn't a machine, after all. It contained a man. And by a man I mean somebody who was capable of thinking and acting on his own."

Man is the salvation of man in *Extinction Bomber*. No one can order another to exterminate humankind. Each and every one of us has the responsibility to prevent our destruction.

297

1957 More and more people took on this individual responsibility. Bertrand Russell and Albert Einstein were point men with their 1955 manifesto, which warned of "the extinction of life on this planet."[336] Linus Pauling's call for a ban on further tests of nuclear weapons was signed by 11,000 scientists that same year.

Meanwhile, the preparations for war went on, undaunted by public opinion. The head of the American army's research department, General James Gavin, testified before a Senate committee in June of 1956. He related that a total American atomic attack against the Soviet Union would spread death and destruction over Asia all the way to Japan and the Philippines. That is, unless the wind was blowing in the other direction. In that case, a hundred million Europeans would be killed instead.

This kind of information did not reassure Europe. In country after country, grassroots movements against nuclear weapons were formed. In the United States, the newly formed National Committee for a Sane Nuclear Policy made the following announcement on November 15, 1957, in the *New York Times*: "We are facing a danger unlike any danger that has ever existed. In our possession and in the possession of the Russians are more than enough nuclear explosives to put an end to the life of man on earth."

This had already been said many times over. It only needed to be made understandable.

298

1957 In Nevil Shute's novel of the future *On the Beach* (1957) the fateful causes have already taken place; only their consequences remain.[337] No one cares anymore how it happened, but it was probably the Chinese who began it. China, desperately overpopulated, struck at the Soviet Union, where large uninhabited regions proved too tempting. The U.S. is bombed by Arabs in Russian planes and believe they have been hit by the Soviet Union. This mistake leads to the extinction of all life in the Northern Hemisphere.

But the causes are no longer interesting. Because now the radioactive fallout is moving inexorably southward. Soon it will reach the last people on Australia's southern coast. Nausea is the first symptom. Then vomiting and bloody diarrhea. Perhaps a few days of improvement, and then the symptoms return, even more intensely. Death comes when the strength needed to survive gives out. An ordinary infection can kill as easily as leukemia. Dogs will outlive us, mice will live even longer, and rabbits will die last. But they, too, will die. By the end of next year there will be nothing living left.

"Couldn't anyone have stopped it?" is the last question. Answer: "I don't know... Some kinds of silliness you just can't stop."

299

Perhaps it was just this sense of resignation that made the novel so enormously successful. Everyone was familiar with that feeling of powerlessness. To serve it up on the well-polished platter of Shute's prose, lightly sentimentalized and at the same time completely inexorable – this was a foolproof recipe for success. We had to live with it, didn't we? The nuclear objectives for the United States were now, at the end of the 1950s, divided into three types: military targets that posed a threat to the U.S., military targets that posed a threat to Europe, and the industrial basis of Soviet military power. But the radioactive fallout would in any case produce such general effects that the choice between different types of targets seemed uninteresting. A 1959 study therefore recommended "random targeting" of weapons over the entire surface of the Soviet Union. This was "area bombing" taken to its ultimate consequence.[338]

The number of estimated deaths rose from year to year. A hundred million dead was no longer sufficient. By 1960 people were already talking about a half-billion dead in the entire Eastern Bloc. A reprisal could hardly be any more massive. The threat to kill another few hundred million would scarcely increase deterrence.

It was clear that the effects of such attacks would not acknowledge national borders. No one could predict how far they might spread. Shute's apocalyptic vision seems probable down to the smallest detail.

The "Last Man" romance had once acquired a new, terrible significance when it became "the last Mohican," "the last Tasmanian," "the last Herero," to name the best known of the peoples destroyed by European expansion.[339] Now that it was a matter of "the last rabbit," it wasn't even Romantic anymore. ➤ **301**

300

1958 In *The Legality of Nuclear Weapons* (1958), George Schwarzenberger, one of Great Britain's leading experts in international law, wonders how much protection was left for civilian populations in the wake of the methods used in the Second World War.

It was obvious that the distinction between combatants and noncombatants had been systematically set aside. In political and military circles, it seemed that large, undefined categories of civilians were now considered legitimate targets. To be counted a civilian today, it is necessary to refrain completely from contributing in any way to the war effort, and put significant distance between yourself and all important target areas.

But not even then can the effects of nuclear war be avoided. A ten-megaton hydrogen bomb has five times as much explosive power as all of the bombs dropped on Germany during the Second World War combined; it will also spread uncontrollable radioactive fallout over huge areas. If such a weapon cannot spare even those who are civilians in the strictest sense of the term, or if the weapon is aimed intentionally at civilians – well, "any such use of nuclear weapons would amount to an illegal form of warfare and the commission of a war crime in the technical sense of the term."[340]

Supposing that nuclear weapons were forbidden in principle, shouldn't their use be allowed in self-defense? If someone breaks the law by beginning a war of aggression, shouldn't the attacked party have the right to defend himself, even with those means otherwise forbidden by law?

No, answers Schwarzenberger. If the victim of aggression is allowed to use forbidden weapons, it will encourage everyone to use them. Because not using them could be interpreted as a tacit admission that you yourself were the aggressor.

Thus a total prohibition of nuclear arms would be justified. But only a dreamer would expect the superpowers to respect such a prohibition in their struggle for survival and world hegemony. What we need, Schwarzenberger says, is not a new law but a new world order. ➤ **304**

301

1959 "The future lay before us, as inalterable as the past." This is the key phrase in detective writer Helen (McCloy) Clarkson's *The Last Day* (1959). We get to know a little family who are on vacation at their island summer cottage. They are half-listening to the radio news which, as so many times before, describes a political crisis in the making.

The next morning they are awakened by a blinding flash of light, and a distant explosion smashes the windows, blows in the doors, and leaves behind a deafening silence. The telephone is dead, as is the radio. No ship can be sighted on the water, no cars come down the road. The children are the first victims of radioactive fallout.

> There is a stage of barbarism where a Genghis Khan will put every enemy to the sword in a conquered city, including the children, or an Agamemnon will sacrifice his own child to a god before sailing to besiege Troy. But we are less innocent. We know better. We have no gods who demand human sacrifice. Yet we sacrifice not one child, as Agamemnon did, not a few thousands as Genghis Khan did, but millions, and we have been preparing for this monstrous act in cold blood for many years.[341]
>
> Why did we let this happen? For one thing we had no imagination. Man cannot believe what he cannot imagine. That's a built-in psychological mechanism – automatic amnesia for the unbearable. Another important factor was fear. We were so paranoically afraid of communism, and fear destroys reason as well as courage. Loyalty to the people? We have let them all be killed. Loyalty to the land? We have let it be burned and poisoned so it cannot be farmed for a generation. Loyalty to democracy? In one sense, nuclear weapons killed democracy before they killed us.

As this is said, there is still someone to say it to. But on the seventh and last day, the book's female narrator is left alone on the island.

> For all I would ever know, I might be the only living thing on earth, and if only earth knew life, I would be the only living thing in the universe.

302

1959 All over the world, women formed the backbone of the resistance. So it was in Sweden, where the Social Democratic Women's Union was the first to take a position against the development of a Swedish atomic weapon in 1956. Only thirty-six percent of the Swedish people were of the same opinion at that time. By October of 1959, the opposition to nuclear weapons had grown to a majority: fifty-one percent.

303

1959 The masterpiece among novels of the future depicting the suicide of the human race is probably *Level 7*, written by Israeli-American author Mordecai Roshwald and published in 1959.

The protagonist, X-127, is sitting in a shelter 1,400 meters under the earth, writing a journal that he believes no one will ever read.

He has been brought from a training camp for push-the-button service to this sealed and automated bunker, where his meal tray comes clattering in on a conveyor belt and all information is given by an impersonal voice from a speaker:

> You are the defenders of truth and justice. To keep us safe from surprise attacks and ready for reprisal, it is of the greatest importance that we protect our protectors. That is why you have been brought down to level 7. Here you can defend our country without being exposed to the slightest danger yourselves. Here you can attack without being attacked yourselves.
>
> The system was locked down as soon as the last of you arrived this morning. You are securely cut off from the face of the earth and from the other six shelter levels.

Once X-127 has completed out his ghastly assignment he realizes – too late – that in the name of freedom and democracy he has carried out orders from a pre-programmed machine that had gone haywire. He is seized by a terrible longing for the humanity he has just liquidated.

His journal begins in March. By August the world has been destroyed down to a depth of thirty meters. Radioactivity seeps progressively farther down, level by level. On September 9, the enemy proposes peace, pointing out that there is no longer anything to fight for: no territory, no riches, no markets – nothing. Peace is concluded via radio on September 27 when only a few cave-dwellers are left on either side of the war.

> 10/2
> The radio transmissions of our ex-enemies have stopped.
>
> 10/3
> The people on Level 7 are deeply depressed. They are afraid to eat and afraid to breathe.
>
> 10/4
> How long will we hold out? Will we survive down here? Raise families? Keep humanity alive until the day a human being crawls out of one of these holes?
>
> 10/7
> It has finally reached us.
>
> 10/9
> Yesterday there were still attempts made to dispose of the corpses, but today no

one seems to care about it, and the bodies lie where they have fallen.

10/11
I have not seen a living person today. For all I know I could be the last living human being on earth.

10/12
Oh friends people mother the sun I I

➤ 312

304

1959 Nagendra Singh, one of India's foremost experts in international law, later chairman of the International Court, takes up the problem in *Nuclear Weapons and International Law* (1959). His point of departure, too, is that the Second World War dismantled the legal protection for civilians. Perhaps senior citizens, infants, and invalids in a large harbor city like Hamburg had to expect that they would be subjected to the merciless consequences of modern war. But even if they should accept that, which is doubtful, "there would still be no justification for using a weapon which would obliterate an area hundreds if not thousands of times larger than Hamburg itself."

Nuclear weapons sweep aside the remnants of difference between combatants and noncombatants and are therefore inconsistent with international law.

But in direst need? If all of humanity runs the risk of being enslaved?

No state of emergency could exist that would give someone the right to destroy entire countries and their inhabitants, answers Singh. "It would indeed be arrogant for any single nation to argue that to save humanity from bondage it was thought necessary to destroy humanity itself."[343]

So, according to Singh, nuclear weapons are already forbidden by international law. But just as chemical and biological weapons were subjects of special treaties, it would be best – for practical, legal, and humanitarian reasons – to make the ban on nuclear weapons an explicit total prohibition.

➤ 310

305

In Algeria, 1,000,000 French ruled 9,000,000 Algerians. On All Saints' Day in 1954, a half-year after the French defeat in Indochina, the Algerians mounted a rebellion in seventy different places around the country. At the time, there were 3,500 French soldiers there. By New Year's Day the number had risen to 20,000. In mid-1955: 180,000. Then the French gave up the neighboring colonies of Tunisia and Morocco, which became independent in 1956, and concentrated their troops in Algeria: 400,000 men. In 1960, France was forced to surrender the rest of its African empire – Benin, Senegal, Chad, and Upper Volta – in order to put everything they had into the war in Algeria, where more than 800,000 Frenchmen now fought to suppress a guerrilla force that had never had more than 40,000 active supporters (though millions sympathized secretly).

The French first followed the examples of Malaya and Kenya. Suspect tribes were forcibly removed to "model villages." The country was cut off from Tunisia and Morocco by 1,800 miles of mines and barbed wire. All civilians were moved out of the border regions, where anything that moved was fair game for bombs and guns.

The battle for the capital was won in 1957 using the same methods that had been used in Nairobi – mass arrests, murders, and torture broke down the resistance movement. This implied grave violations of the 1949 Geneva Convention – but the French had also had a hand in that Convention and had made sure that there was no possibility that war criminals could be punished.[344]

Out in the countryside, the helicopter proved to be the decisive weapon. Not since airplanes had been introduced into combat in the 1920s had a new weapon carrier changed the conditions of guerrilla warfare so dramatically.

General Challe, who took French command in Algeria in January of 1959, organized a helicopter transport of an elite force of 20,000 paratroopers and foreign legionnaires. They struck at dawn with antipersonnel fragmentation bombs, flew in 500 men backed up with fighter helicopters, smoked out the dug-in guerrillas, hunted fleeing men from the air, and were back in their barracks before sunrise. By May of 1960, the guerrillas were down to 12,000 men, divided into small, constantly hounded groups of a dozen or fewer. "We have won," said the military. But the war still cost a billion dollars a year. It still required a half-million men and a thousand airplanes and helicopters to keep the Algerian people in check. The same violence that had won the war had made a continuation of French rule impossible.

Algeria became independent in July of 1962.

306

During the postwar period, the Soviet Union regularly voted in the United Nations for a people's right to self-determination, and supported the anticolonial liberation movements – since this did not imply liberation for their own vassal states.

The U.S. tried to maintain the principle of self-determination for all people – but at the same time they were against all movements supported by the Soviet Union as a matter of course, and they voted in support of the colonial powers, i.e., their NATO allies. More and more, they began to emphasize anti-Communism rather than self-determination.

Neutral Sweden regularly voted against the Soviet Union and for the European colonial powers during the 1940s and 1950s. When the Algerian War first came up at the United Nations in 1955, Sweden voted with France as usual. But the bigger the military operations required to keep the Algerians and other peoples down, the more transparent the fiction became that this was a matter of "police actions" against small groups of "terrorists."[345]

307

An air attack on the Tunisian border village Sakiet-Sidi-Joussef on February 8, 1958, though insignificant enough in itself, proved to be decisive.

It attracted attention because the French planes struck the wrong side of the border, bombing a village in neutral Tunisia. They hit a village full of Algerian refugees who had sought relief from the French bombings in Algeria. They hit a school, killing all of the students.[346] They also hit a Red Cross convoy at the moment when it was handing out clothes and blankets to the refugees. A Swede, Colonel Gösta Heuman, was part of the convoy; his story was printed on the front page of *Dagens Nyheter*:

> For fifty minutes the French planes kept up their dive-bombing over the border village. The machine-gun salvos rattled, the bombs blew up with a loud roar, we saw how the missiles zoomed by on their way to their targets on the ground.
>
> There we stood, despairing, powerless.
>
> Then everything was quiet.
>
> I rushed back to the stricken city as fast as I could. It was a scene of total horror. There the dead and the dying lay, badly injured people were wandering around among the ruins. Children cried out in despair for their mothers, women searched for their children and their families.
>
> These were hours of terror. Everything was so horrifying. And our ability to help the unfortunate victims was so distressingly small. It was heartrending to see the suffering people. Many had horrible wounds.[347]

This had already happened hundreds, even thousands of times during a war that had lasted almost four years. But now it was a Swede telling the story. This brought the war much closer to us. It opened Swedish eyes to the reports of others, as well; for example, the French journalist Servan-Schreiber's reports on how French interrogators tortured Algerians.

The consequences of such methods are obvious, ran the editorial in *Dagens Nyheter*'s editorial a few months later.

> The entire Arab population turns against you, since for every "liquidated" Algerian, twenty rebels are created. Worse, hundreds of thousands of young men, the largest army France has ever sent overseas, are getting an appalling upbringing in "a war that has rotted and threatens to infect France."[348]

That year, Sweden abstained on the Algeria question in the United Nations. And in 1959, Sweden was the first and only Western country to vote against France for an independent Algeria.[349]

308

1960 For each new country that won independence, the power relations in the United Nations were altered. In 1960, the General Assembly approved the so-called Colonial Charter which would be a watershed:

> All peoples have the right to self-determination; by virtue of that right they freely determine their political status and freely pursue their economic, social and cultural development.[350]

The Declaration was approved by all the states except the colonial powers, which abstained. They continued to do so until 1970. Then, a quarter-century after the end of the Second World War, even the former colonial powers voted for "the principle of equal power among peoples and self-determination" in Declaration 2625. This not only acknowledges a principle, but also makes it a duty for the member states to promote its realization.[351]

But the General Assembly's proclamations were only "statements of opinion," without legally binding force. They were incorporated therefore with the two conventions on human rights, which came into effect in 1976 and constitute valid international law for all states.

309

But the wording is not completely clear. Who are the "peoples"? The old colonies often consisted of several different peoples who were considered a single people after independence. And what is "self-determination"? Did all of these peoples have the right to form their own states once they were independent? If not, to what degree of self-government are they entitled? Can the people's God-given right to self-determination be reconciled with the state's just-as-eagerly maintained right to territorial integrity?[352]

The problems left behind by European colonialism were still with us at the turn of the millennium. But Europe no longer tried to solve them with bombs. ➤ **17**

310

1960–1961 Once Schwarzenberger and Singh had broken the ice, the German experts in international law took the floor. In *Die Atomwaffe im Luftkriegsrecht* (*The Atomic Weapon in the Law of Air Warfare*, 1960), Alexander Euler, with impressive scholarship, presents all of the reasons for and against an express prohibition of atomic weapons. His conclusion: "Considering the terrible dangers of an atomic war, criminalization of nuclear weapons through a specific international convention should be required by reason and human dignity."[353]

Eberhard Menzel, in *Legalität oder Illegalität der Anwendung von Atomwaffen* (*Legality or Illegality of the Use of Atomic Weapons*, 1960) joins a group of other experts in international law – Arkadiev, Bartos, Bastid, Bennet, Bogdanow, Castrén, Colombos, Draper, Durdenewski, Franguilis, von Frankenberg, Greenspan, Haug, Harvey Moore, Kleut, Korowin, Koschevnikov, Linster, Neumann, Pritt, Reintanz, Sahovic, Saksena, Sauer, Spetzler, Strebel, Talensky, and Vargehese – all of whom consider nuclear weapons illegal.

The experts who maintain the legality of nuclear weapons refer to the fact that in some cases they can be used against purely military targets – for example, a battleship far out at sea – without causing civilian injuries. But one cannot, argues Menzel, conclude that nuclear weapons in general should be allowed on the basis on such special cases. Menzel emphasizes that the effects of nuclear weapons do not end with the war; the most devastating can show up decades after peace has been concluded – even future generations can be affected. In *Nie wieder Krieg gegen die Zivilbevölkerung, Eine völkerrechtliche Untersuchung des Luftkrieges 1939–1945* (*No More War Against Civilian*

Populations, An Investigation of the Air War 1939–1945,1961) Maximilian Czesany supports this statement with the information that every seventh newborn in Hiroshima up to 1957 had some form of birth defect. Also, 1,046 children had defects in their skeleton, muscles, skin, or nervous system; twenty-five had no brain, and eight had no eyes. The damage done to the genetic inheritance of humankind that would be caused if the nuclear weapons of today were used is grounds enough to forbid them.

311

1961 In 1961, when these studies came out, the General Assembly of the U.N. declared in resolution 1653 that the use of nuclear weapons was a violation of international humanitarian law.

These weapons were directed not only at the enemy, but also

> against mankind in general, since the peoples of the world not involved in such a war will be subjected to all the evils generated by the use of such weapons; any State using nuclear or thermonuclear weapons is to be considered as violating the Charter of the U.N., as acting contrary to the laws of humanity, and as committing a crime against mankind and civilization.

The nuclear powers rejected the resolution and could ignore it with impunity. If you had already made plans to kill several hundred million people in the first round, one resolution more or less wouldn't make much of a difference. ➤ **321**

312

1961 In 1960, the U.S. still controlled the overwhelming majority of the world's nuclear weapons – 10,000 bombs, of which 1,000 were hydrogen bombs. This was at least ten times as many as the Soviet Union had. The U.S. was also far superior in the number of bombers and other weapon carriers, and had a ring of bases from which they could comfortably reach any part of the Soviet Union.[354]

That year, Eisenhower accepted a new, trimmer list of nuclear objectives, characterized by a spirit of compromise. There were only 280 military and political targets, plus 1,000 other objectives in 131 cities.[355]

When Kennedy assumed the presidency in 1961, he was informed of the military's latest creation, the *Single Integrated Operations Plan* (SIOP). This plan was based on the overwhelming military superiority of the U.S. over the Soviet Union, and went on the assumption that the U.S. would be the first to use nuclear weapons. No fewer than 170 atom and hydrogen bombs were directed at Moscow alone in SIOP. The plan offered no possibility of excluding targets in China or eastern Europe, even if these countries were not drawn into the war. From 1961 on, the SAC had a number of bombers in the air around the clock, armed with hydrogen bombs and prepared to deploy SIOP. The cold calculation was that an attack carried out according to plan would kill between 360 and 425 million people.[356]

313

1961 I myself could be counted among those who would be killed with absolute certainty. During the spring of 1961, I was studying Chinese at Peking University, living in one of the student dormitories on campus. The next year, I moved to a little house by Nan He Yuan Nan Kou, next to the Forbidden City, only a few hundred meters from the Communist Party's headquarters and Mao Zedong's residence. No place in the world, with the possible exception of the Kremlin, was the target of so many hydrogen bombs.

314

1961 "How can a government be so irresponsible as to carry on a reckless foreign policy that risks war every day when it has provided no protection to its civilian population whatever?"[357]

This question is posed in Helen Clarkson's *The Last Day* (1959). It was posed in country after country by the movements that question nuclear weapons and which now, in 1961, had reached their apex. Kennedy answered on July 25 in a televised speech, in which he asked the American people to prepare themselves for a war of hydrogen bombs by building family shelters.

"In the coming months," said the President, "I hope to let every citizen know what steps he can take without delay to protect his family in case of an attack."[358]

Twenty-two million copies of a brochure entitled *The Family Fallout Shelter* were distributed. For the first time, bombs became a practical matter for every American family, as they were for me when I was a child. How much shelter can we afford? Do we have room for it? How should we equip it? A violent debate erupted. But it wasn't the mass destruction of entire large cities that aroused interest, but the question of whether the owner of a family shelter would have the right to defend it against his less provident neighbors. "Gun Thy Neighbor?" asked *Time*, quoting a resident of Chicago:

> When I get my shelter finished, I'm going to mount a machine gun at the hatch to keep the neighbors out if the bomb falls. I'm deadly serious about this. If the stupid American public will not do what they have to to save themselves, I'm not going to run the risk of not being able to use the shelter I've taken the trouble to provide to save my own family.

A similar tone was taken all over the country, reported *Time*, describing well-armed and well-equipped shelters full of canned food and ammunition.

315

Kennedy himself wrote the foreword to an issue of the magazine *Life*, which launched a new protective suit for use against radioactive fallout. The journal reassured its readers: "Prepared, you and your family could have ninety-seven chances out of 100 to survive."

The families who had been grilled alive in their "family shelters" in Tokyo had once heard the same message. To actually protect the entire population would have required astronomical sums and implied unacceptable changes in their lifestyle.

In an open letter to the President in November, several hundred professors wrote that bomb shelters promoted a false sense of security. "By buying a shelter program that does not shelter, and thereby believing that we can survive a nuclear war, we are increasing the probability of war."

The social anthropologist Margaret Mead saw the family shelter as a product of a long evolution away from the American ideal. The U.S. was no longer trying to build a safe world, or even a safe country or a safe city. No, the family sought instead an illusory security by creeping into itself and pulling back from the world. The last station on that line was the little hole in the ground where the nuclear family ducked and covered under attack from nuclear weapons. "The armed, individual shelter is the logical end of this retreat from trust and responsibility for others" (Henriksen, 1997).

316

While the debate about family bomb shelters was going on in the United States, Philip Wylie sat down and wrote *Triumph* (1963). He wrote of what really happens when a hydrogen bomb explodes.

As the fireball approaches the earth, writes Wylie, the steel in skyscrapers melts and they collapse. But before they have reached the ground, both the buildings and the ground evaporate, and millions of tons of concrete and bedrock turn into a frothing white light. At the same time the radioactivity streams out at the speed of light in all directions from the center of the explosion, destroying all the life that has not yet evaporated within a miles-wide radius. But worst of all is the flash of light. Everyone sees it, involuntarily – there is no time to blink. The retina burns away in all who see it, and they are blinded forever – even if they only catch a glimpse of it, at a distance of four or five miles. Men, women, and children feel a sudden pain and turn away – but too late. Within a range of thousands of square miles all pilots with unprotected eyes are blinded in their airplanes, and the same happens to bus drivers, train engineers, and ordinary drivers in their cars and everyone else. They can no longer see. They will never see again.

And this is just a fraction of the destructive capability of this weapon. There is still the firestorm to be reckoned with, the familiar old firestorm that they managed to produce by chance in Hamburg, Dresden, and Tokyo, but which now has become entirely certain and will inexorably turn a great city like Moscow or Peking into a crematorium – at the same time that other firestorms consume hundreds, or thousands, or hundreds of thousands of other cities on earth. And finally the radioactive fallout has to be taken into consideration. The heaviest particles fall after an hour, then the lighter ones, and finally the invisible ones. A single bomb can spread radioactive dust over 1,000 square miles, and within a few days or weeks turn all water, air, food, and objects within this area to deadly poison.

Those who have not been evaporated in the fireball or killed by radiation or blinded by the flash or burned in the firestorm might have some chance of surviving the fallout in their family shelter, if the fallout, counter to expectations, remains within a limited area.

317

Why are such weapons required? How can such a defense be defended? Well, says Wylie, the evils of Communism are so profound that the free world has never understood them. "Hitler killed his millions, Stalin his tens of millions. Grovsky [Khrushchev] might easily decide to destroy a billion and more people, including all but a few thousands of his own, to gain the real and basic Red goal: world dominion."

That is why the last surviving human beings in Wylie's tale of the future think that freedom was worth the cost. Deep in their bunker, some Americans are listening to an Australian radio broadcast announcing that the Northern Hemisphere is a single mass grave from Canada in the North to Mexico in the South, and that in the East, the population has been destroyed from Europe to China. "You are the only ones left in all of this area." Australia now takes over the task of organizing a world government. "Men are to become free and equal from now on."

> "Took the extermination of half a world to bring it about. Worth it, though, perhaps, eh?"
>
> "Some price!"
>
> "Righto...Slavs. Japanese – gone. Most Chinese. Quite a high fee for perpetual liberty and individual equality. Paid, though."

318

1962 While Philip Wylie was imagining this future, the Soviet Union exploded a fifty-megaton superbomb, bigger than any exploded to date. This single bomb contained 4,000 Hiroshimas. The fifty-megaton bomb gave a false impression of Soviet military strength, which already had been long overestimated in the U.S. and Europe. From the satellite photographs that were now beginning to pour in, it was clear that the American superiority in nuclear weapons was even more overwhelming than previously believed.

That was what made the Cuban Missile Crisis so dangerous.[359]

If, as was generally believed, each superpower had the capability to destroy its opponent, it hardly mattered that the Soviet Union based nuclear weapons in Cuba. The U.S. had now or in the past positioned nuclear weapons with its allies all around the Soviet border – in Great Britain, Germany, Italy, Turkey, Japan. But now the U.S. and the U.S.S.R. were not of equal strength. The Soviet capability in intercontinental warfare was still minimal. The Russians' nuclear firepower against the U.S. was so weak that it would be doubled or perhaps even tripled by the bases on Cuba.

It was for that reason that these bases were so important to the Russians. And it was for that reason that the Americans could not tolerate them. And that is why, for several days in October of 1962, the world was in a free-fall toward total destruction. We sat waiting and trembling at the thought of hundreds of thousands of Hiroshimas that were already in the air, carried by the wings of bombers, or stood ready to fire in their silos, a few hours or a few minutes away from their targets.

319

Thanks to the recordings made in the White House, today we can follow the discussions between Kennedy and his military and civilian advisers about the crisis in Cuba, line for line.

The chiefs of staff recommended direct military action. Blockades and political sanctions would be like "appeasement at Munich," said LeMay.[360] The Russians would respond with air attacks against the American navy, so that even a blockade would lead straight to war, but with unfavorable conditions for the U.S. "I just don't see any other solution except military intervention *right now*," said LeMay.

A little later the generals were left alone in the room for a few moments, while the tape recorder kept on turning. They rushed up to congratulate LeMay.

> Unidentified general: "You pulled the rug right out from under him [Kennedy]. Goddamn!"
>
> General Shoup: "He finally got around to the word 'escalation.' That's the only goddamn thing that's in the whole trick. Go in [unclear] and get every goddamn one. Somebody's got to keep them from doing the goddamn thing piecemeal. That's our problem. Go in there and friggin' around with the missiles. You're screwed. Go in there and friggin' around with the lift. You're screwed. You're screwed, screwed, screwed. Some goddamn thing, some way, that they either do the son of a bitch and do it right, and quit friggin' around."

320

There was no "massive reprisal." Kennedy was strong enough to hold his trigger-happy generals in check. Khrushchev was humble enough to back down. He took his nuclear weapons home from Cuba and contented himself with a secret promise from Kennedy that the Americans would bring similar nuclear weapons back from Turkey.

Humankind could breathe again. We still had a little way to go to get to the final destruction predicted by Cuvier. ➤ 19

321

1962 The Cuban Missile Crisis in 1962 let the air out of the resistance to nuclear weapons.[361] The relief that nothing had happened eased imperceptibly into the illusion that nothing could happen. To protest the bombs that were actually being dropped on the Vietnamese seemed more vital that protesting the bombs that threatened – but up to now did nothing more than threaten – to exterminate all of humankind. At that time the Second Vatican Council (1962–1965) was discussing what Jesus would have thought about massive versus flexible reprisal. The answer went to the heart of the matter: "Any act of war aimed indiscriminately at the destruction of entire cities or extensive areas along with their population is a crime against God and man himself. It merits unequivocal and unhesitating condemnation."[362] ➤ 339

322

1964 During the summer of 1964 my wife was pregnant with our first child. Her rounder curves and the child's movements inside her body created an erotic wave of joy that flooded our entire existence. I was working on my dissertation in comparative literature and had arrived at a point where all of the threads of my argument could be brought together. It was a wonderful time and only out of the very corner of my eye did I notice that something rather odd was happening in the Gulf of Tonkin.

The North Vietnamese navy, one of the world's weakest, was said to be mounting repeated, unprovoked attacks against the world's strongest, the American navy. Lyndon Johnson responded with air attacks against Vietnamese marine bases. Congress approved the President's decision after the fact and gave him sweeping permission to employ "all necessary measures."[363]

"Strange," I thought, but the episode already seemed a thing of the past. Our son was born in September. The sweet smell of baby poo and mother's milk suddenly filled the apartment. The whole winter I kept him sleeping out on the balcony (a Swedish custom) while I wrote my dissertation. When he awoke I swept the snow off him, carried him in, and cuddled him. I changed his diapers, fed him, burped him, and when he got sleepy I put him out in the snow again and kept on writing.

323

Today we know that the American military planners at the time had begun to doubt the "massive reprisal" concept. It had become so massive that it no longer seemed realistic. If the concrete problem was that North Vietnam was smuggling weapons over the border to South Vietnam in support of a rebel force called FNL – well, in that case it seemed a little much to threaten the destruction of all life on earth. The planners sought a new, more flexible strategy. It could take the form of CINCPAC OPLANS 37–64, a plan in three phases designed to stop the smuggling of weapons to the FNL by using bombers.[364] In the first phase, thirty B-57s would be sent to South Vietnam to bomb the smugglers south of the border. In the second phase, the bombing would take place north of the border; each individual attack would be defended as retaliation for some specific action by the FNL in South Vietnam. Once the world had grown used to this, the third phase would move on to general retaliation; bombing would become the normal state of affairs. The Vietnamese in both the north and the south would soon realize that they themselves could regulate the bombing – if smuggling increased, so would the raids, if it decreased the raids would decrease, and if it stopped entirely, the bombing would stop as well.

That's how flexible the new retaliation plan was – much more reasonable than massive retaliation, and therefore, it was hoped, more threatening in reality.

324

1964 This plan was in place as early as the spring of 1964. The problem was to get it through Congress. The bombing of South Vietnam was already something of a difficulty, since it would happen on behalf of a South Vietnamese government that was chosen by the CIA rather than by the people of Vietnam. Bombing North Vietnam would be an act of war that would definitely require the approval of Congress. The Congress would ask: Is this going to be a new Korean War?

So the repeated North Vietnamese attacks on the American cruiser Maddox came at a very convenient moment. While it was true that no injuries were reported on the American vessel, it was undeniably cheeky to attack it. It was an insult that Congress could not allow to pass. Now the President was immediately granted the powers it had seemed so unlikely he would ever get just a few months earlier, during the drafting of CINCPAC OPLANS 37–64.

325

1965 Precisely according to plan, in the autumn of 1964, thirty B-57s were moved into Bien Hoa in South Vietnam and began to bomb south of the border.[365]

On November 1, FNL guerrillas attacked the Bien Hoa base and destroyed twenty-seven of the thirty B-57s on the ground. The Americans could hardly ask for a better justification for reprisal against North Vietnam.

But nothing happened, because the presidential election was approaching and Lyndon Johnson sought reelection as a dove, posed against the Republican hawk, Barry Goldwater. The American people, who wanted no part of a war in Vietnam, gave Johnson one of the greatest victories in American history.

As soon as Johnson was inaugurated he began to take "all necessary measures." Precisely according to plan, North Vietnam was bombed in February of 1965, first as a specific reprisal for specific attacks against American bases in North Vietnam.

In March, the world had got used to the situation and the bombings had become normal. Then Operation Rolling Thunder was initiated, which aimed at the systematic destruction of North Vietnam, beginning in its southern regions. At the same time, American Marines landed to defend Da Nang and other air bases. It soon became clear that it was unreasonable to expect these Americans to sit around passively in their camps and wait to be attacked. To act offensively, they needed – and got – reinforcement. As the number of American troops rose, North Vietnam, too, began to send regular troops. In December of 1965 the U.S. had 184,000 men in Vietnam to assist 570,000 South Vietnamese in the fight against 100,000 FNL and 50,000 North Vietnamese soldiers.[366]

Each of these stages was described as one of the "necessary measures" that Congress had already granted the President. So, despite of the result of the election, without a declaration of war and without any further decisions from Congress, the U.S. slid into the most catastrophic war of its history. ➤ 328

326

1965 Stimson's description of the decision he had himself helped to make was accepted and became an unquestionable truth. It was twenty years before historical research even began to nibble at it.

The first was Gar Alperovitz with *Atomic Diplomacy* (1965). He came to the same conclusion as the Strategic Bombing Survey: "The atomic bomb was not needed to end the war and save lives." But during the Cold War, this conclusion had become so controversial that Alperovitz had to run the gauntlet of colleagues who found his thesis "implausible, exaggerated, or unsupported by the evidence."[367]

327

1965 At the same time, the bomb was becoming an important theme in Japanese literature, with Kenzaburo Oe's *Notes from Hiroshima* (1965) and Masuji Ibuse's *Black Rain* (1965).[368] Ibuse, who was not at Hiroshima himself, uses documentary journal materials. Two days after the bomb, one of his protagonists, Shigematsu, stands in front of the mirror:

> I peeled off the sticking plaster holding the bandage in place, and cautiously removed the cloth. The scorched eyelashes had gone into small black lumps, like the blobs left after a piece of wool has been burned. The whole left cheek was a blackish-purple color, and the burned skin had shriveled up on the flesh, without parting company with it, to form ridges across the cheek. The side of the left nostril was infected, and fresh pus seemed to be coming from under the dried-up crust on top. I turned the left side of my face to the mirror. Could this be my own face, I wondered. My heart pounded at the idea, and the face in the mirror grew more and more unfamiliar.
>
> Taking one end of a curled-up piece of skin between my nails, I gave it a gentle tug. It hurt a little, which at least assured me that this was my own face. I pondered this fact, peeling off skin a little at a time as I did so. The action gave me a strange kind of pleasure, like the way one joggles a loose tooth that wants to come out, both hating and enjoying the pain at the same time. I stripped off all the curled-up skin. Finally, I took hold of the lump of hardened pus on the side of my nostril with my nails, and pulled. It came away from the top first, then suddenly came clean off, and the liquid yellow pus dropped onto my wrist.[369]

Millions of Japanese saw themselves in Ibuse's mirror. His masterpiece came out in England in 1971, but not until fourteen years later in the U.S. There were three decades between the Japanese and American editions of Nobel Prize-winner Oe's *Notes from Hiroshima*.

➤ 351

328

The two sides in Vietnam fought two completely different wars. The U.S. was fighting against totalitarian tyranny, which had led to the mass murder of many millions of people under Hitler and Stalin and had then spread to the East, swallowed up China, North Korea, and North Vietnam, and now was about to conquer South Vietnam, too, and maybe even all of Southeast Asia. Democracies had fallen to Hitler during the 1930s, but the U.S. had held evil in check in Korea. Now today's Americans must not disappoint their South

Vietnamese comrades – even if they were corrupt, even if they lacked the support of the people, for they were the last outpost of freedom in Asia.

The FNL and North Vietnam were fighting against the foreign domination that the Vietnamese had been living under since France had conquered their country in the middle of the 19th century. The South Vietnamese regime was just one of a series of vassal states set up by the French, the Japanese, and now the Americans – always with the excuse that it was what was best for the Vietnamese people. The FNL uprising was just one in a long series that began with the rebellion of 1885, continued with the Yenbai uprising of 1930, the struggles against the Japanese, and later fights against the French again. In all of these uprisings, the Vietnamese had been beaten bloodily or cheated at the negotiation table. This time they would hold out until they won back their freedom.

329

1965 A few days before the air offensive against North Vietnam began, *Design for Survival* (1965) came out, a book by a retired air force general, Thomas Power. He speaks for the entire American military leadership when he describes how easily the U.S. could have bombed its way to victory in Vietnam: "We would have continued this strategy until the Communists had found their support of the rebels in South Vietnam too expensive and agreed to stop it. Thus, within a few days, and with minimum force, the conflict in South Vietnam would have been ended in our favor."[370]

It was not quite that simple. In December of 1965, the Americans were forced to admit that Rolling Thunder was a failure.[371] Roads and bridges had been repaired quickly by their enemies, and far from stopping the small-scale arms smuggling, they were now replaced by regular military transports.

Bombing had failed in Korea, and now it was failing in Vietnam as well. The American air force prophet Alexander de Seversky foresaw this already in 1942: "Total war from the air upon an undeveloped country or region is well-nigh futile; it is one of the curious features of the most modern weapon that it is especially effective against the most modern type of civilization."[372]

330

But once you have bombers, you can always find a reason to use them. The air war against North Vietnam began to be viewed as a form of psychological warfare. It was hoped that the bombs would show the determination of the U.S., encourage the South Vietnamese government, and thereby have a stabilizing effect on the political situation in South Vietnam.

Bombs were also a way of communicating with Hanoi. Corpses and ruins might not reduce the physical capability of the North Vietnamese to support the FNL, but they provided "a measure of their discomfort."[373]

331

1965 A frequently evoked metaphor was that the bombs were pieces in a board game. They were also seen as a currency that had buying power at the negotiation table. "Thus, if we give up bombing in order to start discussions, we would not have the coins necessary to pay for the concessions required for a satisfactory terminal settlement."[374]

International politics was viewed as a global market where the bombing of Vietnam raised the international price of guerrilla warfare. Those who were thinking about taking up such adventures in the future would always have to reckon with the higher costs that America's bombs entailed. Even if the localized bombing war in Vietnam was a loss, globally it could still represent a profit for the U.S.

332

1965–1967 On November 11, 1965, a young Quaker by the name of Norman Morrison burned himself to death outside the windows of the Secretary of Defense at the Pentagon.

In his memoirs (1995), Robert McNamara relates that at first he did not really understand what intense emotions had been aroused by the war that the American people had been tricked into. He himself shut all of his feelings in, speaking to no one. In this silence his wife and children drifted away from him. People spat at him on the street when they could, and he was forced to run away from enraged students.

In the summer of 1967, he realized that no escalation of the bombing could stop the North Vietnamese support of the FNL unless the entire population were destroyed, "which no one in a responsible position suggested." Maybe no one suggested it openly, but the demands pushed by the military would have taken the U.S. across the line into nuclear war. To his generals, the super-hawk McNamara was a sentimental dove.

The war he waged had become detestable to him; he wrote:

> There may be a limit beyond which many Americans and much of the world will not permit the United States to go. The picture of the world's greatest superpower killing or seriously injuring 1,000 noncombatants a week, while trying to pound a tiny, backward nation into submission on an issue whose merits are hotly disputed, is not a pretty one.[375]

333

"It was as if an enormous scythe had cut through the jungle and felled giant trees like grass," an FNL soldier recounts of the B-52s' area bombing.

> You would come back to where your lean-to and bunker had been, your home, and there would simply be nothing there, just an unrecognizable landscape gouged by immense craters.[376]
>
> The fear these attacks caused was terrible. People pissed and shat in their pants. You would see them coming out of their bunkers shaking so badly it looked as if they had gone crazy.

Even so, the explosive bombs were not the most feared. There was a new kind of bomb, which did not destroy buildings or military materiel but was directed only at living targets. Its sole purpose was to kill people. ➤ 34

334

The possibilities began to be realized during the Korean War. The U.S. was facing an Asian enemy with apparently limitless human resources. The "Asian masses" had to be challenged with a weapon of corresponding mass effect. An alternative to the tactical use of nuclear weapons then became what was called "controlled fragmentation."[377] A metal canister filled with explosives broke into fragments of precisely the right size, number, speed, and distribution upon explosion to kill the largest possible number of people.[378]

This principle was first applied to the construction of a new hand grenade, the M26. It blew up into more than 1,000 pieces of exactly the same size, which were expelled faster than a kilometer per second.

The peak of this development was achieved in Vietnam with the much-feared "cluster bomb," the CBU-24. The bomb consists of a canister that opens in the air and spreads a large number of smaller bombs out over a large area. When these explode, they throw off a total of 200,000 steel balls in every direction.

When the B-52s carpet-bombed, they often dropped explosive bombs first in order to "open the structures," then napalm to burn out the contents, and finally CBU-24s to kill the people who came running to help those who were burning.[379] Sometimes time-release cluster bombs were dropped in order to kill those who did not come before the danger was over – or so they thought.

After the war, the Pentagon reported that during the years 1966–1971 almost a half-million of this type of bomb were deployed, directed only at living targets and carried by B-52s. That was 285 million little bombs altogether, or seven bombs for every man, woman, boy, and girl in all of Indochina.[380]

335

Another much-feared type of bomb used during the Vietnam War was the so-called "Fuel Air Explosive" (FAE). A typical FAE consisted of a canister holding three forty-five-kilo bombs called BLU-73, filled with a very volatile and inflammable gas.

The canister is dropped from a helicopter or slow airplane, opens, and releases the bombs inside. Each bomb produces a cloud fifteen meters wide which, when it hits the ground, detonates with five times as much power as the same amount of trotyl. The explosion can also be delayed, to give the gas time to penetrate deep caves, tunnels, and shelters. The effect is basically the same as when if you open a gas valve, let the gas fill a room, and then try to light a cigarette.

If desired, FAE bombs can be made so large as to bridge the gap between conventional weapons and tactical nuclear weapons.[381]

336

1968 The FNL's offensive in January of 1968, called the Tet Offensive, gave the U.S. plenty of use for its new bombs. Finally the eternally elusive enemy engaged in battle – in sixty-four district capitals, thirty-six provincial capitals, and in the country's capital. Finally the superiority of American firepower could decide the matter.

But military victories do not always bring political gain. The British had enjoyed military victories in Malaya, Aden, and Kenya; even the French in Algeria had achieved military victory. But it was the losers who won.

The Tet Offensive was a political catastrophe for the Johnson administration, because they had lied for so long about the war. They had said that there was no war. Now everyone could see for himself that there was. They had said time and again that the war was almost won. Now that there was a real victory to report, no one believed them. People believed only what they thought they had seen with their own eyes – that a half-million American soldiers could not even prevent the FNL from attacking the American Embassy itself in Saigon. Rarely has a suicide mission enjoyed such success.

337

1968 In retrospect, 1968 has been named the year of insanity, the year when Communist tyranny seduced Paris, and an entire generation of youth became enraptured Maoists.

But 1968 was not only the year of the Paris Spring, but also the Prague Spring. The year in which Solzhenitsyn published *Cancer Ward*, the year in which the inventor of the Soviet hydrogen bomb, Sakharov, began his resistance to the regime.

1968 was the year of the Vietnam demonstrators. It was not Communism that the demonstrators glorified, but the right to self-determination. It was not democracy that they condemned, but the bombs. Lyndon Johnson promised in the end to stop bombing North Vietnam.

338

1969 The halt to bombing in North Vietnam proved to be nothing more than a concession to opinion. It simply meant that the flexible retaliation was moved to Laos, where 230,000 tons of bombs were dropped in 1968 and 1969. The aim was to stop military transports to the FNL. The result was devastating for the 50,000 farmers on the Plain of Jars and 100,000 other farmers in northern Laos. The U.N. observer George Chapelier reported: "Nothing was left standing. The villagers lived in trenches and holes or in caves. They only farmed at night. All of the interlocutors, without any exception, had their villages completely destroyed."[382]

The rule book said of course that civilians were not to be bombed. But for the military, rules were not norms to follow but problems to solve. In August of 1969, the CIA's Air America flew in large transport planes to the Plain of Jars and evacuated 10,000–15,000 survivors by force. "They would be herded together like cattle until they were so squashed together we couldn't close the doors."

USAID took care of the refugees, whose numbers grew to a quarter-million by 1970. One study found that USAID's refugee budget was equal to the cost of two days of bombing with 300 sorties per day.

Who won? In 1971, Laotian guerrillas controlled all of Laos except for the largest cities. The darlings of the CIA were taking care of the opium traffic and heroin factories instead, which had their best customers among the U.S. troops in Southeast Asia. ➤ **340**

339

1969 The nuclear powers objected that what the Vatican Council had to say about God and the U.N. General Assembly's pronouncement on international law were just "expressions of opinion," with no binding effect.

For that reason, the Institute for International Law called a meeting in Edinburgh in 1969 in order to answer once again the question first addressed in 1911 in Madrid. The meeting concluded with an authoritative statement establishing that the obligation to distinguish between military and nonmilitary targets, between combatants and civilians, remains an essential principle in valid international law.

International law prohibits, according to the seventh paragraph of the statement:

> the use of all weapons which, by their nature, affect indiscriminately both military objectives and nonmilitary objects, or both armed forces and civilian populations. In particular, it prohibits the use of weapons the destructive effect of which is so great that it cannot be limited to specific military objectives or is otherwise uncontrollable...
>
> Existing international law prohibits all attacks for whatsoever motive or by whatsoever means for the annihilation of any group, region, or urban center with no possible distinction between armed forces and civilian populations or between military and nonmilitary objectives.[383]

Both paragraphs are directed specifically at weapons of mass destruction, especially nuclear weapons. So the U.S. refused to approve them. And when they were integrated the next year into the great U.N. resolution "Basic Principles for the Protection of Civilian Populations in Armed Conflicts," they could no longer specify a prohibition of weapons of mass destruction, but instead, in order to win the support of the U.S., they had to be formulated in general, non-obligatory language.

The civilian population could not be attacked "as such" in the new wording; "every effort" would be made and "all necessary precautions" would be taken to protect civilians from "the ravages of war."[384]

None of the superpowers objected to the new wording. They were considered fully compatible with existing plans for the use of nuclear weapons, which were now estimated to be sufficient to destroy the population of the earth 690 times over.[385] ➤ **341**

340

1970 My daughter was born in January of 1970. I had bought my parents' home from my father and I used to place her stroller in the garden, next to the wall of the house, and write while she slept.

One day a driver lost control of his car at the busy corner of Långbrodal and Johan Skytte's Roads. The heavy vehicle slid straight across the neighbor's yard and into our garden, where it finally rammed into a cherry tree – with its grille just a few yards from the stroller.

The threat of the extermination of humankind and the sight of burning children in Vietnam and all the other fears and indignation I felt paled before the sudden threat to my own daughter. I borrowed money, had a sturdy foundation poured, and put up a fence that nothing less than a tank could knock down. By the time my fortress was ready, my daughter no longer lay sleeping in her stroller, protected from every danger. She was already running out on the street with the other kids, playing in their yards. ➤ **344**

341

1971 Karl Friedrich von Weizsäcker's *Kriegsfolgen und Kriegsverhütung* (*The Consequences and Prevention of War*, 1971), contains 700 big pages of detailed expert analysis of the consequences that existing NATO plans would imply for the civilian population in West Germany – that is, for the population the plans were first of all intended to defend. It turned out that even the shortest and most limited local variant of nuclear war could mean ten million dead and a complete destruction of German industrial society. A possible or even probable escalation to "blind" use of vailable tactical nuclear weapons could lead to the extinction of all life in Germany.[386]

➤ **356**

342

1972 In Christopher Priest's tale of the future, *Fugue for a Darkening Island* (1972), a nuclear war in Africa has claimed the lives of 5,000,000 people. Millions of sick, frightened, hungry, and desperate people want to escape the disaster area at any price – but they are not welcome anywhere. The conservative British government warns that illegal immigrants will be turned away, by force if necessary.

When the first shiploads of Africans land on the English coast, a large crowd gathers on the beach to show their sympathy with the refugees and protest the government's policy. But when more boatloads continue to arrive month after month, public opinion reverses.

Priest's narrator is a liberal academic, the owner of a townhouse, and a father, vaguely critical of the xenophobic position of his government and his neighbors. He wants the refugees to be taken in and integrated into society legally and systematically.

Now they are arriving illegally instead, by night, often armed or with homemade bombs in their bundles. The neighbors build barricades at the cross-streets and stand watch with shotguns while an endless line of hungry and impoverished blacks stream past in the darkness.

Soon the foreigners simply break into the houses where they think there will be plenty of room, settle in, and take what they want. When more and more streets and entire neighborhoods are occupied, the narrator's sympathy has long since been subsumed by fear and hate.

A bomb that smashes his living room window is the decisive moment. He flees with his wife and daughter in search of shelter in the country. But their England has already been ravaged by race warfare. The air force is bombing concentrations of refugees, but from the air they cannot distinguish friend from foe. The protagonist loses his identity card at a roadblock and his money at another, he is separated from his wife and daughter, and finds them on the last page of the novel, both dead, black, painted with tar. "I slept that night on the beach. In the morning I murdered a young African and stole his rifle."[387] ➤ **370**

343

1972 When the strong return from wars with the weak – what sort of men have they become? What happens to those who have looked into the gaping abyss between the values we officially espouse and those we practice in reality – among "savages and barbarians," in Algeria or Vietnam?

"Eventually we all became *morally neutral.* I would not say cynical. I would say that we became as truly *objective* about the war as we had trained ourselves to be about other problems we had to deal with professionally," writes Leonard Lewin in the novel of the future *Triage* (1972).

"Triage" means "thinning," as in a carrot patch, or "sorting," as of coffee beans or patients in a field hospital.

And it is in a hospital that the book begins. The chronically sick and dying are left lying and take up space, though their medical treatment has been completed. Two doctors discuss how to make politicians take responsibility for people who will hardly be voting in the next election. From an objective standpoint, the dying have to make way for those who can really be cured.

> "So are we going to decide how much to spend on a dying man? X number of dollars, X number of days in the hospital? You can't really mean that."
>
> "That's what we already do."
>
> "Since we sometimes have to play Almighty God we might as well be professional gods? Is that what you mean?"[388]

Before the month is out, the two doctors have "promoted" forty patients in addition to those who are "left on schedule." The sick have been spared suffering, the taxpayers have been spared extra payment, and the personnel have minimized their trouble. Since the result is so welcome, no one wants to believe what everyone has reason to suspect.

Soon, mortality has also climbed among the drug addicts of the metropolis. Heroin, ordinarily taken in a twenty-percent solution, is suddenly pure, so that a normal dose is deadly.

Prisons and other institutions are plagued by inexplicable epidemics. Poisoned drinking water within particular localities reduces the numbers of the chronically unproductive and unemployable. The fire department begins to experience significant difficulty in reaching the slums before fires there have reached catastrophic proportions. The police have similar problems stopping gang wars – let the criminals kill each other, it lets us off the hook. The police also regularly fail to find the militant far-right organizations that practice violence against colored people, leftists, and gays. Military stockpiles become more and more frequent targets for break-ins, and the weapons are seldom recovered. Military transports, even those carrying weapons of mass destruction, meet with mysterious fates in which their materiel is lost.

Once the "Organization" has been active for a time, people tend to accept even the strangest and most provocative events as "part of the natural order of things." Social systems designed to produce results have always been based on the elimination of the unfit and the disorderly. They are locked up in prisons or institutions – buried alive, as cheaply as possible. But it is of course even cheaper to bury them dead. That solution has always come up as the most suitable when the number of rejects and misfits has become as high as it has – according to an objective, morally neutral view – today. Or so Leonard Lewin's tale would have it. ➤ **393**

344

1972 The napalm used in Vietnam was no longer the napalm that had peeled human beings like oranges during the Korean War. Improved research had created new kinds that adhered better, burned more deeply, and caused greater injury.

The amounts used had also increased. During the Second World War, the U.S. had dropped 14,000 tons of napalm, primarily against targets in Japan.

During the Korean War, U.S. planes dropped more than 32,000 tons of napalm. In addition there was the napalm dropped by other countries' air forces and by the navy.

In Vietnam between 1963 and 1971, the U.S. dropped about 373,000 tons of napalm of the new, more effective kind.

The figures are taken from the U.N. General Secretary's napalm report, presented in October of 1972.[389] Napalm was popular with the military because, according to the report, it could "combine area characteristics with high incapacitating power."

345

"Area characteristics," like "area bombing," refers to the fact that the weapon destroys its target by destroying the entire area in which the target lies. Good "area characteristics" means that the pilot can fly higher and faster, thus running less risk of being shot down – and still destroy his target. Of course, everything else is also destroyed and "unavoidably and even deliberately" greater harm will be done to the civilian than to the military sector of society. The risk is passed off to the people on the ground. The pilot and his crew save their own skins.

"High incapacitating power" means that the effects of the weapon will completely eliminate a person even if only a little, peripheral part of the body is hit. Napalm fulfills that requirement. Aside from those who die immediately in the fireball, twenty to thirty percent of those who are just hit by burning droplets will die within a half-hour. And as many as fifty percent will die a slow and painful death within the following six weeks.[390]

The report describes the long-term suffering borne by the survivors, the extraordinary resources required to keep them alive, and the chronic maiming and consequent emotional trauma that result.

The report concludes that while science creates even more effective incendiaries than napalm, the long-cherished principle of noncombatant immunity appears to be receding from military consciousness.

"Clear lines must be drawn between what is permissible in war and what is not permissible." But they could not be drawn as long as the world's leading superpower was using napalm on a daily basis.

346

1975 During the Second World War the U.S. dropped a total of 2,000,000 tons of bombs. In Indochina at least 8,000,000 tons were dropped. The explosive power of these bombs corresponded to about 640 Hiroshimas.[391]

During the Second World War, seventy percent of the U.S. bombs were aimed at individual targets, and only thirty percent at entire areas. In Indochina area bombing made up eighty percent of the attacks. In Germany and Japan twenty-six kilos of bombs per hectare of enemy land were dropped. In Indochina it was 190 kilos.

South Vietnam had to bear the brunt of it. When the war was over there were ten million bomb craters covering a total area of 100,000 hectares.[392]

And yet, flexible reprisal failed. The bombs could prolong the war but not change the outcome. On April 30, 1975 the Saigon regime fell. When the last Americans left the city in helicopters from the roof of the embassy, they looked out over a sea of FNL flags. ➤ **20**

347

More precision was not only unnecessary – it might even be dangerous. As long as the ballistic missile could only hit big cities, its use was limited to genocide. In military terms it was worthless. But the more precision increased, the more possible it became to limit effects primarily to military objectives.

A little waste had to be part of the calculation. Maybe it would cost a few million or a few dozen millions of lives to knock out the enemy's nuclear store. But that figure would decrease as precision increased. And precision improved by a factor of about 100,000 during the thirty years between 1945 and 1975.[393] The increased likelihood of hitting a target made a successful first strike thinkable and tempting. Increased precision thus undermined the balance of terror and made deterrence less dependable.

Paradoxically enough, there was nothing more threatening to the civilian population than the alleged ability to limit a nuclear war to military targets.

348

And up to now, it has never been more than an alleged ability.[394] No hydrogen bomb carried by a ballistic missile has ever been launched from South Dakota and exploded over the Kremlin. No one knows if it really would explode right there, or somewhere else, or not at all.

Hydrogen bombs have obediently exploded where they were supposed to in test situations, but never after sojourning in space and reentering the earth's atmosphere. Unarmed missiles make regular test runs between California and the Marshall Islands. But can the precision achieved on the rifle range really be reproduced if the missile is aimed at other targets? They've only practiced on that one atoll. Will the assumptions used to draw conclusions from the test situation hold up under conditions of real warfare? In war the missiles would be launched over other gravitational fields and exposed to other magnetic disturbances and other, unknown sources for error.

Even from a great distance, nuclear explosions can damage electronic equipment, including the computers that give these missiles their alleged precision. The electromagnetic wave that is released can destroy computer memory and block the channels of command, rendering the continued control of nuclear arms impossible. When an atomic explosion occurs, each event can transform the next in a way that is impossible to calculate in advance.[395]

Fortunately, the "surgical precision" of intercontinental war has never been put to the test in reality.

349

Despite what politicians and civilian experts were saying and writing throughout the 1960s on the topic of "flexible reprisal," the military was still planning for the fatal blow.

Secretary of Defense Schlesinger said as much in response to a direct question at a Senate hearing on nuclear weapons strategy on March 4, 1974.

> A SENATOR: Are you saying that the President does not now have the option of a limited strike against missile silos?[396]
>
> SCHLESINGER: He does hypothetically in that he could ask the SAC to construct such a strike in an emergency... It is ill advised to attempt to do that under the press of circumstances. Rather one should think through problems in advance and put together relevant small packages which a President could choose...
>
> A SENATOR: Hasn't that been suggested earlier? Why hasn't it been carried out, in that case?
>
> SCHLESINGER: Many statements can be found saying that flexibility or selectivity would be desirable. But before this time it has been sort of an aspiration. Now we are consciously basing our deterrent strategy upon the achievement of flexibility and selectivity in the way that was only discussed earlier.

It sounded good. Giving the President of the United States choices other than the immediate destruction of humankind seemed reasonable. But this option soon brought nuclear war closer:

A SENATOR: Do you think it is possible to have a limited nuclear war, just to exchange a couple of weapons?

SCHLESINGER: I believe so.

The little, tailor-made precision packages had made nuclear war less unthinkable, and therefore more likely.

350

In practice, the military surgeons did not place their trust in the precision of the missiles, but rather on the massive effect of increasing numbers of increasingly violent nuclear weapons.

By the middle of the 1970s, the U.S. had 1,200 MIRV warheads mounted on ground-based intercontinental missiles. (MIRV meant that from 1970 on, several hydrogen bombs would be carried on the same missile, but then would separate and reenter the atmosphere individually, each aimed at its own target.) Plus 600 warheads in the one- to two-megaton class, also on ground-based missiles. Plus the navy's 3,840 MIRV warheads in the forty-kiloton class on Poseidon missiles and 528 MIRV warheads of the 100-kiloton class on Polaris missiles. Along with about 400 B-52 bombers (each of which could carry several megaton bombs), to say nothing of a few hundred attack planes armed with nuclear weapons and based on ships and ground bases ringed around the Soviet borders.

On the thirtieth anniversary of Hiroshima, we were no longer measuring the world's nuclear arsenals in Hiroshima terms. But the U.S. alone now had the capability to increase by more than a hundred-thousandfold what had happened in Hiroshima, simultaneously and anywhere on earth.[397] ➤ **352**

351

1975 On the thirtieth anniversary of the first atom bomb, a new historical examination of the decision to drop it came out – Martin Sherwin's *A World Destroyed* (1975). He defended a more cautious form of Alperovitz's thesis: the bomb had not been dropped solely to save lives, but also as a move in a political game between the superpowers.

Several years later Truman's diary from the Potsdam Conference of the summer of 1945 was found, along with his letters to his wife. Here was proof that Truman was completely clear on the political worth of the bomb, that he was aware that Japan wanted to surrender, and that he realized that the entrance of the Soviet Union into the war meant the end for Japan. When he dropped the bomb he knew, in other words, that the bomb was not necessary to end the war.[398] ➤ **364**

352

Precision forced a choice of priorities, not only between civilian and military targets, but also among civilian targets. Whom did they really want to kill? Was it the oppressed non-Russian peoples of the Soviet Empire or the ruling Russians? Surely the effect of deterrence could be heightened with so-called "ethnic targeting." A group of American consultants was asked at the end of the 1970s to research whether increased missile precision could be used to break the Soviet Empire up into small independent national entities. Maybe it would even be possible to spare certain peoples within these entities – say, the Baltic peoples – while destroying those regions of the Baltic states populated primarily by Russians. An ethnic alternative was integrated into the American war plan SIOP.[399] ➤ **357**

353

1977 Earl Turner is a young Nazi from Los Angeles who begins his diary with an account of holding up a liquor store and cutting the throat of a Jew. The diary is published a hundred years after the victory of the Nazi revolution, and it is in this brave new Nazi world that the reader of Andrew MacDonald's *The Turner Diaries* (1977) is supposed to find him- or herself.

At the outset, "the Jews" force passage of a law that robs the American people of their right to bear arms. Half the population become lawbreakers as a consequence and lose all faith in the democratic system. The Nazis recruit more and more members among officials, police, and the military.

At two A.M. one day, it is time to take over. Sixty Nazi battle units strike Los Angeles, and hundreds swarm over other areas in the country. A few minutes later, electricity and water are cut off, airports are closed, highways are impassable, and telephones no longer function. A little group of officers who support the Organization immediately begin to disarm black soldiers under the pretext that blacks in other units have committed mutiny. In some cases, all blacks in uniform are simply shot, which soon turns the lie about black mutiny into truth. All the while, the Nazi radio urges white soldiers to change sides, while other radio broadcasts, faked to sound like they are made by blacks, urge all the blacks to shoot their white officers.

After a few days the Organization has taken over Los Angeles and ethnic cleansing begins. There is quite simply not enough food for everyone, so the food is reserved for the whites. The others are driven away, a million per day. Those who cannot walk are jammed into requisitioned cars. "This whole evacuation amounts to a new form of warfare: demographic war. If the System bosses had the option, they'd turn the niggers back at the border with machine guns. They are trapped by their own propaganda line, which maintains that each of those creatures is an 'equal' with 'human dignity' and so forth, and must be treated accordingly."[400]

354

After a four-days' course on the handling of nuclear weapons, Turner is sent to Washington at the end of August with the assignment of placing a number of hydrogen bombs around the capital city.

The "System" could still have put down the Nazis without difficulty. Turner notes in his diary that "the only thing that's really kept them off us this long has been our threat of nuclear reprisal against New York and Tel Aviv. To protect our nuclear weapons, we will have to distribute them outside California."

The Organization sets off its first nuclear weapon in Miami, where 60,000 are killed, primarily Latinos. "We are in the midst of a nuclear civil war," Turner notes ecstatically in his diary.

When the civil war turns into a world war, Turner considers this, too, a success. By provoking the Russians into attacking, the Organization has inflicted much more serious damage on the System than they themselves could have caused. The two main centers of Judaism, Tel Aviv and New York, are devastated. In practical terms, the U.S. is governed by its generals.

An epilogue relates that it was Turner who ensured the victory of the Organization by blowing up the Pentagon and himself. Since then that day has been celebrated as the Day of the Martyrs.

Fast on the heels of the war came the collapse of the European economy which prepared the ground for the Organization's seizure of power there. The gutters ran with the blood of immigrant workers and race traitors.

Now China is the only center of power still untouched by Nazism. It was easy to take out the primitive Chinese missile system, but the Yellow Peril was more difficult to stop. The Organization solved the problem with chemical, biological, and radiation warfare on a large scale. During a period of four years, the entire area between the Urals and the Pacific became totally sterile, all the way from the Arctic to the Indian Ocean. Thus "The Great Eastern Waste" was formed.

Only now, a hundred years later, have certain areas of this wasteland been opened for colonization. The remaining traces of the original population unfortunately present a threat that must first be eliminated before this enormous region is safe for White Civilization.

355

Priest's and Lewin's novels are concretized thought experiments. The reader does not sense that the authors themselves have experienced the moral meltdown they depict. Neither of them received much public acclaim, either. But *The Turner Diaries*, in contrast, is buoyed by genuine ideological sentiment. The author's pseudonym masks the real-life sect leader William Pierce, a former university lecturer in physics, who had leading positions in a number of neo-Nazi organizations before he founded his own "National Alliance" in 1974. The extermination of "foreign" races is the dominant political goal of the Alliance. The basis of the movement is a mystical doctrine of salvation, called "Cosmotheism," which takes as its point of departure the notion that the entire social system is heading for a breakdown as a result of racial mixing. Total destruction is a necessary prerequisite for a biological and ideological rebirth of humanity.[401]

The Turner Diaries quickly became one of the central texts of American far-right extremists.

➤ 379

356

1977 When in 1970 the International Red Cross called for negotiations in Geneva over a renewal of humanitarian law, especially for the protection of civilians, the initiative met with resistance from the U.S., which skillfully and energetically worked to make sure that the problem would not be taken up.

When it proved to be impossible to stop the initiative, the U.S., Great Britain, and France took part only on the condition that the negotiations would be limited to conventional weapons; if motions for new rules were made, these would under no circumstances be allowed to apply to the use of nuclear weapons.[402]

The international law that 124 countries finally agreed upon on June 10, 1977, was for the first time truly international. It applied to all continents, to all political systems, and to both external and internal conflicts. For the first time it was no longer true that anything would be allowed against savages and barbarians.

The law took the form of two supplements to the protocol of the 1949 Geneva Convention.

Air warfare was regulated in Protocol I. The basic rule says:

> In order to ensure respect for and protection of the civilian population, the Parties to the conflict shall at all times distinguish between the civilian population and combatants and between civilian objects and military objectives and accordingly shall direct their operations only against military objectives.

Article 51 prohibits air attacks that cannot be aimed at specific military targets and therefore cannot distinguish between soldiers and civilians. This article forbids area bombing and the use of any weapon whose effects cannot be limited to military targets. The wording is reminiscent of the rule opposed by Great Britain and France in the 1920s, and which the Western powers had opposed throughout the postwar period.

But more than thirty years after Hamburg, Dresden, and Tokyo, firebombs were still too sensitive a topic to be explicitly named. That prohibition is not mentioned until Protocol III of 1980, where article 2 states:

> It is prohibited in all circumstances to make any military objective located within a concentration of civilians the object of attack by air-delivered incendiary weapons.[403]

But on the subject of nuclear weapons, humanitarian international law still had nothing to say. ➤ **359**

357

1980 In 1980, on the thirty-fifth anniversary of Hiroshima, the two superpowers controlled more than 15,200 warheads on strategic weapon carriers. Both sides had in addition several tens of thousands of smaller nuclear weapons, all of them just as strong or stronger than the bomb that destroyed Hiroshima.[404]

The number had more than doubled in a decade, but it was no longer the number that was decisive. The more important figures concerned the precision and what was called the "yield"; that is, the destructive capability per kilo of nuclear charge.

Precision was measured in Circular Error Probability (CEP) – the radius of the circle around the target within which fifty percent of the weapons aimed at the target would strike. The American air force had once demanded the unreasonable CEP of 500 meters in order to do away with the ballistic missile. Now, thirty years later, the missile system was already down to a CEP of 200 meters at a distance of 13,000 kilometers. The present goal was a CEP of thirty meters.

At the same time, the explosive power per kilo of nuclear charge has increased. The effect of a conventional bomb during the Second World War was about 0.5 times the bomb's weight – that is, the explosive power of the bomb was equivalent to half its weight in trotyl. The Hiroshima bomb weighed four tons and had an effect equivalent to 200,000 tons of trotyl. Thus the effect was 3,000 times the weight of the bomb. By 1980, the effect had climbed to 2,000,000 times the bomb's weight. A single hundred-kilo charge, easy to transport in, say, a little delivery truck, can cause the same effect as 200,000 tons of trotyl, or sixteen times the destruction that occurred in Hiroshima.

Now there were tens of thousands of such weapons, and the Stockholm International Peace Research Institute (SIPRI) calculated that their total explosive power was equivalent to 1,000,000 Hiroshimas.[405]

358

At the beginning of the century, the missile was not a weapon used in real war, but just to terrorize savages and barbarians. C. B. Wallis summarized the 19th-century British practice when he wrote in *West African Warfare* (1906): "Rockets are very useful in setting fire to native towns and should be taken on all river expeditions. They can be fired from a launch or from a boat, and when properly aimed a single rocket is sufficient to set a town on fire."

Now the rocket had returned. It was aimed instead at our cities. Half of the world's nuclear weapons were, according to SIPRI, programmed to destroy targets in or near big cities, primarily in the Northern Hemisphere. On the average, every larger city there could be subjected to the equivalent of thirteen million tons of trotyl, or more than 1,000 Hiroshimas each. The people of those cities would of course die immediately, the population of the surrounding countryside a bit later, and gradually, as a result of radioactive fallout, the savages and barbarians of the Southern Hemisphere would die as well.[406] ➤ **21**

359

1982 After four decades of scientific research one would think that most of the imaginable consequences of nuclear war would be well known. But the height of terror had not yet been reached.

In 1982, two scientists at the Max Planck Institute in Munich calculated that the enormous forest fires created by atomic blasts would pollute the atmosphere with several hundred million tons of soot, which would prevent sunlight from reaching the earth. An

American group added the effect of burning cities, which the Germans had not included in their calculations. The result would be a half-year of darkness and a fall in temperature of about 100 degrees.

When sunlight finally penetrated the nuclear darkness, the joy at its return might be short-lived – for the damaged ozone layer would let in enough ultraviolet light to first blind, then kill.

The primary uncertainty was over how far south the nuclear winter would spread and how many nuclear weapons would be needed to produce it. It was calculated that 5,000 megatons would be more than enough. The entire stockpile of nuclear arms at that point was 13,000 megatons.[407]

360

What did the law say about weapons with such consequences?

As far as conventional weapons were concerned, the answer was crystal clear. Supplemental protocol 1, article 51, paragraph 4 states:

> Indiscriminate attacks are prohibited. Indiscriminate attacks are:
>
> a) those which are not directed at a specific military objective;
> b) those which employ a method or means of combat which cannot be directed at a specific military object; or
> c) those which employ a method or means of combat the effects of which cannot be limited as required by this protocol.[408]

Apparently nuclear winter is an effect that cannot be confined to military targets, but indiscriminately impacts on civilians as well, whole continents, in fact. So apparently hydrogen bombs are "a means of combat the effects of which cannot be limited as required by this protocol." If hydrogen bombs had not been atomic weapons and therefore excluded from the convention, they would naturally have been forbidden. But they had the characteristics that should have placed them under prohibition precisely because they were nuclear weapons – and thus permitted. That was the neat little dead end where international law got stuck for two decades.

361

During these years the experts in international law attempted many times to formulate and solve the question of nuclear weapons and international law.

If a state has accepted the general principle that it should not cause unnecessary suffering and should protect human rights, to what extent can the application of this general principle be applied to create new rules and make them binding, even for the state that is unwilling to admit that these rules are a necessary consequence of the general principle? Allan Rosas, a professor at Turku University in Finland, poses this question in *International Law and the Use of Nuclear Weapons* (1979). And if the state in question is a large power – how far can you go down that road without completely losing sight of political realities?

We ought to at least be able to agree to condemn the side that first uses a nuclear weapon, in Rosas's opinion. To use strategic nuclear arms as a defense and bring mass destruction to an opponent, even though he attacked using only conventional weapons, is illegal without a doubt. It is in violation of (1) the prohibition against causing unnecessary suffering, (2) the prohibition against waging indiscriminate war, (3) our obligation to preserve the environment, and (4) our duty to respect human rights. ➤ **378**

362

1983 As early as the 1950s, a novel form emerged in which the nuclear catastrophe changes the American male into Tarzan. With *The Turner Diaries* a genre is born in which American men consciously cause nuclear catastrophes in order to realize their political aims. In one series of novels after another, nuclear weapons are seen as the far right's golden opportunity to take power and destroy all the other races.

A law setting limits on the possession of guns is the point of departure for William W. Johnstone's *Out of the Ashes* (1983). Here, as in many other American tales of the future, the law provokes a popular rebellion among nice, ordinary Americans. With the help of the generals, they begin an atomic war in order to finally turn America around.

The author's alter ego, Ben Raines, is a Vietnam veteran and former soldier of fortune in Africa. He is also an author, but despite decades behind a desk and at the whisky bottle he still moves with the smoothness of a huge cat and always shoots first.

Ben is one of the lucky few who survives the nuclear war. He sets out on a journey through what is left of America, and everywhere he runs into young, beautiful people who love his books. The rebels have scrawled his name on the walls of buildings. An entire movement is just waiting for him to step forward and take over the Leadership.

In the third part, Ben has allowed himself to be elected governor for life in a free state in the northwestern corner of the U.S. After a couple of years he has established a "real" government by the people, the kind that the U.S. has not had since the Wild West. Criminals are shot on the spot, the young look up to their elders with respect, no labor unions cause trouble, and no benefits are necessary, since rents are low, everyone has work, and schools and hospitals are free.

"A contentment hung in the air; a satisfaction that could almost be felt, as if everyone here had finally found a personal place under the sun and was, oh so happy with it."[409]

Creating this paradise was of course costly. One hundred and fifty million Americans are dead, three-quarters of the earth's population has been destroyed.[410] But so what? A general formulates the book's underlying credo:

> GENERAL: Nobody really likes niggers or Jews or greasers... Deep down, boy, we're the master race. Besides, we've got the guns, most of them.
>
> BOY: What about Russia and China?
>
> GENERAL: Gone. There's nothing left, sonny. Human, that is.[411]

363

"Bang, you're dead," we said. "Now you're dead," we said.

Father is lying on his side in bed with his eyes closed.

His mouth is open, as it often was when he slept.

The body is still warm under the blanket. His hands and head have gone cold. This is not three-quarters of the earth's population. Just one human being, and a very old one, at that. And yet an existential crater opens within me. On the table beside the bed lie the vocabulary lists you were studying last night. You, who had no chance to study during your youth, were still going to school almost every day at ninety-one years of age.

And now you are dead.

How thin the membrane, shivering between us. How close I now am to the gray plastic bag they took you away in. ➤ **394**

364

1985 On the fortieth anniversary of Hiroshima, Ronald Schaffer's *Wings of Judgement* (1985) came out, which places the atom bomb in the history of aerial wars, and shows that Truman's lies were part of a series of untruths used to gradually break down public resistance to attacking civilians. Suddenly and almost simultaneously a number of scholars wrote the literary history of the atom bomb: Thomas D. Clareson (1985), Paul Brians (1987), David Dowling (1987), Carl B. Yoke (1987), Bruce Franklin (1988), Spencer Weart (1988), Martha Bartter (1988), and Millicent Lenz (1990). An important theme, especially in Bruce Franklin's work, is the attempt to show how Truman fulfilled a centuries old American dream – the dream of a superweapon that brings peace.

Hersey's *Hiroshima* came out in a new edition (1985), now with an epilogue that describes the fate of his six survivors over the ensuing forty years. Dr. Sasaki had spent five years operating on the scars left by burns – ugly, thick, rubbery, copper-red growths that formed over the wounds. He found that the scars often came back after the operation, just as swollen and infected as before, and reluctantly he concluded that it would have been better not to operate.

His wife died of cancer, like countless numbers of his other patients. Dr. Sasaki built himself a four-story concrete house and conducted a prosperous private practice. He had long since repressed memories of the bomb, but sometimes he is haunted by the memory of those corpses that he was forced to have cremated without identification one day forty years ago. Could it be that those nameless souls are wandering forever, in search of their bodies?

365

By this time the historians' discussion had developed far beyond Stimson's simplistic image of how the decision was made. But in the mass media, Stimson was still the only voice. On the fortieth anniversary of Hiroshima, all of ABC's stations across America announced:

> What happened over Japan forty years ago was a human tragedy that cost tens of thousands of lives. But what was planned to take place in the war between Japan and the United States would almost certainly have been an even greater tragedy, costing hundreds of thousands of lives.[412]

Here the truth has been turned upside-down. What happened – not over Japan but in Japan – was a human tragedy that really did cost hundreds of thousands of lives. Those who planned this tragedy did it to spare tens of thousands of American lives, lives which in all probability would never have had to be lost, since Japan was offering to surrender without invasion.

➤ **375**

366

1989 If such a "curious figure" ever managed to survive, his "curiousness" did not disappear at the end of the war. In his body the war continued, decade after decade, for the rest of his life.

In the summer of 1989, nearly forty years after the Korean War, the American historian Bruce Cumings interviewed a Korean by the name of Pak Jong Dae. Pak had no face. Where his face had once been, napalm had left behind a gruesome scar. In the middle of the scar, one eye was left. The hand he extended was a shrunken claw. He had long since become used to the fact that others had difficulty shaking his hand and even more difficulty looking at him. He was polite, gentle, and at the same time not without pride. The surgeons had attempted to reconstruct his hands, nose, and lips, and he could speak, though he slurred a bit when he said:

> Everybody has his youth which is precious and important. My youth has gone with thirty-six operations. I had a lot of laughter and hopes for the future. I had two hands with which I could play the accordion. All these the bomb took away from me... I do not think there should be any more victims like me in this world. Never again. Never in this world a victim like me.[413]

➤ **276**

367

1989 For a long time, slavery was considered an obvious necessity. Blood feuds were once a matter of honor. Both of these seemed to be firmly established institutions, part of the foundation of society, deeply anchored in millennia of history, perhaps even part of human nature. And yet in time they grew archaic, despicable, and finally unthinkable. Why shouldn't war go the same way?

The American political scientist John Mueller poses that question in *Retreat from Doomsday, The Obsolescence of Major War* (1989). His thesis is that at least "major wars," wars between great powers or between states in the industrialized world, have become unthinkable because the economies and cultures of these countries have been so closely woven together that war is no longer a serious alternative.

Mueller's thesis seemed to have been supported by the fall of the Berlin Wall and the collapse of the Soviet Union, which took place without the explosion of a single nuclear weapon.

368

1991 The conventional, large-scale war is on its deathbed – this is also the opinion of the Israeli military historian Martin van Creveld in *On Future War* (1991). But the result, in his opinion, will not be peace, but new forms of warfare.

The great powers have gathered four-fifths of the world's military might in their hands. And yet they are suffering from military impotence: their weapons have become so terrible that they are unusable. They are not even good for threats, since everyone can see through the bluff.

Nuclear war seems dirt-cheap. A single atomic submarine with a crew of less than 100 men can destroy every large city in Germany and have weapons enough left over to devastate yet another country of equal size. But who would use such weapons? And against whom?

Even the conventional weapon systems have become so advanced that they are irrelevant. They are dinosaurs – too expensive, too fast, too big, too difficult to maintain, and too powerful for the wars that are actually waged.[414] And so, according to van Creveld, they won't be able to prevent war, either.

369

1990–1991 What about the Gulf War? Iraq's invasion of Kuwait was really stopped by a high-tech war in which the advanced weapon systems proved to be anything but impotent.

On the television screen, the war looked like a computer game, without blood, without civilian injuries. The images were dominated by cruise missiles that sneaked around streetcorners and, with perfect precision, found their military targets. What we saw seemed to be a new kind of war that fulfilled the demands of both humanitarianism and military efficiency – custom-made destruction without messy side-effects. It was only afterward that we found out how tightly controlled that propaganda image really was.[415]

In reality it was the same old bombs striking the same old villages. The French general Pierre Gallois, who visited Iraq immediately after the war, reported: "I drove for 2,500 kilometers in my four-wheel-drive and in the villages everything was destroyed. We found fragments of bomb dating from 1968, left over from the Vietnam War. This was the same kind of bombing I did half a century ago in World War Two."[416]

The great powers had been selling weapons for years to Iraq for its rearmament. They knew perfectly well that Iraq considered Kuwait an Iraqi province that had been separated from its mother country and made an independent state by British oil interests. They also knew that Iraq was a harsh dictatorship that waged war on its own citizens. They knew that Iraq was a threat to Israel. And yet they armed Iraq with the very weapons that they would later go to war to destroy.

That an alliance of five great powers and twenty-one other states managed to defeat a third-rate power in the Third World can hardly be called an outstanding military achievement. That the victory in the Gulf War was portrayed in that light indicates not justifiable self-confidence but low expectations. ➤ 392

370

The wars that have actually been fought since 1945 have been in general what were called "little wars" in the 19th century, and which today are called, quite misleadingly, "low-intensity conflicts."

They have often been waged from the air against people on the ground – but with little success. They have been conducted by developed nations in undeveloped ones – but no one can promise that they will stay there forever. They have been waged by regular, highly qualified troops who have proved to be helpless against irregular forces armed with primitive weapons. The inferior arms have won, as a general rule. Even when they have lost from a military standpoint, they have won politically. War in the true sense of the word requires, according to van Creveld, equal opponents. To fight the weak degrades the strong and undermines his morale. Even when the stronger wins, he has lost. The existence of more than 100 new states offers proof enough.[417]

The colonial powers fought hard for decades to preserve their huge holdings, writes van Creveld.

> They were also, to put it bluntly, utterly ruthless. Entire populations were driven from their homes, decimated, shut in concentration camps or else turned into refugees.
>
> From Algeria to Afghanistan there have been cases when the scale of the operations was so large as to make them look like genocide, yet even so the end of the conflict was by no means guaranteed.[418] ➤ 343

371

Shintoism is nationalism elevated to a religion, in which the highest ritual act is a sacrificial death for the fatherland. Two and a half million Japanese have been killed in wars. Their still-living spirits have found refuge in the Yasukuni Temple, and the temple museum gives the spirits form in photographs, bloodstained uniforms and the fallen hero's last letter to Mother. The problem is that among these fallen heroes are those who attacked China in 1894, 1930, and 1937 – yes, even some who were guilty of the Nanking Massacre, where more than 200,000 Chinese civilians were murdered. Also among the heroes are those who attacked Pearl Harbor in 1941, and those who were convicted of war crimes and executed in 1948. Wars of aggression are believed to have brought "peace to the land" (yasu-kuni), and the spirits of the fallen are still worshipped in the temple.

The museum's textual displays are pure war propaganda. "The Chinese incident," as the fifteen-year war against China is called in Japan, was inevitable because the British and the Americans incited Chinese rebels into anti-Japanese activities. The attack on Pearl Harbor was a question of national survival. The Pacific War was, according to a brochure sold in the museum, "not a war of aggression but just the opposite: it was a holy war to liberate the world from Communism."

The museum glorifies self-sacrifice, especially the sacrificial deaths of kamikaze pilots and "the human torpedoes." The suicide attacks were in fact of no military significance, and even when they were successful, they only managed to prolong an already-lost war. But here they represent the ideological apex.

The message is best expressed on a memorial plaque set up by the Union for the Cause of the Special Attack Forces in 1985 in memory of the attack on Pearl Harbor: "Some 6,000 men died in suicide attacks that were incomparable in their tragic bravery and struck terror in the hearts of our foes. The entire nation sheds tears of gratitude for their unstinting loyalty and selfless sacrifice."[419]

372

It is of course not true that the entire Japanese nation shares these sentiments. Yasukuni has always been a controversial sanctuary.[420]

After Japan's defeat in the Second World War, Shintoism lost its status as the state religion, and the Japanese government's visits to Yasukuni stopped. But when the occupation was over, the Prime Minister began to go there, first privately in a private car, then privately in a government car, and finally in 1986 as an official representative of the government. When I was there in 1995, he had come with 152 conservative members of parliament. Yasukuni is slowly but surely on the way to recovering its place as a national symbol, which is what the extreme right has demanded throughout the postwar period.

If you imagine the German Chancellor on his knees in a temple devoted to the fallen heroes of Germany, including Heinrich Himmler, Hermann Göring, and other convicted war criminals – then you will realize why Yasukuni's rebirth as a symbol of Japanese national identity has become one of the most controversial events in modern Japanese history.

For many Japanese, Yasukuni is an example of how feelings of guilt, if they are never acknowledged, can lead a nation to a collective denial of its past.

373

Another example can be found at Yasukuni's rival for the world's most visited museum: the Smithsonian Air and Space Museum. Fifty years after the first atom bomb, a remarkable battle took place here over what story should be told of Hiroshima.[421]

A model of the first atom bomb, affectionately known as "Little Boy," has always been exhibited at Air and Space. The museum also owned the Enola Gay, the gigantic B-29 from which the bomb was dropped. But the plane had never been exhibited. Military groups demanded that the Smithsonian restore the plane and show it to the public.

As the fiftieth anniversary of the bombing of Hiroshima approached, Martin Harwit, the museum's new director, announced that a memorial exhibit would be mounted with its premiere in May of 1995. The main event would be the unveiling of the Enola Gay's shining fuselage, which would almost completely fill the huge exhibit hall.

374

But Harwit did not want only to glorify military technology and effectiveness. The idea was also to put the bombing of Hiroshima into its historic context, describe the situation at the end of the Pacific War, give the arguments for and against the bombing, and show the effects of the bombing, the human tragedies and the inheritance that the bombing left to the Cold War and armaments race.[422]

These intentions alone sufficed to incite strong feelings. Before the exhibit project had even taken shape on paper, the museum was bombarded with protests from veterans' organizations. 8,000 readers of *Air Force Magazine* signed a protest letter that demanded a "proud and patriotic" exhibit of the Enola Gay. The American Legion condemned the museum for its supposed intention to "depict the U.S. airmen as war criminals."[423]

Even a respected liberal newspaper like the *Washington Post* supported the veterans' demands. The reasons for dropping the bomb did not need to be examined, the effects of the bombs did not need to be shown. Keep the lid on! ➤ **235**

375

1995 Martin Harwit was wrong when he thought that in 1995, fifty years after the fact, it would finally be possible to bring the historical discussion to the public and give a critical and comprehensive image of the decision to drop the bomb. He had underestimated the power of denial.

The veterans had good connections in the Senate, and they were able to push through a unanimous resolution that declared that the as-yet-nonexistent exhibit was "revisionist, unbalanced, and offensive."[424]

The term "revisionist" is interesting. The word is used in Europe primarily about the so-called historians who deny that the Holocaust occurred or attempt to downplay its significance. But Martin Harwit's exhibit project was not intended to deny what had happened in Hiroshima – on the contrary. It was not he but the veterans who were "revisionists."

The word "revisionist" has also been used to brand those who have fallen away from the "true" belief, especially Marxism. In that sense, all good historical research is "revisionist" – it constantly revises earlier conceptions, especially the descriptions that the power apparatus provides of its own actions. Earlier unknown facts are produced, already-known facts are seen in a new light. This kind of "revision" is the primary task of historical research and the museum's task is to bring such revision to the public. Why did the senate want to condemn it?

376

Congress's threat to reduce support not only for the Air and Space Museum, but for the entire Smithsonian Institution, forced Martin Harwit into extensive negotiations with the veterans, who were allowed to sit in judgment over the results of historical research.

First, the entire scholarly debate about the decision to drop the bomb was taken away.

Then the quotes from Eisenhower, MacArthur, and other famous generals who were against the bomb disappeared. Only a single photograph of a dead Japanese was allowed. Only a single victim of radioactive sickness remained – but two images of Americans who studied the victims.

Now the story went that Truman decided to drop the bomb solely to save lives. He believed that Hiroshima was a purely military target. And civilians in the true sense of the word hardly existed in Japan at the time, since even women and children were armed with bamboo spears. Thanks to the bomb, and only to the bomb, the war ended immediately with Japan's unconditional surrender. In short: a large public museum had been forced into unconditional surrender by political interest groups. Bowing and scraping, Martin Harwit had to thank the American Legion "for spending so much time helping to improve the fairness and accuracy of the script...all that had been lost was excessive repetition and excessive gruesomeness."[425]

377

Martin Harwit stood firm on one point only. He categorically refused to state that the bomb had saved a million American lives, when the American chiefs of staff had said 20,000 to 25,000, and the highest contemporary estimate anyone could find had been 63,000.[426]

Furious over this last bit of resistance, the American Legion once again turned to the press and to Congress. Within a few days, eighty politicians had demanded Harwit's resignation and threatened reduced support. Now the lid was really screwed down. In January of 1995, the exhibit was canceled.

The only thing that was shown, "proudly and patriotically," was the body of the airplane – without the slightest indication of what this object had done to hundreds of thousands of once-living human bodies.

For many Americans, this canceled exhibit was an example of how never-expressed feelings of guilt can cause a kind of voluntary cerebral hemorrhage, which erases what a nation has neither the will nor the strength to remember. ➤ 15

378

The superpowers continued to interpret international law according to their own lights, but they became more and more isolated in doing so. Finally, on December 15, 1994, the U.N. General Assembly attempted to resolve the question of the legality of nuclear weapons by requesting a pronouncement from the International Court in The Hague.

The time seemed ripe. The illusions once inspired by nuclear weapons had long since withered.

Throughout the postwar period, military and civilian strategists had tried in vain to find a way to use nuclear weapons without thereby risking the destruction of humanity. Now it was clear to most people that there was no such use. Nuclear weapons are quite simply unusable.

What did the Chinese or Indians achieve with their nuclear weapons? What good was an atom bomb to Israel, in the face of stone-throwing Arabs? The hydrogen bomb had not helped Great Britain or France keep their empires. If any of these countries had tried to use the bomb in self-defense against a superpower, it would have been immediate national suicide.

The Americans, who were first to have the bomb, were also the first to discover the impotence of its omnipotence. The Soviet Union made the same discovery during the 1980s, in Afghanistan.[427] When the Russians finally left Afghanistan in 1989, it was too late. The arms race had broken the Soviet economy, and in 1991 the Soviet empire collapsed from within.

The mutual demonization of the enemy suddenly became unnecessary and ridiculous. The Kremlin had, after all, given up power without even threatening a nuclear holocaust. The two mortal enemies now cooperated nicely about the dismantling of the same lethal weapons that they had recently used to threaten each other. The Russian nuclear weapons were manned by troops paid by Washington.

In this new situation, there seemed to be no reason to use a weapon that could destroy humankind. Therefore, the General Assembly turned to the International Court for an "advisory opinion" on the following question:

"Is the threat of use of nuclear weapons in any circumstance permitted under international law?"

➤ 380

379

1995 The young man who blew up the Oklahoma City Federal Building on April 19, 1995, killing 168 people, fortunately had no access to nuclear weapons. He found the model for his actions in *The Turner Diaries* (1977), which for more than two decades had been a cult book among the far right and had sold, according to the publisher's advertisements, more than 198,000 copies. Timothy McVeigh, who was convicted of the crime, was completely consumed by the novel's message, which had produced a turning point in his life.[428]

American and European tradition have now begun to melt together into something which is "neither European National Socialism or American racist ideology but a new form of militant racism," writes Swedish historian Heléne Lööw. Within this global movement, Turner and his megamurder of the nonwhite races is the great inspiration. A Swedish Nazi tells Lööw, "It's a fantastic book, it tells it just like it is, it hits you right in the heart, when I had read it I became the person I should be. It is the underlying philosophy for [the Swedish neo-Nazi journal] *Storm*, the most important book."[429]

➤ 362

380

1995 The Court invited the U.N. member states to submit written opinions on the question and to then comment on one another's views. Submissions arrived from thirty-five states. In November of 1995, the Court held open hearings with representatives from twenty-four countries.

The Western nuclear powers argued that the Court should leave the question unanswered. It was, they said, vague and abstract, and it touched upon complicated situations that were already being studied by other, more competent U.N. organs. A pronouncement from the Court on a subject as sensitive as this one could even risk undermining results that had already been achieved.

The public was of a different opinion. The case excited greater interest than any other case in the history of the Court. Petitions were signed by more than 3,000,000 people. The flood of letters grew until it became physically impossible for the Court to accept its mail – most of it lay in a warehouse in The Hague while the Court wrestled with the legal problem.

381

1996 The Palace of Peace in The Hague was a gift from an American multimillionaire. It looks like it, too – a modern millionaire's dream of a medieval castle, a peace fortress with towers and pinnacles, a fairy-tale palace in a fairy-tale forest where only the electric fencing serves as a reminder of reality.

Thirteen men and one woman met there on July 6, 1996, all of them dressed in floor-length robes, ready to answer the General Assembly's questions. No Swedish media were there. The destruction of humankind apparently lacked general interest. The following is a summary of their conclusions with brief commentary.

The Court rules:

4A) unanimously, that international law does not contain any specific authorization of the threat or use of nuclear weapons.

5B) [by a vote of] eleven to three, that international law does not contain any comprehensive and universal prohibition of the threat or use of nuclear weapons.

6C) unanimously, that threat or use of nuclear weapons is illegal when it violates the U.N. statute's prohibition of wars of aggression (article 2, paragraph 4) or does not satisfy the requirements which (in article 51) apply to the use of the right of self-defense, especially the requirement of proportionality (to not use more violence than necessary).

382

Three judges from countries in the Third World with no atomic weapons – Abdul Koroma from Sierra Leone, Mohammed Shahabuddeen from Guyana, and Christopher Weeramantry from Sri Lanka – wanted to go further. They maintained that nuclear weapons under any circumstances imply more force than demanded by necessity – or at least that the power that first uses a nuclear weapon employs an unnecessary amount of violence. And even if the first explosion were not a disproportionate use of violence, there is a risk that it will bring about an uncontrollable escalation. Therefore, nuclear weapons do not satisfy the demand for moderation that the U.N. charter requires of its members when they are acting in self-defense.

The court as a whole did not accept the reasoning of the three judges. It contented itself with ruling (#43) that these risks exist and must be taken into account by every state that believes it could use nuclear weapons in self-defense without violating the U.N. statute.

Thus the Court leaves judgment up to the nuclear powers themselves.

383

After that, the Court takes up questions of humanitarian international law, and here it is worthwhile following their argument point by point.

> Paragraph 78: The cardinal principles of humanitarian law are aimed at the protection of the civilian and civilian objects. States must never make civilians the object of attack and must consequently never use weapons that are incapable of distinguishing between civilian and military targets.

These rules are generally accepted, the Court continues.

> Paragraph 79: [They] are to be observed by all States whether or not they have ratified the conventions that contain them, because they constitute intransgressible principles of international customary law.

The fact that nuclear weapons are not named in the 1977 supplement protocol to the Geneva Convention, and that the U.S. and several other states explicitly made an exception for nuclear weapons, does not prevent the protocol's basic principles from applying to all weapons, including nuclear weapons (paragraph 84).

A large majority of both states and experts in international law are agreed that humanitarian international law applies to nuclear weapons. The Court shares this view (paragraphs 85–86).

The principle of neutrality implies that the effects of war must not affect neutral states. The Court finds that this principle also must be taken into account, whatever weapons are used (paragraphs 88–89).

So far, the Court's reasoning is logical and consistent. It results in a clear and unambiguous conclusion, which once and for all puts an end to the long postwar controversy about the application of international law to nuclear weapons.

The Court rules:

> D) unanimously, that threats or use of nuclear weapons should also be compatible with the requirements of the laws of war and especially with the demands of international humanitarian law.

384

But *can* the use of nuclear weapons ever be compatible with international humanitarian law? [Can the effects of nuclear weapons avoid civilians, or be stopped at the borders of neutral states?] This was the question that the General Assembly had posed: Are there any circumstances under which it would be permissible to use nuclear weapons? The Japanese Shigeru Oda, who did not want to answer at all, and the judges from the three Western nuclear powers – the United States, Great Britain, and France – argued that the use of nuclear weapons would not necessarily injure civilians or neutrals, and so under certain circumstances could be compatible with international law. So four judges answered "yes" to the General Assembly's question. Four answered "no." The latter four all came from countries with no nuclear weapons: Sierra Leone, Guyana, Sri Lanka, and Hungary. The Hungarian, Geza Herczegh, offered the clearest articulation of their position: "The fundamental principles of humanitarian international law categorically and without equivocation forbid the use of weapons of mass destruction and, among those, nuclear weapons."

In total, eight judges wanted to answer either "yes" or "no" to the General Assembly's question. Six judges remained – three from the Eastern nuclear powers Russia, China, and India, two from European Union countries, and finally the chairman of the Court, the Algerian judge Mohammed Bedjaoui. These six agreed on a compromise, which was sharply criticized by both the "yes"- and the "no"-sayers, and even to a certain extent by themselves – but with the assistance of the Hungarian, they acquired enough votes to make it the judgment of the Court.

385

On the way to their compromise, the Court first criticizes the "yes" votes. The Court observes that none of the states that consider use of nuclear weapons legal under certain circumstances was able to detail what those circumstances might be in more detail, or how such a justifiable, limited use of nuclear weapons would be prevented from escalating into total nuclear war.

The conclusion, one would think, would be that the Court rejected the opinion of the "yes" votes. But here the reasoning starts to slide. The Court's conclusion is: "The Court does not consider that it has a sufficient basis for a determination on the validity of this view" (paragraph 94). Why not? Wasn't it this type of determination that the Court was assigned to perform?

Then the Court turns to those who voted "no."

According to their view, nuclear weapons, however used, are incompatible with international law because of their uncontrollable effects (paragraph 92). But the Court does not consider itself sufficiently informed to conclude that the use of nuclear weapons under any circumstances would be a violation of the laws of war (paragraph 95).

At that, the Court leaves aside the question of nuclear weapons and humanitarian international law and returns inexplicably to the question of a state's right to survival and self-defense, which had already been discussed in connection with the U.N. charter.

The Court cannot, it maintains, ignore the "policy of deterrence" that has been applied in many states for many years. And here the argument once again begins to slide. It is clear that the Court should not "ignore" the policy of deterrence, even if it no longer enjoys the importance it once had. But the question is not whether the Court ought to ignore this policy or not, but rather: Is it legal?

Deterrence belongs to the realm of politics, not of law, writes the Chinese judge Jiuyong Shi. "The policy of deterrence should be an object of regulation by law, not vice versa."

386

The result of these deliberations was the controversial double paragraph. Its two parts were considered as an indivisible whole, though several judges wanted to vote "yes" to the first part and "no" to the second. The Court rules:

> E) seven to seven and the Chair's deciding vote:
>
> that the threat or use of nuclear weapons would generally be contrary to the rules of international law applicable in armed conflict, and in particular the principles and rules of humanitarian law;
>
> However, in view of the current state of international law, and of the elements of fact at its disposal, the Court cannot conclude definitely whether the threat or use of nuclear weapons would be lawful or unlawful in an extreme circumstance of self-defense, in which the very survival of a state would be at stake.

387

This is not a happy compromise. According to the declarations and dissenting judicial opinions, nobody liked it.

The German judge Karl-August Fleischhauer calls it incomplete and vague, but also points out that the allowance the compromise leaves for the legal use of nuclear weapons is extraordinarily small. According to the International Court's unanimous decision, threat or use of nuclear weapons are legal

1. only if the weapon is used in compliance with the U.N. charter, that is, in self-defense and without using more violence than necessity demands, and
2. only if the weapon is used in compliance with humanitarian international law, that is, without affecting civilians or neutrals.

The Court is also of the opinion, although not unanimously, that threat or use of nuclear weapons can be legal

3. only if the weapon is used in a situation of extreme emergency in which the existence of a state is threatened.

It is difficult to imagine any use of nuclear weapons which fulfills all three of these criteria simultaneously. Hiroshima and Nagasaki certainly do not. None of the plans for nuclear war referred to in this book satisfy the requirements of the International Court.

388

Were the great powers fighting this long legal battle just for the pleasure of being allowed to destroy a solitary warship on the open sea?

Certainly not. Warships can be destroyed in many other, less controversial ways.

What the great powers were fighting for was the right to keep their nuclear arsenals. As long as there was the tiniest possibility for legal use of these weapons, the powers can say that they need their stockpiles for just that eventuality.

That's how they can keep open the physical possibility of doing all those things that have become legally impossible. None of the criminal old plans for war crimes actually need to be abandoned, as long as there is a single permissible target that can function as an alibi for the constant preparation to do something completely different, now unnamable and absolutely forbidden.

Hundreds of thousands of Hiroshimas still come creeping toward us through this narrow, apparently insignificant crack in the law. Naked, skinless, blind, bleeding from their mouths and eyes, they still come creeping through this crack. ➤ **22**

389

1997 Chechaouen glitters in the spring rain when, nearly seventy years after the catastrophe, I knock on the door of the teacher Ali Raisuni. He shows me around room after room filled with brown boxes full of brown envelopes full of documents of the city's history. We drink tea together in his living room, an oval room with seats along the walls, as is the custom here. He draws his naked feet under himself and begins to talk. Beside him sits a little boy who listens with shining eyes. ➤ **120**

390

1997 On April 26, 1997, on the sixtieth anniversary of the city's destruction, the people of Guernica walk in procession through the dark streets with candles in their hands, in remembrance of their dead.

But the evening is not somber, it is warm and lively; cafes and restaurants are full, the streets echo with the bright voices of children and their enchanted cries as balloons fly into the sky. There is a feeling of victory and liberation in the air.

The memorial Mass at the cemetery concludes as usual with each person taking the hand of his or her neighbor. This year, the sign of reconciliation includes the perpetrators as well, for the German ambassador is there with a message from the president of his country. He asks forgiveness for what the Germans did sixty years earlier. ➤ **156**

391

1998 During the summer of 1998, I traveled around England to see how British museums, fifty years after the Second World War, accounted for the results of the Bomber Command's war effort. My guidebook was Bob Ogden's *Aircraft Museums and Collections of the World, Part 2: Great Britain and Ireland*, which in its second, revised edition describes 160 museums and collections. I saw many of the small, private museums and all of the large, official ones: the Imperial War Museum in Duxford, the RAF Museums in Hendon and Cosford, the Army's Museum in Middle Wallop, and the Navy's in Yeovilton. None of them, as it turned out, wanted to acknowledge what the British had actually bombed.

A gigantic gallery in Hendon is devoted to the Bomber Command. Both the planes and the bombs are there, enormous and overwhelming. But what did these planes and bombs do? A little corner of the room shows the destruction of an industrial work site. The result of residential bombing is never shown.

In this exhibit, no human being was ever harmed by British bombers – except in one showcase on the atom bomb, but that was of course not a British bomb. And even there, images of material damage predominate. Only at the very bottom of the case can you catch a glimpse of a human being. If you get down on your knees, you can see that the image portrays a man with a naked chest, photographed from behind so that his face is invisible. The text informs us that the burns on his back are being treated.

How nice, you think, that the only person to suffer injury from bombing – not British bombing of course, but Allied bombing all the same – how nice that he was so well cared for.

➤ **200**

392

1998 Even if nuclear weapons have really become forever unusable, they are still dangerous. They can still cause accidents with catastrophic consequences. The weapons or the raw materials from which they are made can fall into the hands of extremists and criminals.

Many Russian stockpiles of highly concentrated uranium are unguarded today, stored in areas with no fences, surveillance cameras or detectors, says William Potter, the head of the Center for Nonproliferation Studies, in a 1998 article in the *Washington Post*.[430] He had just returned from a research trip to fifteen Russian nuclear facilities. The guards, who had not been paid in months, had turned off the alarms.

An invasion of Russian tanks across European frontiers had long been unlikely and today is unthinkable. But an invasion of Russian refugees after a nuclear catastrophe is not as improbable. How will we find a place for them?

No European power today would wage war against India or Pakistan. It is far more likely that a nuclear war between those two countries will render them uninhabitable and cast out waves of refugees over the world. How will human rights and compassion fare then?

➤ **342**

393

One of van Creveld's many controversial theses is that the existence of the state is justified by its ability to wage war.

It was not the social-welfare system that created the modern state, but its military effectiveness in comparison to that of other warfaring organizations. Now the state's monopoly is about to be lost – both upward, to supranational organizations, and downward, to commercial, political, and criminal ones. Conventional wars will cease with this change, but at the same time, the power of the state will decay and the result will be a new kind of war.

A state that cannot wage war cannot, according to van Creveld, offer its citizens the possibility of life, or even an acceptable reason to die. It has played out its role.

Instead, the security business will blossom and become the dominant industry. Like the *condottieri* of yore, it may one day even completely supplant the state.

The war of the future will be fought between tribes and sects, by terrorists, bandits, guerrillas, and pirates.[431] Distinct frontlines will be replaced by improvised roadblocks manned by hooligans. This has already begun in Asia, Africa, and Latin America. It will continue in the former Soviet Union, China, and India – and in the U.S. and Europe if the growing tide of violence is not stopped.

Wars will not disappear – instead they will be longer, bloodier, and more terrible. They will be waged by private armies, motorcycle gangs, Nazi groups, security guards, moonlighting policemen, and soldiers who haven't been paid. The bomb of the future is not the intercontinental missile, but explosives in a purse; not the bomb from the air, but the car bomb and the letter bomb. ➤ **353**

394

1999 Johnstone's *Out of the Ashes* enjoyed a great success and had many imitators. "Saturating Johnstone's works," writes Brians (1987) "and making them typical of the type, is a pornographic concentration on extreme violence, in his case particularly on rape and sexual torture, especially of children. Johnstone takes sadistic sex further than any of the other new novelists of nuclear violence but he is not atypical of the rest in his emphasis on rape. These are quintessentially masculine novels aimed at a male audience."[432]

In Volume 27 of the series, *Triumph in the Ashes* (1998), Ben Raines cleanses Africa of black murderers who lack the slightest trace of conscience or mercy, "mindless maniacs bent on total annihilation."

In Volume 28, *Hatred in the Ashes* (1999) he returns to the U.S. in order to overthrow America's first woman president and once again rebuild the society of the free and the brave on the ruins of the nuclear holocaust.

More than 7,000,000 copies of the series have been sold. Similar series by other authors are *Survivalist* (twenty-four volumes), *Phoenix, Wasteworld, Traveler, Overload, Deathland, Wingman, Guardian, Endworld, Zone, Casca*, and *Doomsday Warrior* (twenty-seven volumes).[433]

An entire industry lives on the hope that war, in particular nuclear war, will prove to be a shortcut to a paradise of masculinity.

395

People do not necessarily begin wars in order to achieve certain goals, writes van Creveld. Often the opposite is the case: people pick their goals in order to have an excuse to wage war. The utility of war is questionable, but "its ability to entertain, to inspire and to fascinate has never been in doubt."[434]

It is primarily men who are entertained. For them, war is temptation, pleasure, and proof of their masculinity. "One suspects," writes van Creveld, "that should they ever be faced with such a choice, men might very well give up women before they gave up war."[435]

If the lust to kill in many men is even stronger than sexual lust, future wars are probably inevitable. But shouldn't it be a little problematic, even for these men, that their pleasures demand the death of so many children? That the war that proves their masculinity at the same time maims and kills children by the thousands?

No, van Creveld sees no problem there. With apparent approval, he writes in his book's conclusion: "One very important way in which men can attain joy, freedom, happiness, even delirium and ecstasy, is by not staying home with wife and family, even to the point where, often enough, they are only too happy to give up their nearest and dearest in favour of – war!"[436]

396

"I don't think about stuff like that," says Ruben.

We are waiting at a red light, and I stretch out my hand, though he has recently got too big to hold it.

"War and bombs and that kind of stuff," he says, "I don't think about it. We play monsters, we play knights and castles and fantasy games, not bombs."

He is silent for a while.

"But of course...what if there were...there's always a 'what if...' "

397

"Nothing left, sonny. Human, that is," the general said when the Chinese had once again been wiped out. How many times did that make? Ever since William Hay had all non-Europeans killed off in 1881, tales of the future have exterminated countless millions of Jews, Communists, blacks, other coloreds – and the climax has always been the marvellous destruction of the Chinese.

These genocidal fantasies recur with striking regularity, independent of conjunctures and political constellations. It cannot be denied that they are almost always written by men and read by men, or that they exhibit a thoroughly masculine character.

And yet it is not this perverted masculinity that scares me most. I am more afraid of the interdependence that John Mueller – and many others – believe will be the cause of peace.

Because dependence also creates vulnerability. An economic crisis in Thailand pushes Indonesia under, which shakes up Korea, which in its turn shoves Japan to the brink of ruin. When the Japanese can no longer afford to carry the Russians on their backs, Brazil, too, is affected, and when Brazil... Even more unchecked than a century ago, the economic crises roll from continent to continent, crushing the dreams of millions of people, casting them brutally back into poverty.

Does that sound like a recipe for peace?

398

Both economic growth and population growth are usually given in percentages, which hides the essential fact: economic growth as manifested in products and services occurs primarily in the already-wealthy world, while population growth as manifested in numbers of people takes place in the poor countries. More and more people are being born into poverty, ignorance, and hunger. More and more people are born superfluous, worthless to the interdependent economy, yet still vulnerable to its effects. More and more are born for whom violence is the only way out.

All of the methods we have tried up to now to provide for more people and raise their standard of living use up the earth's limited resources and pollute the air, ground, and water with waste. Throughout this century, it has been clear that the standard of living enjoyed in industrial countries cannot be extended to the world's population. We have created a way of life that must always be limited to a few.

These few can make up a broad middle class in a few countries and a small upper class in the rest. The members know each other by their buying power. They have a common interest in preserving their privileges, by force if necessary. They, too, are born into violence.

Out of this violence, both that which has already been committed and that which is still dormant, the century's dreams of genocide emerge. The injustice we defend forces us to hold on to genocidal weapons, with which our fantasies can be realized whenever we like. Global violence is the hard core of our existence.

➤ **1**

399

And what is now yet to come.

➤ **10**

NOTES

[1] Ziegler 1994, paragraph 14.

[2] Needham 1986, 180.

[3] Needham 1986, 168.

[4] Howard 1994, introduction, Stacey 1994. But the distinction is older than the Romans: cf Schwarzenberger 1976, 81. Gong 1984, chapter 3.

[5] Grotius (1625) 1950, chapter 11. Helm 1962. Hartigan 1982, chapter 8. Ziegler 1994, paragraph 32.

[6] Strehl 1962, chapter 1.

[7] Montesquieu 1748, part I, chapter 3. Rousseau 1762, part 1, chapter 4. Kotzsch 1956, chapter 3. Helm 1962. Weigley 1973, chapter 8. Howard 1979, 5. Best 1980, chapter 2:6, 3:7. Selsky 1994. Allen 1994 chapters 1–2.

[8] *The Iliad*, song 6, verse 55ff. Markusen 1995, chapter 3. Waswo 1997.

[9] Baker 1994. Heyne cited in Kennett 1982, chapter 1.

[10] Malthus, 1982, Book I, chapter 1.

[11] Lindqvist 1996, 97–107.

[12] Majevski 1963, 114ff. Sambrook 1966, 25ff.

[13] Shelley 1994, xii. Wagar 1962, chapters 1–2.

[14] Mackenzie 1990, chapter 2.

[15] This section and the three following are based on Spaight 1930, chapters 3–4. Cf Best 1980, chapter 7.

[16] Hartigan 1982, chapter 9. Walzer 1992, chapter 2. Green 1993.

[17] Weigley 1973, chapter 8. Gong 1984, chapter 3.

[18] Ziegler 1994, paragraph 42.

[19] Green 1993.

[20] Dilke 1869, I:109, chapter 28.

[21] Cf Lindqvist 1992, paragraphs 100–135. Lindqvist 1995, 52–91, 119–143.

[22] Hay 1881, chapters 1 and 10.

[23] Cf Boyle 1962, 576ff. Cf Bond 1985: "British admirals displayed an unedifying propensity to bombard enemy ports at the least excuse throughout the 19th century...but since most of these incidents took place in what would now be called the Third World...Britain suffered less criticism than the major land powers."

[24] Hornung 1885, 544, 552. 1886, 188.

[25] Farrer 1885, chapter 6.

[26] Kennedy 1988, 150.

[27] Spetzler 1956, 134–136.

[28] Caldwell 1990, 22, 26ff. Cf De Moor 1989, introduction.

[29] McCurdy 1997, 112ff.

[30] When no other source is given, all information on Goddard is taken from Coil 1992.

[31] Winter 1990.

[32] Ellis 1993, chapters 1, 3, 4.

[33] Clarke 1966, chapter 4. Travers 1979, 264–286. Gat 1992, 109ff. Ellis 1993, chapter 3. Crook 1994. Cooper 1991, chapter 6.

[34] Odell 1898, chapter 2. Franklin 1988, chapter 2.

[35] Odell 1898, 74, 152.

[36] Odell 1898, chapter 15.

[37] Waterloo 1898, 243.

[38] Waterloo 1898, 259. Franklin 1988, chapter 2.

[39] Serviss 1898, chapter 15. Franklin, chapter 3.

[40] Serviss 1898, chapter 17.

[41] October 7, 1899. Watt in Howard 1979.

[42] Cole 1900, chapter 1, chapter 13ff, 202ff.

[43] Shiel 1898, chapter 2.

[44] Shiel 1898, 290. Wagar 1982, chapter I:10.

[45] Shiel 1898, chapter 33. Franklin 1988.

[46] Wagar 1982, chapter I:8.

[47] Corn 1983.

[48] MacKenzie 1990, chapter 2.

[49] MacKenzie 1990, 34, 141.

[50] Biddle 1994.

[51] Corn 1983, 4.

[52] Corn 1983, 39f.

[53] Norton 1908, chapter II:11, Franklin 1988, chapter 2. Bartter 1988, chapter 1.

[54] Godfrey 1908, 53. Franklin 1988, chapter 2.

[55] Sedberry 1908, chapter 59. Franklin 1988, chapter 2.

[56] Hearne 1910, 183f.

[57] Kennett 1982, chapter 1. Warleta Carillo 1984. Kunz and Müller 1990, chapter 2.

[58] Annuaire 1911. Garner 1920, paragraph 308.

[59] *L'Italia in Africa* 1964. Segre 1974. Smith 1976. Wright 1983.

[60] Paris 1992, chapter 3. Thodes 1957. Joll 1960, chapter 3. Ingold 1978. Morrow 1993.

[61] *Times* and *The Chronicle* cited in Askew 1942. *L'Italia* 1964. Irace 1912, chapter 10. McClure 1913. Paris 1992, chapter 3.

[62] *L'Italia* 1964. Saundby 1961, chapter 1. Liddell Hart 1947, 80ff.

[63] In Swedish: *Lögnerna* 1912. Paris 1992, chapter 2.

[64] Fisch 1984, 294ff.

[65] Cf Morrow 1993.

[66] Cf Weart 1988, chapter 3.
[67] Warleta Carillo 1984. Kunz and Müller 1990, chapter 2.
[68] Prokosh 1995, chapter 1.
[69] Wells 1926, preface. Weart 1988, chapter 2.
[70] Friedman 1985, chapter 6.
[71] Wells 1926, 83–88.
[72] Train 1915, 132, 214f. Franklin 1988, chapter 2. Bartter 1988, chapter 1.
[73] Barney 1915, 410ff. Franklin 1988, chapter 2.
[74] Lanchester 1915, 191f.
[75] Lanchester 1915, 194f. Cf Quester 1966, chapter 3.
[76] Boyle 1962, 312ff.
[77] Townshend 1986.
[78] Fisch 1984. Grewe 1988, parts 4–5. Korman 1996.
[79] Korman 1996, chapter 5.
[80] Bring 1992, chapter 7.
[81] Longmate 1983, chapter 1. Schaffer 1985, chapter 2.
[82] Boyle 1962, chapter 12. Killingray 1984.
[83] Dobson 1986. Jones 1987, chapters 10–11. Jardine 1928, chapter 9. Clayton 1986, 220. Dean 1986, chapter 2.
[84] Grey 1941, 65–67. As early as 1912, Grey had wanted to use the air force "for impressing European superiority on an enormous native population." Morrow 1993.
[85] Harris 1947, chapter 1.
[86] Liddell Hart 1932, chapter 7. Groves 1934, chapter 15. Grey 1941, chapters 7–8, Slessor 1956. Asprey 1975, chapter 29. Groehler 1977, chapter 2. Robinson 1982, 13ff. Killingray 1984, 429–444. Clayton 1986, 78ff, 112ff, 175ff, 218ff. Dean 1986, chapter 2. Townshend 1986. De Moor and Wesseling 1989. Towle 1989, chapter 1. Omissi 1990, chapters 1–7. Meilinger 1995.
[87] Boyle 1962, 389–390.
[88] Westring 1936. Sigaud 1941. Earle 1944, chapter 20. Schaffer 1985, chapter 2. *Dizionario* 1992. Morrow 1993. Friedrich 1995, chapter 10. Gat 1998, 52ff.
[89] Garner 1920, chapter 11, paragraphs 296 and 310.
[90] Omissi 1990, chapter 8.
[91] Townshend 1986.
[92] SWAA 1836:5, National Archives, Windhoek, Namibia.
[93] Killingray 1984.
[94] Hamilton 1922, 1928, chapter 3.
[95] Anderson Graham 1923, chapters 3, 14, 22.
[96] Fuller 1923, chapter 7.
[97] Charlton 1931.
[98] Saward 1984. Messenger 1984. Towle 1989, chapter 1.
[99] Charlton 1931.
[100] Saward 1984.
[101] Cf Weigley 1973, chapter 14. Clayton 1986, 25.
[102] Moore 1924, chapter 5.
[103] Spaight 1924, chapter 1.
[104] Harris 1927, chapter 5.
[105] Kunz and Müller 1990, chapter 7.
[106] Harris 1927, 300. French Chechaouen = Arabic Shawan = Spanish Xauen = English Sheshuan.
[107] Harris 1927, chapters 5–6. Woolman 1969, 139ff.

[108] Preston 1993.
[109] Wright 1926, 263–280.
[110] Gat 1998.
[111] Crane 1993, chapter 2. Miller 1982.
[112] Mitchell 1925. Schaffer 1985, chapter 2.
[113] Desmond 1926, chapters 23, 27, 46.
[114] Glossop 1926, chapter 17.
[115] Neufeld 1995, chapter 1.
[116] Gail 1928, chapter II:2.
[117] Noyes 1927, chapter 20.
[118] Noyes 1927, chapter 25. Franklin 1988, chapter 8. Bartter 1988, chapter 2.
[119] Nowlan 1928, chapter 18.
[120] Nowlan 1928, epilogue.
[121] Omissi 1990, chapter 8. Bermann 1986.
[122] Kennett 1982, chapter 3. Douhet 1942, Book 2, chapter 4.
[123] "Libya," in Cannistraro 1982. Gordon 1987. Towle 1989.
[124] Neufeld 1995, chapter 2.
[125] Spohr cited by Franklin 1988, chapter 8.
[126] Chase 1929, chapter 17.
[127] Gobsch 1933, chapter 26.
[128] Spaight 1947, chapter 10. Towle 1989, chapter 1. Omissi 1990, chapter 8.
[129] SIPRI 1972.
[130] Dalton 1934, 310–315.
[131] Macilraith and Connolly 1934, 118ff, 136ff, 297, 302ff, 317. Cf Campbell 1937, 61–63.
[132] Oppenheim and Lauterpacht 1935, paragraph 214. Wording unchanged since 1944, made somewhat milder in 1952.
[133] The term was coined by Leon Daudet, who wrote *La guerre totale* inspired by Alphonse Seché's *Les guerres d'enfer* (1915), in which the conclusion states: "Modern conflicts tend more and more to destruction, to extermination." Markusen 1995, chapter 3.
[134] Ludendorff 1935, chapter 1. Earle 1944, chapter 13.
[135] Clayton 1986, 80f, 380f. Towle 1989, chapter 1.
[136] Omissi 1990, chapter 8.
[137] Townshend 1986.
[138] *Dagens Nyheter* 1936. Mörner 1936, 120f.
[139] Agge 1936, 106f.
[140] Negus 1936. Smith 1976, chapter 5.
[141] Groehler 1977, chapter 3.
[142] Smith 1976, chapter 5.
[143] *Indiscriminate* 1937.
[144] Auden and Isherwood 1939.
[145] O'Neill 1936, chapter 10.
[146] Pollard 1938, chapter 5.
[147] *Durango* 1937. Thomas and Morgan-Witts 1975. Whealey 1989.
[148] Steer's article reprinted in Oppler 1988.
[149] *Dagens Nyheter* 1937 4/28, 5/4, 5/8.
[150] *Dagens Nyheter* 1962 4/27.
[151] Stanley Baldwin 1932 11/12. Longmate 1983, chapter 4. Royse 1928, chapter 5.
[152] Oppler 1988.
[153] Gotthard Johansson in *Svenska Dagbladet* 1938 3/9.
[154] Spaight 1944, chapter 5. Snow 1942, 174f.

[155] Spaight 1947, chapter 11. Cf Liddell Hart 1947, 85–95.

[156] Sherwin 1975, chapter 1. Friedman 1985, chapter 6.

[157] Fuller 1948, chapter 7.

[158] Spaight 1944, chapter 3. Cf Quester 1966, chapter 11.

[159] Spaight 1947, chapter 11. Spetzler 1956, 223ff. Cf Sherry 1987, 71. Boog 1995.

[160] Veale 1953, chapter 6. Cf Rumpp 1961, chapter 1. For information on Veale, see Best 1980, introduction, and Roberts in Howard 1994.

[161] Nürnberg 36:329, 4:143, cited by Roberts in Howard 1994. Howard 1979: "Hitler attacked both Poland and the Soviet Union with the intention of destroying their societies and reconstructing them as German colonies." Howard 1994, introduction.

[162] *Akten zu Deutschen Auswärtigen Politik 1918–1945*, Serie D, Baden-Baden 1956, Vol. VII, 171f. Cited in Czech 1989.

[163] Cf Wright 1942, 811–812. Bartov 1985.

[164] Spaight 1947, chapter 11. Sallagar 1969, chapter 11. Longmate 1983, chapter 26. Markusen 1995, chapter 8.

[165] Garrett 1993, 11.

[166] Sherman cited in Weigley 1973, 149.

[167] Artillery called it "zone fire." According to Kennett 1982, chapter 3, it was the French who invented area bombing during the 1920s. But the concept was already proposed by Grahame-White 1912, chapter 13. "Absolute precision would not always be an essential," as long as a large number of projectiles could be counted upon to "do damage over a given area."

[168] Longmate 1978, especially chapters 3, 13, 14, 16. Friedrich 1995, chapter 8.

[169] Grey 1941, chapter 8.

[170] Bills 1990, introduction.

[171] Prokosh 1995, chapter 1. According to Grey 1941, "personnel bombs" were invented during the Spanish Civil War, while Kunz and Müller 1990, chapter 2, claim that they were used in Morocco as early as 1913.

[172] Franklin 1980. Bartter 1988, chapter 7.

[173] Bester (1941) 1976.

[174] Heinlein (1941) 1980, 118. Franklin 1988, chapter 8.

[175] Heinlein (1941) 1980, 128.

[176] Liddell Hart 1947, 23f.

[177] Longmate 1983, chapter 10.

[178] Garrett 1993, chapter 6.

[179] Garrett 1993, chapter 3.

[180] Headland 1992, chapter 9.

[181] Breitman 1998.

[182] Svanberg and Tydén 1997, chapter 14. Czech 1989.

[183] Zuckerman 1978, chapter 7.

[184] Harris 1947. Robinson 1982, 13ff. Longmate 1983, chapter 11. Messenger 1984, chapter 2. Saward 1984. Towle 1989, chapter 1. Omissi 1990, chapter 6. Boog 1995.

[185] Neufeld 1995, chapter 5.

[186] Gordon 1984, chapter 4. Svanberg and Tydén 1997, chapter 10.

[187] Longmate 1983, chapter 16. Beck 1986, chapter 1. Taylor 1987. Boog 1995.

[188] Fieser 1964, chapter 1.

[189] Werrell 1996, chapter 1.

[190] Schaffer 1985, chapters 4–5. Crane 1993, introduction and chapters 1, 2, 8.

[191] Szilard 1978, chapter 5.

[192] Hastings 1979, 180.

[193] Hastings 1979, 173.
[194] Hastings 1979, 171f.
[195] Middlebrook 1980. Sherry 1987, chapter 6.
[196] Middlebrook 1980, 244.
[197] Markusen 1995, chapter 8.
[198] Middlebrook 1980, 264–269.
[199] Garrett 1993, chapter 1.
[200] Dyson 1984.
[201] Englund 1998, 196. Cf Boog 1995. Cf Markusen and Kopf 1995, chapter 1.
[202] Englund 1998, 217.
[203] Svanberg 1997, chapter 11ff. Breitman 1998. According to Breitman, many Jewish lives could have been saved if the British had published what they already knew in 1941. Quester 1966: A transition to precision bombing could have been used "to deter other obnoxious practices in Nazi Germany" (157). Does Quester mean to imply that a halt in the bombing of German civilians would have been a possible way to rescue Jews?
[204] Wasserstein 1979, 306f. Breitman 1998, 170.
[205] Wyman 1984, 105.
[206] Middlebrook 1980, 360.
[207] Longmate 1983, chapter 26.
[208] Goebbels 6/17 1942: "Germany would repay blow by blow by mass extermination of Jews in reprisal for the Allied air bombings of German cities." Cited by Wyman 1984.
[209] Neufeld 1995, chapter 5 and epilogue.
[210] Garrett 1993, chapter 7. Walzer 1992, chapter 16. Best 1980, chapter 4:4: "From the moment the bombing of cities starts up again in the summer of 1944, the raids are indefensible."
[211] Schaffer 1985, chapter 5.
[212] Bergander (1977) 1994.
[213] McKee 1982, chapter 10.
[214] McKee 1982, 46.
[215] McKee 1982, chapter 10.
[216] McKee 1982, chapter 8.
[217] Longmate 1983.
[218] Longmate 1983, chapter 16.
[219] Longmate 1983, chapter 16. Schaffer 1985, chapter 5. Garrett 1993, chapter 2. Bond 1996, chapter 7, defends the attack on Dresden.
[220] Rodenberger 1955.
[221] Fieser 1964, chapter 3.
[222] Schaffer 1985, chapter 6. Werrell 1996, chapter 2.
[223] Schaffer 1985, chapter 5. Background: Iriye 1972.
[224] Schaffer 1985, chapters 4, 8.
[225] Sherry 1987, chapter 8.
[226] *New York Times* 1/9 1943. Dower 1986, chapter 3. Cf Crane 1993, chapter 9.
[227] Sherry 1987, chapters 2, 3. Werrell 1996, chapter 2.
[228] Seversky 1942, chapter 5. Weigley 1973, chapter 11. Franklin 1988, chapter 6.
[229] Sherry 1987, chapter 5.
[230] Werrell 1996, 116f, 136–139, 150–159.
[231] Guillain 1981.
[232] Sherry 1987, chapter 9.
[233] Schaffer 1985, chapter 7.
[234] Guillain 1981.
[235] Edoin 1987, chapter 8.

[236] Edoin 1987, chapter 9.
[237] Sigal 1988, chapter 6.
[238] Schaffer 1985, chapter 7. Crane 1993, chapter 9.
[239] Sherry 1987, chapter 9. Crane 1993, chapter 9.
[240] Sherry 1987, chapter 10. Werrell 1996, 163–168.
[241] Crane 1993, chapter 9.
[242] Werrell 1996, 227.
[243] Weigley 1973, chapter 15. Sherry 1987, chapter 10. Walzer 1992, chapter 16.
[244] Bills 1990, chapter 2. Clayton 1994, 30ff.
[245] Bills 1990, chapter 2.
[246] Franklin 1988, chapter 9.
[247] Szilard 1978, chapter 6.
[248] Wittner 1993, 25f.
[249] Schaffer 1985, chapter 8.
[250] Skates 1994, chapter 16f. Holloway 1994, chapter 6.
[251] Smithsonian 1994, EG:400.
[252] Lifton 1995, 4.
[253] Lifton 1995, 27f.
[254] Braw 1986. Wittner 1993, chapter 3. Weart 1988, chapter 12.
[255] Hastings 1993, chapter 1.
[256] Hastings 1993, chapter 1.
[257] Best 1994, chapter 6. Markusen 1995, chapter 4. Paech 1995.
[258] Friedrich 1995, chapter 10.
[259] Final Report, cited in Friedrich 1995, chapter 10.
[260] Lifton 1995, 47ff. Boyer 1985, chapter 16.
[261] Laurence 1946, chapter 16.
[262] Lifton 1995, 65.
[263] Lifton 1995, 267.
[264] *Charter of the United Nations*, Chapter 1, Article 1:2.
[265] Hawthorn 1991, chapter 3.
[266] Hastings 1993, chapter 1.
[267] Hastings 1993, chapter 1.
[268] Gaddis 1997, 70–84. Holloway 1994, chapter 13.
[269] Hastings 1993, chapter 2.
[270] Boyer 1985, chapters 4–5. Brians 1987, chapter 11. Franklin 1988, chapter 11. Wittner 1993, chapter 14, Holloway 1994, 162.
[271] Franklin 1988, chapters 7, 12. Brians 1987, chapter 12.
[272] Jenkins 1946, chapter 11. Franklin 1988, chapter 10.
[273] Boyer 1985, chapter 17.
[274] Lifton 1995, 83.
[275] Lifton 1995, chapter 7. Alperovitz 1995, 446ff, 520.
[276] Sturgeon (1947) 1997, 125–149. Franklin 1988, chapter 13.
[277] Spaight 1947, chapter 2.
[278] Neufeld 1995, epilogue. Mackenzie 1990, chapter 6.
[279] Rosenberg 1982. Bracken 1983. Schaffer 1985, epilogue. Holloway 1994, chapter 11. Markusen 1995, chapter 11.
[280] Wittner 1993, chapter 4.
[281] Schaffer 1985, epilogue.
[282] Markusen 1995, chapter 11.
[283] Best 1994, 111.

[284] Best 1994, 116.
[285] Best 1994, 158–179. Cf Pictet 1985, 51–58.
[286] Mackenzie 1990, 113ff.
[287] Mackenzie 1990, 134ff.
[288] Towle 1989, chapters 1, 4.
[289] Towle 1989, chapter 3. Armitage 1983, chapter 3.
[290] Cutterbuck 1966. Rawlings 1984. Postgate 1992.
[291] Clayton 1994, chapter 5.
[292] Wittner 1993, chapter 14. Franklin 1988, chapter 11.
[293] "Gulf" cited in Franklin 1980.
[294] Brians 1987, chapters 1, 4.
[295] Merril 1950, chapter 2.
[296] Merril 1950, chapter 29.
[297] Franklin 1988, chapter 13.
[298] What I was reading in New York in 1950 is more or less encapsulated by Lowe 1986, chapter 7. Background material can be found in various sources, including Hastings 1993, chapter 1.
[299] Hawthorn 1991, chapter 3.
[300] Hastings 1993, chapter 3.
[301] Hastings 1993, chapter 14.
[302] Crane 1993, chapter 10.
[303] Veale 1953, foreword.
[304] See section 256, above.
[305] Prokosh 1995, chapter 2. Walzer 1992, chapter 9.
[306] Walzer 1992, chapter 7.
[307] *Manchester Guardian* 3/1 1952. SIPRI: Napalm 1972. Cf Walzer 1992, chapter 9.
[308] "Korean War," in *Nationalencyklopedien.*
[309] Schaffer 1985, epilogue.
[310] Weigley 1973, chapter 17. Walzer 1992, chapter 17.
[311] SIPRI 1974, appendix 5A.
[312] Markusen 1995, chapter 11.
[313] Edgerton 1990, chapter 1.
[314] Rosberg and Nottingham 1966, chapter 9. Furedi 1989.
[315] Towle 1989, chapter on Mau Mau.
[316] Armitage 1983, chapter 3.
[317] Barnett and Njama 1966, 409–410.
[318] Towle 1989.
[319] Edgerton 1990, chapter 3.
[320] Edgerton 1990, chapter 5.
[321] See note 256.
[322] Towle 1989, chapter 3. Armitage 1983, chapter 3.
[323] Walzer 1992, chapter 6.
[324] Gaddis 1997, chapter 8.
[325] Rosenberg 1982, document 1. Schaffer 1985, epilogue.
[326] Gaddis 1997, chapter 8.
[327] Holloway 1994, chapter 15.
[328] Gaddis 1997, 232.
[329] Lindqvist (1955) 1981, 30.
[330] Rosenberg 1982, document 2. Rosenberg in Howard 1994.
[331] Myrdal 1976, 112f.

[332] Myrdal 1976, chapter 3. Holloway 1994, chapter 15.
[333] LeMay in April 1956 at the Naval War College, cited by Rhodes *Dark Sun*, 566.
[334] SIPRI 1973, chapter 5. SIPRI 1972.
[335] Schwarzenberger 1958, introduction.
[336] Wittner 1997, 6, 37–39, 3, 52f.
[337] Brians 1987, chapters 1, 4. Weart 1988 chapter 12.
[338] Bracken 1983, chapters 1953–61.
[339] Lindqvist 1996, 122-160. Lindqvist 1997, chapters 9–12, chapters 18–21.
[340] Schwarzenberger 1958, 22.
[341] Clarkson 1959, 118ff. Brians 1987, chapter 3.
[342] Wittner 1997, 21, 216–218. Rudling 1975.
[343] Singh 1959, 242f.
[344] See note 256. Towle 1989, chapter 4. Armitage 1983, chapter 4. Andreopoulos in Howard 1994.
[345] Demker 1996.
[346] *Dagens Nyheter* 1958 2/9.
[347] *Dagens Nyheter* 1958 2/10.
[348] *Dagens Nyheter* 1958 4/6.
[349] Demker 1996, 25.
[350] Bring 1992, 231ff.
[351] Bring 1992, 418.
[352] Bring 1992, 235ff.
[353] Euler 1960, Abstract.
[354] Dyer 1985, chapter 9.
[355] Schaffer 1985, epilogue.
[356] Dyer 1985, chapter 10.
[357] Clarkson 1959, fifth day.
[358] Henriksen 1997, chapter 6.
[359] Gaddis 1997, chapters 8, 9.
[360] May and Zelikow 1997, 178.
[361] Boyer 1985, epilogue. Weart 1988, chapter 12.
[362] Bailey 1972, chapter 1.
[363] Goulden 1969.
[364] Gibson 1988, chapter 9.
[365] Gibson 1988, chapter 9.
[366] Towle 1989, chapter "The War in South Vietnam." Weigley 1973, chapter 18.
[367] Lifton 1995, 271.
[368] Treat 1995, chapters 7–8.
[369] Ibuse 1965, 143–44.
[370] Power cited in Franklin 1988, chapter 7.
[371] Gibson 1988, chapter 10.
[372] De Seversky cited in Hastings 1993, chapter 14.
[373] Gibson 1988, chapter 9.
[374] Gibson 1988, chapter 10.
[375] McNamara 1995, 216ff, 286, 269.
[376] Towle 1989.
[377] Prokosh 1995, chapter 2.
[378] Prokosh 1995, chapter 4.
[379] Gibson 1988, chapter 11.
[380] Prokosh 1995, chapter 4.

[381] SIPRI 1977, chapter 1. Prokosh 1995, chapter 7.
[382] Gibson 1988, chapter 12.
[383] Green 1993, Edinburgh Resolution, points 7 and 8.
[384] Resolution 2675, Bailey 1987, appendix 9.
[385] Jules Moch, according to Myrdal 1976, chapter 2.
[386] Weizsäcker 1971, 46.
[387] Priest 1972, 125.
[388] Lewin 1972, chapter 2.
[389] SIPRI 1973, 147–150.
[390] SIPRI 1973, 150.
[391] Franklin 1988, chapter 7. Gibson 1988, chapter 9.
[392] SIPRI 1978, chapter 3.
[393] Mackenzie 1990, chapter 4.
[394] Mackenzie 1990, chapter 7.
[395] According to Fred C. Iklé in a Senate hearing, 1974 9/5, cited in SIPRI 1975.
[396] SIPRI 1975, 43.
[397] SIPRI 1974, introduction.
[398] Lifton 1995, 272f.
[399] Dyer 1985, chapter 10. Cattell 1986. Markusen 1995, chapter 11: "Put bluntly, ethnic targeting meets the precise definition of genocide because it singles out for destruction a specific group on the basis of its ethnic background."
[400] MacDonald 1995, 155.
[401] Whitsel 1998. Lööw 1998, 375ff.
[402] Myrdal 1976, chapter 8. Best 1994, 269f.
[403] Protocol III, article 2:2. Green 1993, chapter 9.
[404] SIPRI 1981, introduction.
[405] SIPRI 1977, introduction. SIPRI 1979, introduction.
[406] SIPRI 1979, introduction.
[407] Dyer 1985, chapter 9.
[408] Article 51:4.
[409] Johnstone 1983, chapter III:1.
[410] Johnstone 1983, chapter II:17.
[411] Johnstone 1983, chapter II:10.
[412] Lifton 1995, 270.
[413] Cumings 1992, 223.
[414] van Creveld 1991, 1, 19, 32.
[415] Taylor 1998.
[416] Toffler 1994, 82. Cf *Needless Deaths* 1991 passim. Cf Crane 1993, chapter 10.
[417] van Creveld 1991, chapter 6.
[418] van Creveld 1991, 22, 29.
[419] Buruma 1994, 223.
[420] Bosworth 1993.
[421] Lifton 1995. Linenthal and Engelhardt 1996. Harwit 1996.
[422] Smithsonian Institution: "The Crossroads," "The End of WWII," "The Atomic Bomb," and "The Cold War," January 1994. (Internal document.)
[423] Lifton 1995, 280f.
[424] Lifton 1995, 285.
[425] Lifton 1995, 292.
[426] Smithsonian 1994, EG:200.54. Lifton 1995, 293.
[427] Lindqvist 1985.

[428] Whitsel 1998.

[429] Lööw 1998, 379. Cf Hamm 1993, 50ff. Barkun 1994, chapter 11. Kaplan 1998, chapters 3, 8.

[430] *Washington Post* cited in *Expressen* 1998 11/20: "Not Even a Fence Offers Protection from Terrorists."

[431] van Creveld 1991, chapter 7. Cf Bjorgo, Tor, ed.: "Terror from the extreme right," special issue of *Terrorism and Political Violence*, 7:1, Spring 1995.

[432] Brians 1987, chapter 5.

[433] Clute 1995, 1188, with additional information from the publishers taken from the Internet.

[434] van Creveld 1991, epilogue.

[435] van Creveld 1991, chapter 7.

[436] van Creveld 1991, epilogue.

BIBLIOGRAPHY

Abd el Krim: *Memoiren: Mein Krieg gegen Spanien und Frankreich*, Dresden, 1927.

Adams, James: *The Next World War: The Warriors and Weapons of the New Battlefield in Cyberspace*, London, 1998.

Agge, Gunnar: *Med röda korset i fålt, Minnen och intryck från svenska abessinienambulansen 1935–1936*, Stockholm, 1936.

Allen, Theodore W.: *The Invention of the White Race: Racial Oppression and Social Control*, London, 1994.

Alperovitz, Gar: *Atomic Diplomacy: Hiroshima and Potsdam: The Use of the Atomic Bomb and the American Confrontation with Soviet Power*, New York, 1965.

Alperovitz, Gar: *The Decision to Use the Atomic Bomb and the Architecture of an American Myth*, London, 1995.

Anderson Graham, P.: *The Collapse of Homo Sapiens*, London, 1923.

Annuaire de l'Institut de Droit International, Brussels 1911. Vol. 24. Session de Madrid, April 1911.

Armitage, M. J. and Mason, R. A.: *Air Power in the Nuclear Age, 1945–1982. Theory and Practice*, London, 1983.

Askew, William C.: *Europe and Italy's Acquisition of Libya 1911–1912*, Durham, 1942.

Asprey, Robert B.: *War in the Shadows: The Guerrilla in History*, 1–2, New York, 1975.

Auden, W. H., and Isherwood, Christopher: *Journey to a War*, New York, 1939.

Bailey, Sidney D.: *Prohibitions and Restraints in War*, Oxford, 1972.

Baker, David: *Flight and Flying: A Chronology*, New York, 1994.

Balke, Ulf: *Der Luftkrieg in Europa, part 2, Der Luftkrieg gegen England und über dem Deutschen Reich 1941–45*, Koblenz, 1990.

Barnett, Donald L. and Njama, Karari: *Mau Mau from Within*, London, 1966.

Barney, John Stuart: *L. P. M.: The End of the Great War*, New York, 1915.

Barron, Neil: *Anatomy of Wonder: A Critical Guide to Science Fiction*, third ed., New York, 1987.

Bartter, Martha A.: *The Way to Ground Zero: The Atomic Bomb in American SF*, New York, 1988.

Beck, Earl R.: *Under the Bombs: The German Home Front 1942–1945*, Lexington, 1986.

Bell, Neil: *Valiant Clay*, London, 1934.

Bergander, Götz: *Dresden im Luftkrieg, Vorgeschichte, Zerstörung, Folgen* (1977), Weimar, 1994.

Bergman, Bo: *Samlade dikter*, Stockholm, 1951–52.

Bermann, Karl: *Under the Big Stick: Nicaragua and the U.S. Since 1848*, Boston, 1986.

Best, Geoffrey: *Humanity in Warfare: The Modern History of the International Law of Armed Conflicts*, London, 1980.

Best, Geoffrey: *War and Law Since 1945*, Oxford, 1994.

Bester, Alfred: "Adam and No Eve" (1941), in *Star Light, Star Bright: The Great Short Fiction of Alfred Bester*, New York, 1976.

Biddle, Tami Davis: "Air Power" in Howard, 1994.

Bills, Scott L.: *Empire and Cold War: The Roots of U.S.–Third World Antagonism 1945–47*, London, 1990.

Bjorgo, Tor (ed.): "Terror from the Extreme Right," Special issue of *Terrorism and Political Violence*, Vol. 7, no. 1, Spring 1995.

Black, Jeremy: *Why Wars Happen*, London, 1998.

Black, Ladbroke: *The Poison War*, London, 1933.

Bleiler, Everett F.: *Science-fiction: The Early Years*, London, 1990.

Bluntschli, Johann Caspar: *Das moderne Völkerrecht der zivilisierten Staaten als Rechtsbuch dargestellt* (1868), Zweite mit Rücksicht auf die Ereignisse von 1868 bis 1872 ergänzte Auflage, Nördlingen, 1872.

Bond, Brian: *War and Society in Europe 1870–1970*, Bath, 1985.

Bond, Brian: *The Pursuit of Victory: From Napoleon to Saddam Hussein*, Oxford, 1996.

Boog, Horst: "*Harris – A German View*." In Harris, Arthur T.: *Dispatch on War Operations*, London, 1995.

Boog, Horst (ed.): *The Conduct of the Air War in the Second World War: An International Comparison*, New York, 1992.

Bosworth, R. J. B.: *Explaining Auschwitz and Hiroshima: History Writing and the Second World War 1945–1990*, London, 1993.

Boyer, Paul: *By the Bomb's Early Light: American Thought and Culture at the Dawn of the Atomic Age*, New York, 1985.

Boyle, Andrew: *Trenchard, Man of Vision*, London, 1962.

Bracken, Paul: *The Command and Control of Nuclear Forces*, New Haven, 1983.

Bradbury, Ray: *The Martian Chronicles* (1950), New York, 1984.

Braw, Monica: *The Atomic Bomb Suppressed: American Censorship in Occupied Japan*, Malmö, 1986.

Breitman, Richard: *Official Secrets: What the Nazis Planned, What the British and Americans Knew*, New York, 1998.

Brians, Paul: *Nuclear Holocausts: Atomic War in Fiction 1895–1984*, Kent, Ohio, 1987.

Bring, Ove: *FN-stadgans folkrätt*, Stockholm, 1992.

Burgess, Michael: *Reference Guide to Science Fiction, Fantasy and Horror*, San Bernardino, Calif., 1992.

Caldwell, Colonel C. E.: *Small Wars: Their Principle and Practice*, HMSO 1896 new edition 1899, revised 1906. I cite the 1906 edition: *Small Wars: A Tactical Textbook for Imperial Soldiers*, London, 1990.

Campbell, Sir Malcolm: *The Peril from the Air*, London, 1937.

Cannistraro, Philip V.: *Historical Dictionary of Fascist Italy*, London, 1982.

Cattell, David T. and Quester, George H.: *Ethnic Targeting: Some Bad Ideas*, in: Ball, Desmond and Richelson, Jeffrey (eds.): *Strategic Nuclear Targeting*, Ithaca, 1986.

Charlton, Lionel: *Charlton*, London, 1931.

Chase, Stuart: *Men and Machines*, New York, 1929.

Clareson, Thomas D.: *Some Kind of Paradise: The Emergence of American SF*, Westport, Connecticut, 1985.

Clarke, I. F.: *The Tale of the Future: From the Beginning to the Present Day; A Checklist...1644–1960*, London, 1961.

Clarke, I. F.: *Voices Prophesying War 1763–1984*, London, 1966.

Clarke, I. F.: *The Tale of the Next Great War, 1871–1914: Fictions of Future Warfare and of Battles Still-to-come*, Liverpool, 1995.

Clarkson, Helen (McCloy): *The Last Day*, New York, 1959.

Clausewitz, Karl von: *On War*, Princeton, 1976.

Clayton, Anthony: *The British Empire as Superpower 1919–1939*, London, 1986.

Clayton, Anthony: *The Wars of French Decolonization*, London, 1994.

Clute, John and Nicholls, Peter: *The Encyclopaedia of Science Fiction*, New York, 1995.

Coil, Suzanne M.: *Robert Hutchings Goddard: Pioneer of Rocketry and Space Flight*, New York, 1992.

Cole, Robert W.: *The Struggle for Empire*, London, 1900.

Committee for the Compilation of Materials on Damage Caused by the Atomic Bombs: *Hiroshima and Nagasaki – The Physical, Medical and Social Effects of the Atomic Bombings*, New York, 1981.

Cooper, Alan W.: *Target Dresden*, Bromley, 1995.

Cooper, Sandi E.: *Patriotic Pacifism: Waging War on War in Europe 1815–1914*, New York, 1991.

Corn, Joseph J.: *The Winged Gospel: America's Romance with Aviation, 1900–1950*, New York, 1983.

Crane, Conrad C.: *Bombs, Cities and Civilians: American Airpower Strategy in World War II*, Lawrence, Kansas, 1993.

Cumings, Bruce: *The Origins of the Korean War*, 1–2, Princeton, 1981–90.

Cumings, Bruce: *War and Television*, London, 1992.

Cutterbuck, Richard: *The Long, Long War: The Emergency in Malaya 1948–1960*, London, 1966.

Czesany, Maximilian: *Nie wieder Krieg gegen die Zivilbevölkerung, Eine völkerrechtliche Untersuchung des Luftkrieges 1939–1945*, Graz, 1961.

Dagens Nyheter 1911 2/11. 1936 2/1. 1937 28/4, 4/5, 8/5. 1956 20/10. 1962 27/4. 1965 9/6.

Dalton, M.: *The Black Death*, London, 1934.

Dean, David J.: *The Air Force Role in Low Intensity Conflict*, Washington, D.C., 1986.

Demker, Marie: *Sverige och Algeriets frigörelse 1954–1962, Kriget som förändrade svensk utrikespolitik*, Stockholm, 1996.

De Moor, J. A. and Wesseling, H. L.: *Imperialism and War: Essays on Colonial Wars in Asia and Africa*, Leiden, 1989.

Desmond, Shaw: *Ragnarok*, London, 1926.

Dilke, Charles: *Greater Britain: A Record of Travels in English-Speaking Countries During 1866 and 1867*, 1–2, Philadelphia, 1869.

Dizionario biografico degli italiani, no. 41, Rome, 1992.

Dobson, Christopher and Miller, John: *The Day We Almost Bombed Moscow: The Allied War in Russia 1918–1920*, London, 1986.

Dominik, Hans: *Djinghis Khans spår, En roman från tjugoförsta århundradet*, Stockholm, 1926.

Douhet, Giulio: *Luftherrschaft* (1921) 1935. *The Command of the Air* (1942) Washington, 1983.

Douhet, Giulio: *The Probable Aspects of the War of the Future*, April 1928. English translation in *The Command of the Air*, New York, 1942.

Dower, John: *War Without Mercy: Race and Power in the Pacific War*, London, 1986.

Dowling, David: *Fictions of Nuclear Disaster*, London, 1987.

Durango – martyrstaden, Ett tyskt bombardemang–dess orsaker och verkningar, Stockholm, 1937.

Dyer, Gwynne: *War*, London, 1985.

Dyson, Freeman: *Weapons and Hope*, New York, 1984.

Earle, Edward M.: *Makers of Modern Strategy: Military Thought from Machiavelli to Hitler*, Princeton, 1944.

Edgerton, Robert B.: *Mau Mau: An African Crucible*, London, 1990.

Edoin, Hoito: *Tokyo Burned*, New York, 1987.

Ellis, John: *The Social History of the Machine Gun* (1976), London, 1993.

Englund, Peter: *Brev från nollpunkten* (1996), Stockholm, 1998.

Euler, Alexander: *Die Atomwaffe im Luftkriegsrecht*, Köln/Berlin, 1960.

Eyffinger, Arthur: *The International Court of Justice 1946–1996*, The Hague, 1996.

Falconer, Jonathan: *RAF Bomber Command in Fact, Film and Fiction*, Frome, Somerset, U.K., 1996.

Farrer, James Anson: *Military Manners and Customs*, London, 1885.

Fisch, Jörg: *Die Europäische Expansion und der Völkerrecht, Die Auseinandersetzungen um den Status der Überseeischen Gebiete vom 15. Jahrhundert bis zur Gegenwart*, Stuttgart, 1984. (Beiträge zur Kolonial – und Überseegeschichte; Bd 26).

Franke, Henning: *Der politisch-militärische Zukunftsroman in Deutschland 1904–1914*, Frankfurt/Main, 1985.

Franklin, H. Bruce: *Robert A. Heinlein: America as SF*, New York, 1980.

Franklin, H. Bruce: *Star Wars: The Superweapon and the American Imagination*, Oxford, 1988.

Friedman, Alan J. and Donley, Carol C.: *Einstein as Myth and Muse*, Cambridge, U.K., 1985.

Friedrich, Jörg: *Das Gesetz des Krieges, Das deutsche Heer in Russland 1941–45, Der Prozess gegen das Oberkommando der Wehrmacht*, Munich, 1995.

Fuller, J. F. C.: *The Reformation of War*, London, 1923.

Furedi, Frank: *The Mau Mau War in Perspective*, London, 1989.

Gaddis, John Lewis: *We Now Know: Rethinking Cold War History*, Oxford, 1997.

Gail, Otto Willi: *Med raket genom världsrymden*, Stockholm, 1928.

Garner, James Wilford: *International Law and the World War*, London, 1920.

Garrett, Stephen A.: *Ethics and Airpower in World War II: The British Bombing of German Cities*, New York, 1993.

Gat, Azar: *The Development of Military Thought: The Nineteenth Century*, Oxford, 1992.

Gat, Azar: *Fascist and Liberal Visions of War: Fuller, Liddell Hart, Douhet and other Modernists*, Oxford, 1998.

Gibson, James William: *The Perfect War* (1986), New York, 1988.

Glossop, Reginald: *The Orphan of Space: A Tale of Downfall*, London, 1926.

Glubb, John Bagot: *War in the Desert: An R.A.F. Frontier Campaign*, New York, 1961.

Gobsch, Hanns: *Europa inför avgrunden*, Stockholm, 1933.

Goddard, Robert H.: "A Method of Reaching Extreme Altitudes," in *The Papers of Robert H. Goddard*, Vol. 1, New York, 1970.

Godfrey, Hollis: *The Man Who Ended War*, New York, 1908.

Goldstein, Laurence: *The Flying Machine and Modern Literature*, Bloomington, 1986.

Gong, Gerrit W.: *The Standard of "Civilization" in International Society*, Oxford, 1984.

Gordon, John W.: *The Other Desert War: British Special Forces in North Africa 1940–1943*, New York, 1987.

Gordon, Sarah: *Hitler, Germans, and the "Jewish Question,"* Princeton, 1984.

Goulden, Joseph C.: *Truth Is the First Casualty: The Gulf of Tonkin Affair – Illusion and Reality*, Chicago, 1969.

Grahame-White, Claude: *The Aeroplane in War*, London, 1912.

Grainville, Cousin de: *Le dernier homme*, Paris, 1806.

Grand-Carté, John and Deltei, Leo: *Conquête de l'Air vue par l'image 1495–1909*, Paris, 1909.

Green, L. C.: *The Contemporary Law of Armed Conflict*, Manchester and New York, 1993.

Grewe, Wilhelm G.: *Epochen der Völkerrechtsgeschichte* (1944), Baden-Baden, 1988.

Grey, Charles G.: *Bombers*, London, 1941.

Groehler, Olaf: *Geschichte des Luftkriegs 1910–1970* (1975), Berlin, 1977.

Grotius, Hugo: *De jure belli ac pacis* (1625), Tübingen, 1950.

Groves, P. R. C.: *Behind the Smoke Screen*, London, 1934.

Guillain, Robert: *I Saw Tokyo Burning: An Eyewitness Narrative from Pearl Harbor to Hiroshima*, London, 1981.

Hamilton, Cicely: *Theodore Savage*, London, 1922 (revised and reissued in 1928 as *Lest Ye Die*).

Harris, Arthur: *Bomber Offensive*, London, 1947.

Harris, Walter B.: *France, Spain and the Rif*, London, 1927.

Hartigan, Richard Shelly: *The Forgotten Victim: A History of the Civilian*, Chicago, 1982.

Harwit, Martin: *An Exhibit Denied: Lobbying the History of Enola Gay*, New York, 1996.

Hastings, Max: *The Korean War*, London (1987), 1993.

Hastings, Max: *Bomber Command*, London, 1979.

Hawthorn, Geoffrey: *Plausible Worlds: Possibility and Understanding in History and the Social Sciences*, Cambridge, 1991.

Hay, William D.: *Three Hundred Years Hence*, London, 1881.

Headland, Ronald: *Messages of Murder: A Study of the Reports of the Einsatzgruppen of the Security Police and the Security Service 1941–1943*, London, 1992.

Hearne, R. P.: *Airships in Peace and War: Being the Second Edition of Aerial Warfare with Seven New Chapters*, London, 1910.

Heinlein, Robert A.: "Solution Unsatisfactory" (1941), in *Expanded Universe: The New Worlds of Robert A. Heinlein*, New York, 1980.

Helm, Johann Georg: "Der Schutz der Zivilbevölkerung im europäischen Kriegsrecht in der Zeit vom 17. Jahrhundert bis zum ersten Weltkrieg," *Zeitschrift für das gesamte Familienrecht*, s. 234ff, 1962.

Henriksen, Margot A.: *Dr Strangelove's America: Society and Culture in the Atomic Age*, Berkeley, 1997.

Hersey, John: *Hiroshima* (1946), London, 1985.

Holloway, David: *Stalin and the Bomb: The Soviet Union and Atomic Energy 1939–1956*, New Haven, 1994.

Hornung, Joseph: "Civilisés et barbares," *Révue de droit international*, 1885, pp. 5–18, 447–470, 539–560; 1886, pp. 188–206.

Hough, Stanley B.: *Extinction Bomber*, London, 1956.

Howard, Michael: *Restraints on War*, Oxford, 1979.

Howard, Michael, et al.: *The Laws of War: Constraints on Warfare in the Western World*, New Haven, 1994.

Howorth, Muriel: *Pioneer Research on the Atom: The Life Story of Frederick Soddy*, London, 1958.

Human Rights Watch: *Needless Deaths in the Gulf War: Civilian Casualties During the Air Campaign and Violations of the Laws of War*, New York, 1991.

Ibuse, Masuji: *Black Rain* (1965), New York, 1984.

Indiscriminate Aerial Bombing of Non-Combatants in China by Japanese, Shanghai, 1937.

Ingold, Felix Philipp: *Literatur und Aviatik, Europäische Flugdichtung 1909–1927*, Basel and Stuttgart, 1978.

International Court of Justice: *Legality of the Threat or Use of Nuclear Weapons*, Advisory Opinion 8 July 1996. (General List No. 95).

Irace, Chevalier Tullio: *With the Italians in Tripoli: The Authentic History of the Turco-Italian War*, London, 1912.

Iriye, Akira: *Pacific Estrangement: Japanese and American Expansion 1897–1911*, Cambridge, Mass., 1972.

L'Italia in Africa: *L'Opera dell'aeronautica*, Tomo 1, Eritrea-Libia, Rome, 1964.

Janson, Gustaf: *Lögnerna*, Stockholm, 1912. Extract in Clarke, 1995.

Jardine, Douglas: *The Mad Mullah of Somaliland*, London, 1928.

Jenkins, Will F.: *The Murder of the U.S.A.*, New York, 1946.

Johnstone, William: *Hatred in the Ashes*, New York, 1999. *Out of the Ashes*, New York, 1983. *Triumph in the Ashes*, New York, 1998.

Joll, James: *Intellectuals in Politics*, London, 1960.

Jones, H. A.: *Over the Balkans and South Russia 1917–1919: Being the History of No. 47 Squadron Royal Air Force* (1923) Reprint Elstree, 1987 (Vintage Aviation Library 14).

Kahn, Herman: *Tankar om det otänkbara* (1962) Stockholm, 1963.

Kennett, Lee: *A History of Strategic Bombing*, New York, 1982.

Killingray, David: "A Swift Agent of Government": Air Power in British Colonial Africa, 1916–1939. *Journal of African History*, 1984, pp. 429–444.

Kipling, Rudyard: "As Easy as ABC," in *A Diversity of Creatures*, London, 1912.

Kleen, Rickard: *Krigets historia ur folkrättslig synpunkt i kort sammandrag*, Stockholm, 1906.

Korman, Sharon: *The Right of Conquest: The Acquisition of Territory by Force in International Law and Practice*, Oxford, 1996.

Kotzsch, Lothar: *The Concept of War in Contemporary History and International Law*, Geneva, 1956.

Kretz, Åke: *Flyganfall! Hur skall jag handla?* Motala, Sweden, 1939.

Kunz, Rudibert and Müller, *Rolf-Dieter: Giftgas gegen Abd el Krim, Deutschland, Spanien und der Gaskrieg in Spanisch-Marocko 1922–1927, Einzelschriften zur Militärgeschichte 34, Militärgeschichtliches Forschungsamt, Freiburg im Breisgau*, 1990.

Kurki, Allan W.: *Operation Moonlight Sonata: The German Raid on Coventry*, London, 1995.

Lanchester, F. W.: *Aircraft in Warfare*, London, 1915.

Laurence, William L.: *Dawn Over Zero: The Story of the Atomic Bomb*, New York, 1946.

LeMay, Curtis E.: *America Is in Danger*, New York, 1968.

Lenz, Millicent: *Nuclear Age Literature for Youth: The Quest for a Life-Affirming Ethic*, Chicago, 1990.

Lewin, Leonard: *Triage*, New York, 1972.

Liddell Hart, B. H.: *Paris, or the Future of War*, London, 1925.

Liddell Hart, B. H.: *The British Way in Warfare*, London, 1932.

Liddell Hart, B. H.: *The Revolution in Warfare*, New Haven, 1947.

Lifton, Robert Jay and Mitchell, Greg: *Hiroshima in America: Fifty Years of Denial*, New York, 1995.

Lindqvist, Sven: *Elefantens fot, Resa i Baluchistan och Afghanistan*, Stockholm, 1985.

Lindqvist, Sven: *Ett förslag* (1955), Stockholm, 1981.

Lindqvist, Sven: *Exterminate All the Brutes* (1992), New York, 1996.

Lindqvist, Sven: *The Skull Measurer's Mistake* (1995), New York, 1997.

Linenthal, Edward T. and Engelhardt, Tom: *History Wars, The Enola Gay and Other Battles for the American Past*, New York, 1996.

Littauer and Uphof: *Air War in Indochina*, Boston, 1972.

London, Jack: "The Unparalleled Invasion," in *Curious Fragments* (1910), London, 1975.

Longmate, Norman: *The Bombers: The RAF Offensive against Germany 1939–1945*, London, 1983.

Longmate, Norman: *Air Raid, The Bombing of Coventry, 1940* (1976), London, 1978.

Lowe, Peter: *The Origins of the Korean War* (1986), New York, 1995.

Lööw, Heléne: *Nazismen i Sverige 1980–1997, Den rasistiska undergroundrörelsen: musiken, myterna, riterna*, Stockholm, 1998.

Ludendorff, Erich: *Der totale Krieg*, Munich, 1935.

MacDonald, Andrew (Pierce, William): *The Turner Diaries*, Hillsboro, West Virginia (1977), 1995.

Mackenzie, Donald: *Inventing Accuracy: A Historical Sociology of Nuclear Missile Guidance*, Cambridge, Mass., 1990.

Macilraith, F. and Connolly, R.: *Invasion from the Air*, London, 1934.

Majevski, Henry F.: "Grainville's Le Dernier Homme," *Symposium*, 1963.

Malthus, Thomas: *An Essay on the Principle of Population* (1803), London and New York, 1982.

Marinetti, F. T.: *La Bataille de Tripoli* (26 Octobre 1911) vécue et chantée par F. T. Marinetti, Milan, 1912.

Markusen, Eric and Kopf, David: *Holocaust and Strategic Bombing: Genocide and Total War in the 20th Century*, Boulder, 1995.

May, Ernest R. and Zelikow, Philip D.: *The Kennedy Tapes: Inside the White House during the Cuban Missile Crises*, Cambridge, Mass., 1997.

McClure, W. K.: *Italy in North Africa: An Account of the Tripoli Enterprise*, London, 1913.

McCurdy, Howard E.: *Space and the American Imagination*, Washington, D.C., 1997.

McKee, Alexander: *Dresden 1945: The Devil's Tinderbox*, New York, 1982.

McNamara, Robert: *In Retrospect: The Tragedy and Lessons of Vietnam*, New York, 1995.

Meilinger, Philip S.: "Proselytizer and Prophet: Alexander P. de Seversky and American Airpower." in Gooch, John (ed): *Airpower, Theory and Practice*, London, 1995.

Menzel, Eberhard: *Legalität oder Illegalität der Anwendung von Atomwaffen, Recht und Staat in Geschichte und Gegenwart 225–226*, Tübingen, 1960.

Merril, Judith: *Shadow on the Hearth* (1950), London, 1953.

Messenger, Charles: *"Bomber" Harris and the Strategic Bomber Offensive 1939–1945*, London, 1984.

Meyer, Alex: *Völkerrechtlicher Schutz der friedlichen Personen und Sachen gegen Luftangriffe, Das geltende Kriegsrecht*, Königsberg, 1935. (Verkehrsrechtliche Schriften IV.)

Middlebrook, Martin and Everitt, Chris (eds.): *Bomber Command War Diaries: An Operational*

Reference Book 1939–1945, Harmondsworth, England and New York, 1996.

Middlebrook, Martin: *The Battle of Hamburg, London*, 1980.

Mitchell, William: *Winged Defense: The Development and Possibilities of Modern Air Power – Economic and Military*, New York, 1925.

Montesquieu, Charles de: "Esprit des lois" (1748), in *Ouevres complètes*, Paris, 1964.

Moore, John Bassett: *International Law and Some Current Illusions, and Other Essays*, New York, 1924.

Mörner, Håkan: *Afrikansk oro, Upplevelser i Abessinien, Somaliländerna, Sudan, Egypten och Palestina*, Helsinki, 1936.

Morrow, John H., Jr.: *The Great War in the Air: Military Aviation from 1909 to 1921*, Washington, D.C., 1993.

Mueller, John: *Retreat from Doomsday: The Obsolescence of Major War*, New York, 1989.

Myrdal, Alva: *Spelet om nedrustningen*, Stockholm, 1976.

Nagl, Manfred: *Science Fiction in Deutschland*, Tübingen, 1972.

Needham, Joseph: *Science and Civilisation in China*, Vol. 5:7, *The Gunpowder Epic*, Cambridge, 1986.

Negus: *Negus anklagar, Sanningen om det italiensk-abessinska kriget*, Stockholm, 1936.

Neufeld, Michael J.: *The Rocket and the Reich: Peenemünde and the Coming of the Ballistic Missile Era*, Cambridge, Mass., 1995.

Norton, Roy: *The Vanishing Fleets*, New York, 1908.

Nowlan, Philip F.: *Armageddon 2149 A.D.*, New York (1928), 1962.

Noyes, Pierrepont B.: *The Pallid Giant* (1927), London, 1928, *Gentlemen, You Are Mad* (1947).

Oberth, Hermann: *Die Rakete zu den Planetenraumen* (1923), Nuremburg, 1960.

Odell, Samuel W.: *The Last War, or The Triumph of the English Tongue*, London, 1898.

Oe, Kenzaburo: *Hiroshima Notes*, New York, 1965.

Ogden, Bob: *Aircraft Museums and Collections of the World, Part 2. Great Britain and Ireland*, Woodley, 1994.

Omissi, David E.: *Air Power and Colonial Control: The Royal Air Force 1919–1939*, Manchester, 1990.

O'Neill, Joseph: *The Day of Wrath*, London, 1936.

Oppler, Ellen C. (ed.): *Picasso's* Guernica, New York, 1988.

Paech, Norman: "Nürnberg und die Nuklearfrage", in: Handel, Gerd and Stuby, Gerhard (hg): *Strafgerichte gegen Menschheitsverbrechen, Zum Völkerstrafrecht 50 Jahre nach den Nürnberger Prozessen*, Hamburg, 1995.

Paret, Peter et al.: *Persuasive Images: Posters of War and Revolution from the Hoover Institution Archives*, Princeton, 1992.

Paris, Michael: *Winged Warfare: The Literature and Theory of Aerial Warfare in Britain 1859–1917*, Manchester, 1992.

Parker, Geoffrey: Early Modern Europe. In Howard, 1994.

Pictet, Jean: *Development and Principles of International Humanitarian Law*, Geneva, 1985.

Pollard, Captain A.O.: *Air Reprisal*, London, 1938.

Postgate, Malcolm: *Operation Firedog: Air Support in the Malayan Emergency*, London HMSO, 1992.

Preston, Paul: *Franco*, London, 1993.

Priest, Christopher: *Fugue for a Darkening Island*, London, 1972.

Prokosh, Eric: *The Technology of Killing: A Military and Political History of Antipersonnel Weapons*, London, 1995.

Quester, George H.: *Deterrence before Hiroshima: The Airpower Background of Modern Strategy*, New York, 1966.

Rawlings, D.R.: *The History of the Royal Air Force*, London, 1984.

Re(s)tif de la Bretonne, Nicolas Edme: *La découverte australe, par en homme-volant*, 1–4, Paris, 1781. In German 1784: *Der fliegende Mensch.*

Rhodes, Anthony: *The Poet As Superman: A Life of Gabriele D'Annunzio*, London, 1957.

Rhodes, Richard: *Dark Sun: The Making of the Hydrogen Bomb*, New York, 1995.

Rhodes, Richard: *The Making of the Atomic Bomb* (1986), London, 1988.

Roberts, Adam and Guelff, Richard (eds.): *Documents on the Laws of War*, Oxford (1989), 1995.

Robinson, Anthony: *Aerial Warfare*, London, 1982.

Rodenberger, Axel: *Der Tod von Dresden*, Frankfurt, 1955.

Rosas, Allan: *International Law and the Use of Nuclear Weapons, Essays in Honour of Erik Castrén*, Helsinki, 1979.

Rosberg, Carl G., Jr. and Nottingham, John: *The Myth of "Mau Mau,"* New York, 1966.

Rose, Horace: *The Maniac's Dream: A Novel of the Atomic Bomb*, London, 1946.

Rosenberg, David Alan: "A Smoking Radiating Ruin at the End of Two Hours," *Documents on American Plans for Nuclear War with the Soviet Union 1954–55*, New York, 1982.

Roshwald, Mordecai: *Level* 7, New York, 1959.

Rousseau, Jean-Jacques: *The Social Contract*, 1762.

Royse, M. W.: *Aerial Bombardment and the International Regulation of Warfare*, New York, 1928.

Rubinstein, William D.: *The Myth of Rescue*, London, 1997.

Rudling, Anna: *Kampen mot atomvapen*, Stockholm, 1975.

Rumpp, Hans: *Das war der Bombenkrieg, Deutsche Städte im Feuersturm, Ein Dokumentarbericht*, Oldenburg and Hamburg, 1961.

Russell, Bertrand: *Power: A New Social Analysis*, London, 1938.

Sadoul, Jacques: *Histoire de la science-fiction moderne (1911–1984)*, Paris, 1984.

Sallagar, Frederick M.: *The Road to Total War*, New York, 1969.

Sambrook, A. J.: "A Romantic Theme: The Last Man," *Forum for Modern Language Studies*, 1966.

Saundby, Sir Robert: *Air Bombardment: The Story of its Development*, London, 1961.

Saward, Dudley: *Bomber Harris*, London, 1984.

Schaffer, Ronald: *Wings of Judgment: American Bombing in World War II*, Oxford, 1985.

Schwarzenberger, George: *The Legality of Nuclear Weapons*, London, 1958.

Sedberry, J. Hamilton: *Under the Flag of the Cross*, Boston, 1908.

Segre, Claudio G.: *Fourth Shore: The Italian Colonization of Libya*, Chicago, 1974.

Selsky, Harold E.: "Colonial America" in Howard, 1994.

Serviss, Garrett P.: *Edison's Conquest of Mars*, London, 1898.

Seversky, Alexander P. de: *Victory Through Air Power*, New York, 1942.

Shanks, Edward: *People of the Ruins*, London, 1920.

Shelley, Mary Wollstonecraft: *The Last Man* (1826), Oxford, 1994.

Sherry, Michael S.: *The Rise of American Air Power: The Creation of Armageddon*, New Haven, 1987.

Sherwin, Martin J.: *A World Destroyed: The Atomic Bomb and the Great Alliance*, New York, 1975.

Shiel, Matthew: *The Yellow Danger*, London, 1898.

Shiel, Matthew: *The Purple Cloud*, London, 1901.

Shute, Nevil: *On the Beach* (1957), London, 1990.

Sigal, Leon V.: *Fighting to a Finish: The Politics of War Termination in the U.S. and Japan, 1945*, Ithaca, 1988.

Sigaud, Louis A.: *Douhet and Aerial Warfare*, New York, 1941.

Singh, Nagendra: *Nuclear Weapons and International Law*, London, 1959.

Skates, John Ray: *The Invasion of Japan: Alternative to the Bomb*, Columbia, S.C., 1994.

Slusser, George and Rabkin, Eric S. (eds.): *Fights of Fancy: Armed Conflict in Science Fiction and Fantasy*, Athens, 1993.

Smith, Denis Mack: *Mussolini's Roman Empire*, London, 1976.

Snow, Edgar: *Striden om Asien*, Stockholm, 1942.

Soddy, Frederick: "Some Recent Advances in Radioactivity, An account of the researches of Professor Rutherford and his co-workers at McGill University," *The Contemporary Review*, May 1903.

Soddy, Frederick: *The Interpretation of Radium* (1909), London, 1912.

Spaight, J. M.: *Air Power and War Rights* (1924), London, 1947.

Spaight, J. M.: *Air Power and the Cities*, London, 1930.

Spaight, J. M.: *Bombing Vindicated*, London, 1944.

Spetzler, Eberhard: *Luftkrieg und Menschlichkeit, Die Völkerrechtliche Stellung der Zivilpersonen im Luftkrieg*, Göttingen, 1956.

Spiers, Edward M.: "The Use of the Dum Dum Bullet in Colonial Warfare," *The Journal of Imperial and Commonwealth History*, October 1975, 3–14.

Spohr, Carl W.: "The Final War," in *Wonder Stories 1932*, cited in Franklin, 1988.

Stacey, Robert C.: "The Age of Chivalry," in Howard, 1994.

Stockholm International Peace Research Institute (SIPRI) *Napalm and Incendiary Weapons: Legal and Humanitarian Aspects*, Interim report, Stockholm, 1972.

SIPRI *Yearbook* 1968–1998.

Strehl, Rolf: *Der Himmel hat keine Grenzen*, Berlin, 1962.

Sturgeon, Theodore: "Thunder and Roses" (1947), in *The Complete Stories of Theodore Sturgeon, Vol IV, Thunder and Roses*, Berkeley, 1997, 125–149.

Star, The, Johannesburg 1922. 7/6 "Abraham Morris Reported Dead." 10/6 "Wonderful Work of Our Airmen in the South West." 13/6 "Problem of the Hottentot. Is Extermination to Be Fate of the Race?"

Svanberg, Ingvar and Tydén, Mattias: *Sverige och förintelsen, Debatt och dokument om Europas judar 1933–1945*, Stockholm, 1997.

Svenska Dagbladet 1938 9/3.

Szilard, Leo: *His Version of the Facts: Selected Recollections and Correspondence*, Spencer R. Weart and Gertrud Weiss Szilard (eds.), Cambridge, Mass, 1978.

Tambaro, Dr. (Neapel): "Das Recht, Krieg zu führen," *Zeitschrift für internationales Recht*, Band 24, s. 41ff, Munich and Leipzig, 1914.

Taylor, Eric: *Operation Millennium: Bomber Harris's Raid on Cologne, May 1942*, London, 1987.

Taylor, Philip M.: *War and the Media: Propaganda and Persuasion in the Gulf War*, Manchester, 1998.

Tennant, J. E.: *In the Clouds above Baghdad: Being the Records of an Air Commander*, London, 1920.

Thomas, Gordon and Morgan-Witts, Max: *The Day Guernica Died*, London, 1975.

Toffler, Alvin and Heidi: *War and Anti-War: Survival at the Dawn of the 21st Century*, London, 1994.

Torres, Anita: *La science-fiction française*, Paris, 1997.

Towle, Philip Anthony: *Pilots and Rebels: The Use of Aircraft in Unconventional Warfare 1918–1988*, London, 1989.

Townshend, Charles: "Civilization and 'Frightfulness': Air Control in the Middle East Between the Wars," in *Warfare, Diplomacy and Politics, Essays in Honour of A. J. P. Taylor*, Chris Wrigley (ed.), London, 1986.

Train, Arthur Cheney and Wood, Robert W.: *The Man Who Rocked the Earth*, New York, 1915.

Travers, T. H. E.: "Technology, Tactics and Morale: Jean de Bloch, the Boer War and British Military Theory 1900–1914." I: *Journal of Modern History* 51, June 1979.

Treat, John Whittier: *Writing Ground Zero: Japanese Literature and the Atomic Bomb*, Chicago, 1995.

Trenn, Thadeus J.: *The Self-Splitting Atom: The History of the Rutherford-Soddy Collaboration*, London, 1977.

van Creveld, Martin: *On Future War*, London, 1991.

Veale, F. J. P.: *Advance to Barbarism: How the Reverse to Barbarism in Warfare and War-Trials Menaces Our Future*, Madison, 1953.

Verne, Jules: *Ingenjör Roburs luftfärd* (1886), Stockholm, 1911.

Wagar, W. Warren: *Terminal Visions: The Literature of Last Things*, Bloomington, 1982.

Wallis, C. Braithwaite: *West African Warfare*, London, 1906.

Walzer, Michael: *Just and Unjust Wars: A Moral Argument with Historical Illustrations* (1977), New York, 1992.

Warleta Carillo, José: Los Comienzos belicos de la aviation espanola, *Révue Internationale d'Histoire Militaire*, No. 56, 1984.

Wasserstein, Bernard: *Britain and the Jews of Europe 1939–1945*, Oxford, 1979.

Waterloo, Stanley: *Armageddon*, London, 1898.

Watt, Donald Cameron: "Restraints on War in the Air Before 1945," in Howard, 1979.

Weart, Spencer R.: *Nuclear Fear: A History*, Cambridge, Mass., 1988.

Weigley, Russell F.: *The American Way of War*, New York, 1973.

Weizsäcker, Carl Friedrich von (ed.): *Kriegsfolgen und Kriegsverhütung*, Munich, 1971.

Wells, H. G.: *The World Set Free*, New York (1914), 1926.

Wells, H. G.: *The War in the Air*, New York (1908), 1926.

Westring, G. A.: *Luftkrig, En sammanställning av 'Douhetismen' och andra teorier samt några fakta och reflexioner rörande nutida luftförsvar*, Stockholm, 1936.

Whealey, Robert H.: *Hitler and Spain: The Nazi Role in the Spanish Civil War 1936–1939*, Lexington, 1989.

Whitsel, Brad: "The Turner Diaries and Cosmotheism: William Pierce's Theology of Revolution," *Nova Religio*, April 1998.

Winter, Frank H.: *The First Golden Age of Rocketry*, Washington, D.C., 1990.

Wittner, Lawrence S.: *The Struggle against the Bomb, Vol. 1: One World or None: A History of the World Nuclear Disarmament Movement Through 1953*, Stanford, 1993.

Wittner, Lawrence S.: *The Struggle against the Bomb, Vol. 2: Resisting the Bomb: A History of the World Nuclear Disarmament Movement 1954–1970*, Stanford, 1997.

Woolman, David S.: *Rebels in the Rif: Abd el Krim and the Rif Rebellion*, London, 1969.

Wright, John: *Libya: A Modern History*, London, 1983.

Wright, Quincy: "The Bombardment of Damascus," in *The American Journal of International Law*, Vol. 20, Washington, D.C., 1926, pp. 263–280.

Wright, Quincy: *A Study of World War I*, Chicago, 1942.

Wylie, Philip: *Tomorrow!* New York, 1954.

Wylie, Philip: *Triumph*, New York, 1963.

Wyman, David S.: *The Abandonment of the Jews: America and the Holocaust 1941–1945*, New York, 1984.

Yoke, Carl B.: "Phoenix from the Ashes: The Literature of the Remade World": *Contributions to the Study of Science Fiction and Fantasy*, 30, New York, 1987.

Zanetti, J. Enrique: *Fire from the Air: The ABC of Incendiaries*, New York, 1941.

Ziegler, Karl-Heinz: *Völkerrechtsgeschichte*, Munich, 1994.

Zuckerman, Solly: *From Apes to Warlords: The Autobiography 1904–1946 of Solly Zuckerman*, London, 1978.

AFTERWORD TO 2012 EDITION

A History of Bombing takes the bombing story up to the end of the 20th century. What has happened since then?

September 11, 2001 is often talked about as if history had been forever changed by Osama bin Laden. The use of fuel-loaded civilian airliners in co-ordinated kamikaze attacks on civilian and military targets on the US mainland was, of course, a disgusting criminal and military innovation. But it was hardly a turning point in history. Rather, a logical development of the suicide bomb.

It gave us one more reminder of the vulnerability of modern, high-tech society and of the utter impotence of military machines to defend it.

More than twenty years ago the Israeli military historian Martin Van Creveld, in his *The Future of War*, rejected modern sophisticated weapon systems as "dinosaurs" – too big, too expensive, too complicated and, above all, too destructive to be used in the wars that are actually waged. The bomb of the future, he said, is not the intercontinental missile but the car bomb, the letter bomb and the suicide bomb.

The nuclear threat remains, although almost forgotten today, and combines with the terrorist threat. The great powers still have enough nuclear weapons on active duty to kill us all. Great powers still do most of the bombing. They seldom bomb peoples of their own race and culture. Before, during, between and after the two world wars, in whichever period you chose to look at, the majority of bombs were always used against peoples of other races and cultures. This is still the case.

A great majority of UN member states won their independence after 1945. Many of them did in fact use terrorist methods in their fight for liberation, and even if they didn't, they were almost without exception labelled "terrorist". Nelson Mandela used to be an "international terrorist" almost up to the day he became an international statesman and winner of the Nobel Peace Prize.

So the "war against terrorism" is not new. It has been waged for a century, with very little success on the whole. Bombing from the air has been an important part of it, especially in Afghanistan, which has always been an uncomfortable battleground for foreign troops.

Bombing seemed easier. The British bombed "terrorists" in Kabul as early as 1919. It was here that Arthur "Bomber" Harris scored his first civilian hits. In the 1980s the Soviet Union bombed "terrorists" in Afghanistan for nearly ten years. The war ended in a Russian defeat that contributed to the downfall of the Soviet Union. The US is now bombing the same Afghan "terrorists" they trained and financed as "freedom fighters" twenty-five years ago.

Is anything new in this seemingly endless repetition of past mistakes?

Yes, what is new is that the majority of American aircraft in the wars against terrorism are now unmanned "drones". Pilots and bombers do not need to be personally present at the killings. They sit safely in their offices in Nevada, USA, bombing live targets they have never seen, except on the screen.

From bow and arrow to intercontinental missile, new pieces of military hardware have tended to increase the distance between the soldier and his enemy. During the Second World War bomber crews sometimes incinerated tens of thousands of human beings in a single night. Few of them could have done the same with a flame-thrower; very few could have done it if they had actually seen and heard and smelled the suffering they were causing.

Many studies have shown that killing becomes easier the further you are from your victim. To sit secure in your Nevadan office while killing in Afghanistan makes it abstract, even boring, sometimes enjoyable, like a video game. A good read about this robotics revolution in warfare is P. W. Singer's *Wired for War* (2009).

Drones have depersonalized and dehumanized war. The robot bomber is the ideal soldier – never tired, never angry, never afraid, never hungry. Never forgets its orders. Feeling no compassion and no guilt, the bombing drone acts without intention and without mercy.

The drone war is the unmanned opposite of the mass armies of the Great War. Convenient – as long as the other side hasn't got the drone. But remember – for the price of a jet fighter you can buy eighty-five Predator drones. They are dirt cheap. What if the drone becomes every man's or at least every state's weapon? Will it not be too easy to wage war, if all you risk are machines, not soldiers?

Some military men are afraid that the computer memory will ensnare the robot warrior. If every bomb is registered and documented so that it can afterwards be scrutinized for compatibility with the laws of war – who will then dare to bomb? Who will dare to wage war?

Even more relevant is the question: who is responsible?

Some drones act only on direct orders from the human being in Nevada. Others start and land with human assistance but once in the air fly themselves.

Others get a certain mission but independently chose how to accomplish it. The fully independent drone, yet to be created, decides within its framework, without orders from Nevada, where to go and what to accomplish.

To varying degrees, they all pose the question of responsibility. A machine, however smart, cannot be charged with war crimes. If a machine kills my child, is it the operator, the programmer, the engineer, the manufacturer, the buyer, the military top brass, or perhaps the political decision-makers who are to blame?

And what will happen if this new unmanned, dehumanized, irresponsible warfare combines with the old, almost forgotten nuclear threat? Remember that the hydrogen bomb, once designed to deter Soviet expansion, is still with us, long after the Soviet Union has been dissolved and its expansion is but a memory.

Enormous stocks of nuclear weapons potent enough to kill every child on earth are still with us, more dangerous than the forgotten dangers from which they were once supposed to protect us.